The University Libraries at Penn State
and the Penn State University Press, through the
Office of Digital Scholarly Publishing, produced
this volume to preserve the informational content
of the original. This reprint edition was created
by means of digital technology and is printed on
paper that complies with the permanent Paper
Standard issued by the National Information
Standards Organization (z39.48-1984).

2008

DEDICATION.

TO THE
SURVIVING SUFFERERS
OF THE
APPALLING CALAMITY AT JOHNSTOWN
AND
NEIGHBORING VILLAGES
THIS WORK
WHICH RELATES THE THRILLING STORY
OF THE GREAT DISASTER
IS DEDICATED.

THE
JOHNSTOWN HORROR!!!
OR
VALLEY OF DEATH,
BEING
A COMPLETE AND THRILLING ACCOUNT OF THE AWFUL FLOODS AND THEIR APPALLING RUIN.

CONTAINING

Graphic Descriptions of the Terrible Rush of Waters; the great Destruction of Houses, Factories, Churches, Towns, and Thousands of Human Lives; Heart-rending Scenes of Agony, Separation of Loved Ones, Panic-stricken Multitudes and their Frantic Efforts to Escape a Horrible Fate.

COMPRISING

THRILLING TALES OF HEROIC DEEDS; NARROW ESCAPES FROM THE JAWS OF DEATH; FRIGHTFUL HAVOC BY FIRE; DREADFUL SUFFERINGS OF SURVIVORS; PLUNDERING BODIES OF VICTIMS, ETC.

TOGETHER WITH

Magnificent Exhibitions of Popular Sympathy; Quick Aid from every City and State; Millions of Dollars Sent for the Relief of the Stricken Sufferers.

By JAMES HERBERT WALKER,
THE WELL KNOWN AUTHOR.

FULLY ILLUSTRATED WITH SCENES OF THE GREAT CALAMITY.

CHICAGO, ILLS.:
U. S. PUBLISHING HOUSE,

Copyrighted, 1889.

PREFACE

THE whole country has been profoundly startled at the Terrible Calamity which has swept thousands of human beings to instant death at Johnstown and neighboring villages. The news came with the suddenness of a lightning bolt falling from the sky. A romantic valley, filled with busy factories, flourishing places of business, multitudes of happy homes and families, has been suddenly transformed into a scene of awful desolation. Frightful ravages of Flood and Fire have produced in one short hour a destruction which surpasses the records of all modern disasters. No calamity in recent times has so appalled the civilized world. What was a peaceful, prosperous valley a little time ago is to-day a huge sepulchre, filled with the shattered ruins of houses, factories, banks, churches, and the ghastly corpses of the dead.

This book contains a thrilling description of this awful catastrophe, which has shocked both hemispheres. It depicts with graphic power the terrible scenes of the great disaster, and relates the fearful story with masterly effect.

The work treats of the great storm which devastated the country, deluging large sections, sweeping away bridges, turning rivulets to rivers, prostrating forests, and producing untold damage to life and property; of the sudden rise in the Conemaugh River and tributary streams, weakening the dam thrown across the fated valley, and endangering the lives of 50,000 people; of the heroic efforts of a little band of men to stay the flood and avert the direful calamity; of the swift ride down the valley to warn the inhabitants of their impending fate, and save them from instant death; of the breaking away of the imprisoned waters after all efforts had failed to hold them back; of the rush and roar of the mighty torrent, plunging down the valley with sounds like advancing thunder, reverberating like the booming of cannon among the hills; of the frightful havoc attending the mad flood descending with incredible velocity, and a force which nothing could resist; of the rapid rise of the waters, flooding buildings, driving the terrified inhabitants to the upper stories and roofs in the desperate effort to escape their doom; of hundreds of houses crashing down the surging river, carrying men, women and children beyond the hope of rescue; of a night of horrors, multitudes dying amid the awful terrors of flood and fire, plunged under the wild torrent, buried in mire, or consumed in devouring flames; of helpless creatures rending the air with pitiful screams crying aloud in their agony, imploring help with outstretched hands, and finally sinking with no one to save them.

Whole families were lost and obliterated, perishing together in a watery tomb, or ground to atoms by floating timbers and wreck; households were suddenly bereft—some of fathers, others of mothers, others of children, neighbors and friends; frantic efforts were made to rescue the victims of the flood, render aid to those who were struggling against death mitigate the terrors of the horrible disaster. There we acts of heroism, strong men and frail women and children putting their own lives in peril to save those of their loved ones.

The terrible scene at Johnstown bridge, where thousands were consumed was the greatest funeral pyre known in the history of the world. It was ghastly work—that of recovering the bodies of the dead; dragging them from the mire in which they were imbedded, from the ruins in which they were crushed, or from the burning wreck which was consuming them. Hundreds of bodies were mutilated and disfigured beyond the possibility of identifying them, all traces of individual form and features utterly destroyed. There were multitudes of corpses awaiting coffins for their burial, putrefying under the sun, and filling the air with the sickening stench of death. There were ghouls who robbed the bodies of the victims, stripping off their jewels—even cutting off fingers to obtain rings, and plundering pockets of their money.

Summary vengeance was inflicted upon prowling thieves; some of whom were driven into the merciless waters to perish, while others were shot or hanged by the neck until they were dead. The burial of hundreds of the known and unknown, without minister or obsequies, without friend or mourner, without surviving relatives to take a last look or shed a tear, was one of the appalling spectacles. There was the breathless suspense and anxiety of those who feared the worst, who waited in vain for news of the safety of their friends, and at last were compelled to believe that their loved ones had perished.

The terrible shock attending the horrible accounts of the great calamity, was followed by the sudden outburst and exhibition of universal grief and sympathy. Despatches from the President, Governors of States, and Mayors of Cities, announced that speedy aid would be furnished. . The magnificent charity that came to the rescue with millions of dollars, immense contributions of food and clothing, personal services and heroic efforts, is one impressive part of this graphic story. Rich and poor alike gave freely, many persons dividing their last dollar to aid those who had lost their all.

These thrilling scenes are depicted, and these wonderful facts are related, in THE JOHNSTOWN HORROR, by eye-witnesses who saw the fatal flood and its direful effects. No book so intensely exciting has ever been issued. The graphic story has an awful fascination, and will be read throughout the land.

CONTENTS.

PAGE.

CHAPTER I.
The Appalling News, ... 17

CHAPTER II.
Death and Desolation, ... 50

CHAPTER III.
The Horrors Increase, ... 74

CHAPTER IV.
Multiplication of Terrors, ... 104

CHAPTER V.
The Awful Work of Death 116

CHAPTER VI.
Shadows of Despair, ... 129

CHAPTER VII.
Burial of the Victims, ... 146

CHAPTER VIII.
Johnstown and its Industries, ... 154

CHAPTER IX.
A View of the Wreck, ... 164

CHAPTER X.

Thrilling Experiences, ... 182

CHAPTER XI.

New Tales of Horror, ... 208

CHAPTER XII.

Pathetic Scenes, ... 246

CHAPTER XIII.

Digging for the Dead, ... 270

CHAPTER XIV.

Hairbreadth Escapes, ... 288

CHAPTER XV.

Terrible Pictures of Woe, ... 334

CHAPTER XVI.

Stories of the Flood, ... 380

CHAPTER XVII.

One Week after the Great Disaster, ... 432

CHAPTER XVIII.

A Walk Through the Valley of Death, . . . 455

CHAPTER XIX.

A Day of Work and Worship, ... 479

CHAPTER XX.

Millions of Money for Johnstown, ... 489

RECOVERING THE BODIES OF VICTIMS.

THE BREAK IN THE SOUTH FORKS DAM.

IN THE PACK-SADDLE, ON THE CONEMAUGH, PENNSYLVANIA RAILROAD.

RUINS IN MAIN STREET, JOHNSTOWN.

RELIEF CORPS CROSSING THE ROPE BRIDGE.

IDENTIFYING THE DEAD.

A GRAVEL-TRAIN RUNS AWAY FROM THE ADVANCING FLOOD.

RESCUED BY RAILROAD MEN.

SOURCE OF THE CONEMAUGH RIVER.

FRIGHTFUL STRUGGLES FOR LIFE.

THE FLOOD STRIKES THE CAMBRIA IRON WORKS.

HOUSES AND HUMAN BEINGS LOST IN THE FLOOD.

TEARING DOWN HOUSES IN JOHNSTOWN.

SOLDIERS GUARDING A HUNGARIAN THIEF.

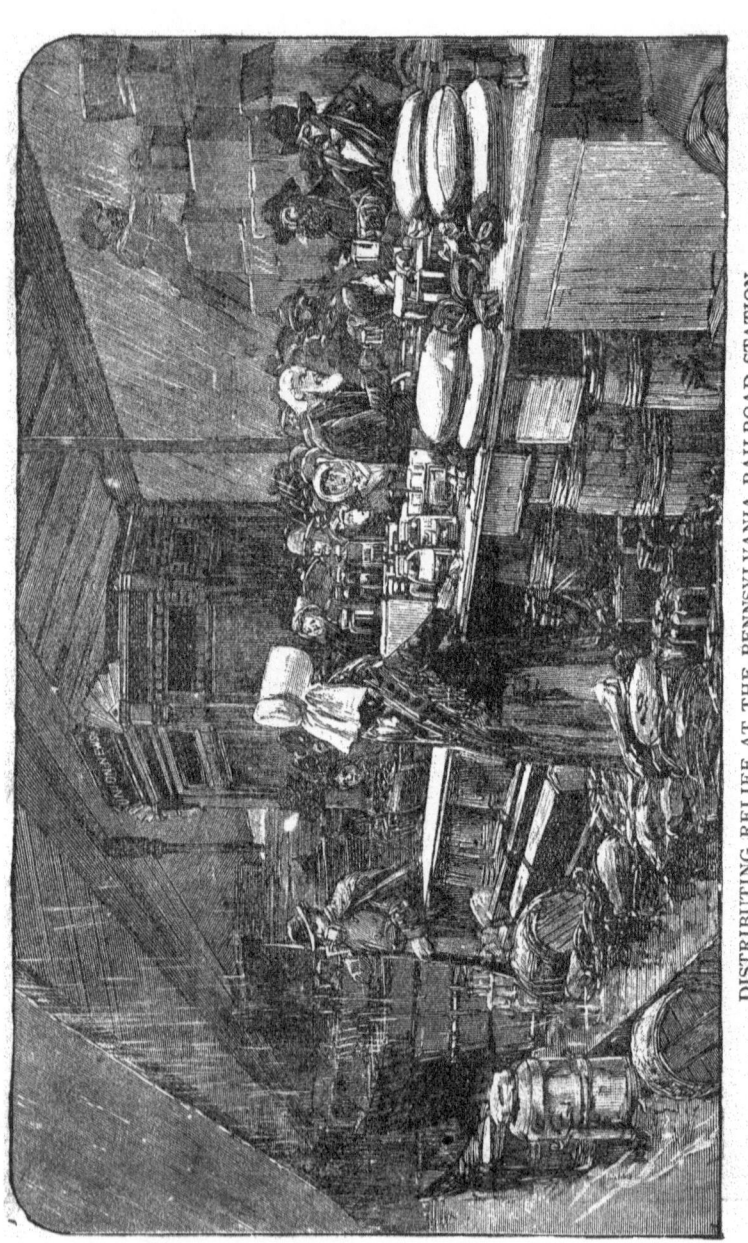

DISTRIBUTING RELIEF AT THE PENNSYLVANIA RAILROAD STATION.

MAIN STREET, JOHNSTOWN, IN FRONT OF MERCHANT'S HOTEL.

SEARCHING FOR LOST RELATIVES.

THE JOHNSTOWN HORROR

OR

Valley of Death.

CHAPTER I.

The Appalling News.

On the advent of Summer, June 1st, the country was horror-stricken by the announcement that a terrible calamity had overtaken the inhabitants of Johnstown, and the neighboring villages. Instantly the whole land was stirred by the startling news of this great disaster. Its appalling magnitude, its dreadful suddenness, its scenes of terror and agony, the fate of thousands swept to instant death by a flood as frightful as that of the cataract of Niagara, awakened the profoundest horror. No calamity in the history of modern times has so appalled the civilized world.

The following graphic pen-picture will give the reader an accurate idea of the picturesque scene of the disaster:

Away up in the misty crags of the Alleghanies some tiny rills trickle and gurgle from a cleft in the mossy rocks. The drippling waters, timid perhaps in the bleak and lonely fastness of the heights, hug and coddle one another until they flash into a limpid pool. A score of rivulets from all the mountain side babble hither over rocky beds to join their companions. Thence in rippling current they purl and tinkle down the gentle slopes, through bosky nooks sweet with the odors of fir tree and pine, over meads dappled with the scarlet snap-dragon and purple heath buds, now pausing for a moment to idle with a wood encircled lake, now tumbling in opalescent cascade over a mossy lurch, and then on again in cheerful, hurried course down the Appalachian valley.

None stays their way. Here and there perhaps some thrifty Pennsylvania Dutchman coaxes the saucy stream to turn his mill-wheel and every league or so it fumes and frets a bit against some rustic bridge. From these trifling tourneys though, it emerges only the more eager and impetuous in its path toward the towns below.

The Fatal River.

Coming nearer, step by step, to the busy haunts of men, the dashing brook takes on a more ambitious air. Little by little it edges its narrow banks aside, drinks in the waters of tributaries, swells with the copious rainfall of the lower valley. From its ladder in the Alleghanies it catches a glimpse of the steeples of Johnstown, red with the glow of the setting sun. Again it spurts and spreads as if conscious of its new importance, and the once tiny rill expands into the dignity of a river, a veritable river, with a name of its own. Big with this sounding symbol of prowess it rushes on as if to sweep by the teeming town in a flood of majesty. To its vast surprise the way is barred. The hand of man has dared to check the will of one that up to now has known no curb save those the forest gods imposed. For an instant the waters, taken aback by this strange audacity, hold themselves in leash. Then, like erl king in the German legends, they broaden out to engulf their opponent. In vain they surge with crescent surface against the barrier of stone. By day, by night, they beat and breast in angry impotence against the ponderous wall of masonry that man has reared, for pleasure and profit, to stem the mountain stream.

The Awful Rush of Waters.

Suddenly, maddened by the stubborn hindrance, the river grows black and turgid. It rumbles and threatens as if confident of an access of strength that laughs at resistance. From far up the hillside comes a sound, at first soft and soothing as the fountains of Lindaraxa, then rolling onward it takes the voluminous quaver of a distant waterfall. Louder and louder, deeper and deeper, nearer and nearer comes an awful crashing and roaring, till its echoes rebound from the crags of the Alleghanies like peals of thunder and boom of cannon.

On, on, down the steep valley trumpets the torrent into the river at Jamestown. Joined to the waters from the cloud kissed summits of its source, the exultant Conemaugh, with a deafening din, dashes its way through the barricade of stone and starts like a demon on its path of destruction.

Into its maw it sucks a town. A town with all its hundreds of men and women and children, with its marts of business, its homes, its factories and houses of worship. Then, insatiate still, with a blast like the chaos of worlds dissolved, it rushes out to new desolation, until Nature herself, awe stricken at the sight of such ineffable woe, blinds her eyes to the uncanny scene of death, and drops the pall of night upon the earth.

Destruction Descended as a Bolt of Jove.

A fair town in a western valley of Pennsylvania, happy in the arts of peace and prospering by its busy manufactures, suddenly swept out of existence by a gigantic flood and thousands of lives extinguished as by one fell stroke—such has been the fate of Johnstown.

Never before in this country has there happened a disaster of such appalling proportions. It is necessary to refer to those which have occurred in the valleys of the great European rivers, where there is a densely crowded population, to find a parallel.

The Horrors Unestimated.

At first the horror was not all known. It could only be imperfectly surmised. Until a late hour on the following night there was no communication with the hapless city. All that was positively known of its fate was seen from afar. It was said that out of all the habitations, which had sheltered about twelve thousand people before this awful doom had befallen, only two were visible above the water. All the rest, if this be true, had been swallowed up or else shattered into pieces and hurled downward into the flood-vexed valley below.

What has become of those twelve thousand inhabitants? Who can tell until after the waters have wholly susided?

Of course it is possible that many of them escaped. Much hope is to be built upon the natural exaggeration of first reports from the sorely distressed surrounding region and the lack of actual knowledge, in the absence of direct communication. But what suspense must there be between now and the moment when direct communication shall be opened!

Heedless of Fate.

The valley of the Conemaugh in which Johnstown stood lies between the steep walls of lofty hills. The gathering of the rain into torrents in that region is quick and precipitate. The river on one side roared out its warning, but the people would not take heed of the danger impending over them on the other side —the great South Fork dam, two and a half miles up the valley and looming one hundred feet in height from base to top. Behind it were piled the waters, a great, ponderous mass, like the treasured wrath of fate. Their surface was about three hundred feet above the deserted town.

If Noah's neighbors thought it would be only a little

shower the people of Johnstown were yet more foolish. The railroad officials had repeatedly told them that the dam threatened destruction. They still perversely lulled themselves into a false security. The blow came, when it did, like a flash. It was as if the heavens had fallen in liquid fury upon the earth. It was as if ocean itself had been precipitated into an abyss. The slow but inexorable march of the mightiest glacier of the Alps, though comparable, was not equal to this in force. The whole of a Pyramid, shot from a colossal catapult, would not have been the petty charge of a pea shooter to it. Imagine Niagara, or a greater even than Niagara, falling upon an ordinary collection of brick and wooden houses.

An Inconceivable Force.

The South Fork Reservoir was the largest in the United States, and it contained millions of tons of water. When its fetters were loosened, crumbling before it like sand, a building or even a rock that stood in its path presented as much resistance as a card house. The dread execution was little more than the work of an instant.

The flood passed over the town as it would over a pile of shingles, covering over or carrying with it everything that stood in its way. It bounded down the valley, wreaking destruction and death on each hand and in its fore. Torrents that poured down out of the wilds of the mountains swelled its volume.

All along from the point of its release it bore débris

and corpses as its hideous trophies. In a very brief time it displayed some of both, as if in hellish glee, to the horrified eyes of Pittsburg, seventy-eight miles west of the town of Johnstown that had been, having danced them along on its exultant billows or rolled them over and over in the depths of its dark current all the way through the Conemaugh, the Kiskiminitas and the Allegheny river.

It was like a fearful monster, gnashing its dripping jaws in the scared face of the multitude, in the flesh of its victims.

One eye-witness of the effects of the deluge declares that he saw five hundred dead bodies. Hundreds were counted by others. It will take many a day to make up the death roll. It will take many a day to make up the reckoning of the material loss.

If any pen could describe the scenes of terror, anguish and destruction which have taken place in Conemaugh Valley it could write an epic greater than the "Iliad." The accounts that come tell of hairbreadth escapes, heartrending tragedies and deeds of heroism almost without number.

A Climax of Horror.

As if to add a lurid touch of horror to the picture that might surpass all the rest a conflagration came to mock those who were in fear of drowning with a death yet more terrible. Where the ruins of Johnstown, composed mainly of timber, had been piled up forty feet high against a railroad bridge below the town a fire was started and raged with eager fury. It is said that scores of persons were burned alive, their piercing cries appealing for aid to hundreds of spectators who stood on the banks of the river, but could do nothing

Western Pennsylvania is in mourning. Business in the cities is virtually suspended and all minds are bent upon this great horror, all hearts convulsed with the common sorrow.

Heartrending Scenes and Heroic Struggles for Life.

Another eye-witness describes the calamity as follows: A flood of death swept down the Alleghany Mountains yesterday afternoon and last night. Almost the entire city of Johnstown is swimming about in the rushing, angry tide. Dead bodies are floating about in every direction, and almost every piece of movable timber is carrying from the doomed city a corpse of humanity, drifting with the raging waters. The disaster overtook Johnstown about six o'clock last evening.

As the train bearing the writer sped eastward, the reports at each stop grew more appalling. At Derry a group of railway officials were gathered who had come from Bolivar, the end of the passable portion of the road westward. They had seen but a small portion of the awful flood, but enough to allow them to imagine the rest. Down through the Packsaddle came the rushing waters. The wooded heights of the Alleghanies looked down in wonder at the scene of the most terrible destruction that ever struck the romantic valley of the Conerraugh

The water was rising when the men left at six o'clock
at the rate of five feet an hour. Clinging to improvised
rafts, constructed in the death battle from floating
boards and timbers, were agonized men, women and
children, their heartrending shrieks for help striking
horror to the breasts of the onlookers. Their cries
were of no avail. Carried along at railway speed on
the breast of this rushing torrent, no human ingenuity
could devise a means of rescue.

With pallid face and hair clinging wet and damp to
her cheek, a mother was seen grasping a floating timber, while on her other arm she held her babe, already
drowned. With a death-grip on a plank a strong man
just giving up hope cast an imploring look to those on
the bank, and an instant later he had sunk into the
waves. Prayers to God and cries to those in safety
rang above the roaring waves.

The special train pulled into Bolivar at half-past
eleven last night, and the trainmen were there notified
that further progress was impossible. The greatest
excitement prevailed at this place, and parties of citizens are out all the time endeavoring to save the poor
unfortunates that are being hurled to eternity on the
rushing torrent.

Attempts at Rescue.

The tidal wave struck Bolivar just after dark, and
in five minutes the Conemaugh rose from six to forty
feet and the waters spread out over the whole country.
Soon houses began floating down, and clinging to the
debris were men, women and children shrieking for

aid. A large number of citizens at once gathered on the county bridge, and they were reinforced by a number from Garfield, a town on the opposite side of the river.

They brought a number of ropes and these were thrown over into the boiling waters as persons drifted by in efforts to save some poor beings. For half an hour all efforts were fruitless, until at last, when the rescuers were about giving up all hope, a little boy, astride a shingle roof, managed to catch hold of one of the ropes. He caught it under his left arm and was thrown violently against an abutment, but managed to keep hold, and was successfully pulled on to the bridge amid the cheers of the onlookers. His name was Hessler and his rescuer was a trainman named Carney. The lad was at once taken to the town of Garfield and was cared for. The boy was aged about sixteen. His story of the frightful calamity is as follows:

The Alarm.

"With my father I was spending the day at my grandfather's house in Cambria City. In the house at the time were Theodore, Edward and John Kintz, and John Kintz, Jr.; Miss Mary Kintz, Mrs. Mary Kintz, wife of John Kintz, Jr.; Miss Treacy Kintz, Mrs. Rica Smith, John Hirsch and four children, my father and myself. Shortly after five o'clock there was a noise of roaring waters and screams of people. We looked out the door and saw persons running. My father told us to never mind, as the waters would not rise further.

"But soon we saw houses being swept away, and

then we ran up to the floor above. The house was three stories, and we were at last forced to the top one. In my fright I jumped on the bed. It was an old fashioned one, with heavy posts. The water kept rising and my bed was soon afloat. Gradually it was lifted up. The air in the room grew close and the house was moving. Still the bed kept rising and pressed the ceiling. At last the posts pushed against the plaster. It yielded and a section of the roof gave way. Then suddenly I found myself on the roof, and was being carried down stream.

Saved.

"After a little this roof began to part, and I was afraid I was going to be drowned, but just then another house with a shingle roof floated by, and I managed to crawl on it, and floated down until nearly dead with cold, when I was saved. After I was freed from the house I did not see my father. My grandfather was on a tree, but he must have been drowned, as the waters were rising fast. John Kintz, Jr., was also on a tree. Miss Mary Kintz and Mrs. Mary Kintz I saw drown. Miss Smith was also drowned. John Hirsch was in a tree, but the four children were drowned. The scenes were terrible. Live bodies and corpses were floating down with me and away from me. I would see persons, hear them shriek, and then they would disappear. All along the line were people who were trying to save us, but they could do nothing, and only a few were caught."

This boy's story is but one incident, and shows

what happened to one family. No one knows what has happened to the hundreds who were in the path of the rushing water. It is impossible to get anything in the way of news save meagre details.

An eye-witness at Bolivar Block Station tells a story of unparalleled heroism that occurred at the lower bridge which crosses the Conemaugh at this point. A. Young, with two women was seen coming down the river on a part of the floor. At the upper bridge a rope was thrown down to them. This they all failed to catch. Between the two bridges he was noticed to point towards the elder woman, who, it is supposed, was his mother. He was then seen to instruct the women how to catch the rope that was lowered from the other bridge. Down came the raft with a rush. The brave man stood with his arms around the two women.

Unavailing Courage.

As they swept under the bridge he seized the rope. He was jerked violently away from the two women, who failed to get a hold on the rope. Seeing that they would not be rescued, he dropped the rope and fell back on the raft, which floated on down the river. The current washed their frail craft in toward the bank. The young man was enabled to seize hold of a branch of a tree. He aided the two women to get up into the tree.

He held on with his hands and rested his feet on a pile of driftwood. A piece of floating débris struck the drift, sweeping it away. The man hung with his body immersed in the water. A pile of drift soon collected and he was enabled to get another insecure footing. Up the river there was a sudden crash, and a section of the bridge was swept away and floated down the stream, striking the tree and washing it away. All three were thrown into the water and were drowned before the eyes of the horrified spectators just opposite the town of Bolivar.

Early in the evening a woman with her two children was seen to pass under the bridge at Bolivar clinging to the roof of a coal house. A rope was lowered to her, but she shook her head and refused to desert the children. It was rumored that all three were saved at Cokeville, a few miles below Bolivar. A later report from Lockport says that the residents succeeded in rescuing five people from the flood, two women and three men. One man succeeded in getting out of the water unaided. They were taken care of by the people of the town.

A Child's Faith.

A little girl passed under the bridge just before dark. She was kneeling on a part of a floor and had her hands clasped as if in prayer. Every effort was made to save her, but they all proved futile. A railroader who was standing by remarked that the piteous appearance of the little waif brought tears to his eyes. All night long the crowd stood about the ruins of the bridge which had been swept away at Bolivar. The water rushed past with a roar, carrying with it parts of houses, furniture and trees. The flood had evidently spent its force up the valley. No more living persons were being carried past. Watchers with lanterns remained along the banks until daybreak, when the first view of the awful devastation of the flood was witnessed.

Along the bank lay remnants of what had once been dwelling houses and stores; here and there was an uprooted tree. Piles of drift lay about, in some of which bodies of the victims of the flood will be found. Rescuing parties are being formed in all towns along the railroad. Houses have been thrown open to refugees, and every possible means is being used to protect the homeless.

Wrecking Trains to the Rescue.

The wrecking trains of the Pennsylvania Railroad are slowly making their way east to the unfortunate city. No effort was being made to repair the wrecks, and the crews of the trains were organized into rescuing parties, and an effort will be made to send out a mail train this morning. The chances are that they will go no further east than Florence. There is absolutely no news from Johnstown. The little city is entirely cut off from communication with the outside world. The damage done is inestimable. No one can tell its extent.

The little telegraph stations along the road are filled with anxious groups of men who have friends and relatives in Johnstown. The smallest item of news is eagerly seized upon and circulated. If favorable they have a moment of relief, if not their faces become more gloomy. Harry Fisher, a young telegraph operator who was at Bolivar when the first rush began, says:— "We knew nothing of the disaster until we noticed the river slowly rising and then more rapidly. News then reached us from Johnstown that the dam at South Fork had burst. Within three hours the water in the river rose at least twenty feet. Shortly before six o'clock ruins of houses, beds, household utensils, barrels and kegs came floating past the bridges. At eight o'clock the water was within six feet of the roadbed of the bridge. The wreckage floated past without stopping for at least two hours. Then it began to lessen, and night coming suddenly upon us we could see no more. The wreckage was floating by for a long time before the first living persons passed. Fifteen people that I saw were carried down by the river. One of these, a boy, was saved, and three of them were drowned just directly below the town. It was an awful sight and one that I will not soon forget."

Hundreds of animals lost their lives. The bodies of horses, dogs and chickens floated past. The little boy who was rescued at Bolivar had two dogs as companions during his fearful ride. The dogs were drowned just before reaching the bridge. One old mule swam past. Its shoulders were torn, but it was alive when swept past the town.

Saved from a Watery Grave to Perish by Flames.

After a long, weary ride of eight or nine miles over the worst of country roads New Florence, fourteen miles from Johnstown, was reached. The road bed between this place and Bolivar was washed out in many places. The trackmen and the wreck crews were all night in the most dangerous portions of the road.

The last man from Johnstown brought the information that scarcely a house remained in the city. The upper portion above the railroad bridge had been completely submerged. The water dammed up against the viaduct, the wreckage and débris finishing the work that the torrent had failed to accomplish. The bridge at Johnstown proved too stanch for the fury of the water. It is a heavy piece of masonry, and was used as a viaduct by the old Pennsylvania Canal. Some of the top stones were displaced.

The story reached here a short time ago that a family consisting of father and mother and nine children were washed away in a creek at Lockport. The mother managed to reach the shore, but the husband and children were carried out into the Conemaugh to drown. The woman is crazed over the terrible event.

A Night of Horror.

After night settled down upon the mountains the horror of the scenes was enhanced. Above the roar of the water could be heard the piteous appeals from the unfortunate as they were carried by. To add also to the terror of the night, a brilliant illumination lit up the sky. This illumination could be plainly seen from this place.

A message received from Sang Hollow stated that this light came from a hundred burning wrecks of houses that were piled upon the Johnstown Bridge.

A supervisor from up the road brought the information that the wreckage at Johnstown was piled up forty feet above the bridge.

The startling news came in that more than a thousand lives had been lost. This cannot be substantiated. By actual count one hundred and ten people had been seen floating past Sang Hollow before dark. Forty-seven were counted passing New Florence and the number had diminished to eight at Bolivar. The darkness coming on stopped any further count, and it was only by the agonizing cries that rang out above the waters that it was known that a human being was being carried to death.

An Irresistible Torrent.

The scenes along the river were wild in the extreme. Although the water was subsiding, still as it dashed against the rocks that filled the narrow channel of the Conemaugh its spray was carried high up on the shore. The towns all along the line of the railroad from Johnstown west had received visitations. Many of the houses in New Florence were partially under water. At Bolivar the whole lower part of the town was submerged.

The ride over the mountain road gave one a good idea of the cause of this disaster. Every creek was a rushing river and every rivulet a raging torrent. The ground was water soaked, and when the immense mountain district that drains into the Conemaugh above South Fork is taken into consideration the terrible volume of water that must have accumulated can be realized. Gathering, as it did, within a few minutes, it came against the breast of the South Fork dam with irresistible force. The frightened inhabitants along the Conemaugh describe the flood as something awful. The first rise came almost without warning, and the torrent came roaring down the mountain passes in one huge wave, several feet in height. After the first swell the water continued to rise at a fearful rate.

Daylight Brings No Relief.

The gray morning light does not seem to show either hope or mitigation of the awful fears of the night. It has been a hard night to everybody. The overworked newspaper men, who have been without rest and food since yesterday afternoon, and the operators who have handled the messages are already preparing for the work of the day. There has been a long wrangle over the possession of a special train for the press between rival newspaper men, and it has delayed the work of others who are anxious to get further east.

Even here, so far from the washed-out towns, seven bodies have been found. Two were in a tree, a man and a woman, where the flood had carried them. The country people are coming into the town in large numbers telling stories of disaster along the river banks in sequestered places.

Floating Houses.

John McCarthey, a carpenter, who lives in Johnstown, reached here about four o'clock. He left Johnstown at half-past four yesterday afternoon and says the scene then was indescribable. The people had been warned early in the morning to move to the highlands, but they did not heed the warning, although it was repeated a number of times up to one o'clock, when the water poured into Cinder street several feet deep. Then the houses began rocking to and fro, and finally the force of the current carried buildings across streets and vacant lots and dashed them against each other, breaking them into fragments. These buildings were full of the people who had laughed at the cry of danger. McCarthey says that in some cases he counted as many as fifteen persons clinging to buildings. McCarthey's wife was with him. She had three sisters, who lived near her. They saw the house in which these girls lived carried away, and then they could endure the situation no longer and hurried away. The husband feared his wife would go crazy. They went inland along country roads until they reached here.

It is said to be next to impossible to get to Johnstown proper to-day in any manner except by rowboat. The roads are cut up so that even the countrymen refuse to travel over them in their roughest vehicles. The only hope is to get within about three miles by a special train or by hand car.

The Dead Cast Up.

Nine dead bodies have been picked up within the limits of this borough since daylight. None of them has yet been recognized. Five are women. One woman, probably twenty-five years old, had clasped in her arms a babe about six months old. The body of a young man was discovered in the branches of a huge tree which had been carried down the stream. All the orchard crops and shrubbery along the banks of the river have been destroyed.

The body of another woman has just been discovered in the river here. Her foot was seen above the surface of the water and a rope was fastened about it.

A Roof as a Raft.

John Weber and his wife, an old couple, Michael Metzgar and John Forney were rescued near here early this morning. They had been carried from their home in Cambria City on the roof of the house. There were seven others on the roof when it was carried off, all of whom were drowned. They were unknown to Weber, having drifted on to the roof from floating débris. Weber and wife were thoroughly drenched and were almost helpless from exposure. They were unable to walk when taken off the roof at this place. They are now at the hotel here.

Hundreds of people from Johnstown and up river towns are hurrying here in search of friends and relatives who were swept away in last night's flood. The most intense excitement prevails. The street corners are crowded with pale and anxious people who tell of the calamity with bated breath. Squire Bennett has charge of the dead bodies, and he is having them properly cared for. They are being prepared for burial, but will be held here for identification.

Four boys have just come from the river bank above here. They say that on the opposite side a number of bodies can be seen lying in the mud. They found the body of a woman on this side badly bruised.

R. B. Rodgers, Justice of the Peace at Nineveh, has wired the Coroner at Greensburg that one hundred dead bodies have been found at that place, and he asks what is to be done with them. From this one can estimate that the loss of life will reach over one thousand.

A report has just been received that twenty persons are on an island near Nineveh and that men and women are on a partly submerged tree.

A report has just reached here that at least one hundred people were consumed in the flames at Johnstown last night, but it cannot be verified here. The air is filled with thrilling and most incredible stories, but none of them have as yet been confirmed. It is certain, however, that even the worst cannot be imagined.

Warnings Remembered Too Late.

It is very evident that more lives have been lost because of foolish incredulity than from ignorance of the danger. For more than a year there have been fears of an accident of just such a character. The foundations of the dam were considered to be shaky early last spring and many increasing leakages were reported from time to time.

According to people who live in Johnstown and other

towns on the line of the river, ample time was given to the Johnstown folks by the railroad officials and by other gentlemen of standing and reputation. In dozens, yes, hundreds of cases, this warning was utterly disregarded, and those who heeded it early in the day were looked upon as cowards, and many jeers were uttered by lips that now are cold among the rank grass beside the river.

There has grown up a bitter feeling among the surviving sufferers against those who owned the lake and dam, and damage suits will be plentiful by and by.

The dam in Stony Creek, above Johnstown, broke about noon yesterday and thousands of feet of lumber passed down the stream. It is impossible to tell what the loss of life will be, but at nine o'clock the Coroner of Westmoreland county sent a message out saying that 100 bodies had been recovered at Nineveh, halfway from here to Johnstown. Sober minded people do not hesitate to say that 1,200 is moderate.

Fire's Awful Work.

"How can anybody tell how many are dead?" said a railroad engineer this morning. "I have been at Long Hollow with my train since eleven o'clock yesterday, and I have seen fully five hundred persons lost in the flood."

J. W. Esch, a brave railroad employee, saved sixteen lives at Nineveh.

The most awful culmination of the awful night was the roasting of a hundred or more persons in mid-flood. The ruins of houses, old buildings and other structures swept against the new railroad bridge at Johnstown, and from an overturned stove or some such cause the upper part of the wreckage caught fire.

There were crowds of men, women and children on the wreck, and their screams were soon heard. They were literally roasted on the flood. Soon after the fire burned itself out other persons were thrown against the mass. There were some fifty people in sight wher the ruins suddenly broke up and were swept under the bridge into the darkness.

The latest news from Johnstown is that but two houses could be seen in the town. It is also said that only three houses remain in Cambria City.

The first authentic news was from W. N. Hays, of the Pennsylvania Railroad Company, who reached New Florence at nine o'clock. He says the valley towns are annihilated.

Destruction at Blairsville.

The flood in the Conemaugh River at this point is the heaviest eyer known here. At this hour the railroad bridge between here and Blairsville intersection has been swept away, and also the new bridge at Coketon, half a mile below. It is now feared that the iron bridge at the lower end of this town will go. A living woman and dead man, supposed to be her husband, were seen going under the railroad bridge. They were seen to come from under the bridge safely, but shortly disappeared and were seen no more.

A great many families lose their household goods. The river is running full of timber, houses, goods, etc.

The loss will be heavy. The excitement here is very great. The river is still rising. There are some families below the town in the second story of their houses who cannot get out. It is feared that if the water goes much higher the loss of life will be very great. The railroad company had fourteen cars of coal on their bridge when it went down, and all were swept down the river.

The town bridge has just succumbed to the seething floods, whose roar can be heard a long distance. The water is still rising and it is thought that the West Pennsylvania Railroad will be without a single bridge. It is reported that a man went down with the Blairsville bridge while he was adjusting a headlight.

Havoc about Altoona.

The highest and most destructive flood that has visited this place for fifty years occurred yesterday. It has been raining continuously for the past twenty-four hours. The Juniata river is ten feet above low water mark and is still rising. The lower streets of Gaysport bordering on the river bank are submerged, and the water is two feet deep on the first floors of the houses there. The water rose so rapidly that the people had to be removed from the houses in boats and wagons. Three railroad trestles and a number of bridges over the streams have been carried away, and railroad travel between this place and the surrounding towns has been interrupted.

Property of all kinds was carried off. The truck gardens and grain fields along the river were utterly destroyed, and the fences carried away. The iron furnaces and rolling mills at this place and Duncanville were compelled to shut down on account of the high water. Keene & Babcock lost 300,000 brick in the kiln ready to burn, G. W. Rhodes 350,000, and Joseph Hart 15,000. It is estimated that the flood has done over $50,000 damage in this vicinity. The fences of the Blair County Agricultural Society were destroyed.

Alarm at York.

Last night was one of great alarm here. It rained steadily all day, some of the showers being severe. The great flood of 1884 is forcibly recalled. Many families are moving out. At half-past one A. M. a general alarm was sounded on the bells of the city.

The flood in the Susquehanna River here reached its greatest height about six o'clock this morning, when all bridges save one were under water. Business places and residences in the low section were flooded to a great extent, and the damage in this city alone amounts to $25,000 so far. The injury to the Spring Grove paper mills near this city is heavy. By noon the water had fallen sufficiently to restore travel over nearly all the bridges.

A number of bridges in the county have been swept away, and the loss in the county exclusive of the city is estimated at $100,000.

In attempting to catch some driftwood James McIlvaine lost his balance and fell into the raging current and was drowned.

Seven bodies have been taken from the water and débris on the river banks at New Florence. One body has also been taken from the river at this point, that of a young girl. None of them have been identified.

The whole face of the country between here and New Florence is under water, and houses, bridges and buildings fill the fields and even perch upon the hillside all the way to Johnstown. Great flocks of crows are already filling the valley, while buzzards are almost as frequently seen. The banks of the river are lined with people who are looking as well for booty as for bodies. Much valuable property was carried away in the houses as well as from houses not washed away.

The river has fallen again into its channel, and nothing in the stream itself except its red, angry color shows the wild horror of last night. It has fallen fully twenty feet since midnight, and by to-night it will have attained its normal depth.

Painful Scenes.

At all points from Greensburg to Long Hollow, the limit of the present trouble, scores of people throng the stations begging and beseeching railroad men on the repair trains to take them aboard, as they are almost frenzied with anxiety and apprehension in regard to their friends who live at or near Johnstown. Strong men are as tearful as the women who join in the request.

Pitiable sights and scenes multiply more and more

rapidly. The Conemaugh is one great valley of mourning. Those who have not lost friends have lost their house or their substance, and apparently the grief for the one is as poignant as for the other.

They Were Warned.

The great volume of water struck Johnstown about half-past five in the afternoon. It did not find the people unprepared, as they had had notice from South Fork that the dam was threatening to go. Many, however, disregarded the notice and remained in their houses in the lower part of the city and were caught before they could get out.

Superintendent Pitcairn, of the Pennsylvania Railroad, who has spent the entire day in assisting not only those who were afflicted by the flood, but also in an attempt to reopen his road, went home this morning. Before he left he issued an order to all Pennsylvania Railroad employees to keep a sharp lookout for bodies, both in the river and in the bushes, and to return them to their friends.

Assistant Superintendent Trump is still on the ground near Lone Hollow directing the movements of gravel and construction trains, which are arriving as fast as they can be fitted up and started out. The roadbeds of both the Pennsylvania and the West Pennsylvania railroads are badly damaged, and it will cost the latter, especially from the Bolivar Junction to Saltsburg, many thousands of dollars to repair injuries to embankments alone.

44   THE JOHNSTOWN HORROR.

In Pittsburg there was but one topic of conversation, and that was the Johnstown deluge. Crowds of eager watchers all day long besieged the newspaper bulletin boards and rendered streets impassable in their vicinity. Many of them had friends or relatives in the stricken district, and "Names!" "Names!" was their cry. But there were no names. The storm which had perhaps swept away their loved ones had also carried away all means of communication and their vigil was unrewarded. It is not yet known whether the telegraph operator at Johnstown is dead or alive. The nearest point to that city which can be reached to-night is New Florence, and the one wire there is used almost constantly by orders for coffins, embalming fluid and preparing special cars to carry the recovered dead to their homes.

Along the banks of the now turbulent Allegheny were placed watchers for dead bodies, and all wreckage was carefully scanned for the dead. The result of this vigilance was the recovery of one body, that of a woman floating down on a pile of débris. Seven other bodies were seen, but could not be reached owing to the swift moving wreckage by which they were surrounded.

A Heartrending Sight.

A railroad conductor who arrived in the city this morning said:—"There is no telling how many lives are lost. We got as far as Bolivar, and I tell you it is a terrible sight. The body of a boy was picked up by some of us there, and there were eleven bodies recovered altogether. I do not think that anyone got into Johnstown, and it is my opinion that they will not get in very soon. No one who is not on the grounds has any idea of the damage done. It will be at least a week before the extent of this flood is known, and then I think many bodies will never be recovered."

Assistant Superintendent Wilson, of the West Pennsylvania Railroad, received the following despatch from Nineveh to-day:—

"There appears to be a large number of people lodged in the trees and rubbish along the line. Many are alive. Rescuing parties should be advised at every station."

Another telegram from Nineveh said that up to noon 175 bodies had been taken from the river at that point.

The stage of water in the Allegheny this afternoon became so alarming that residents living in the low-lying districts began to remove their household effects to a higher grade. The tracks of the Pittsburgh and Western Railroad are under water in several places, and great inconvenience is felt in moving trains.

Criminal Negligence.

It was stated at the office of the Pennsylvania Railroad early this morning that the deaths would run up into the thousands rather than hundreds, as was at first supposed. Despatches received state that the stream of human beings that was swept before the floods was pitiful to behold. Men, women and children were carried along frantically shrieking for help. Rescue was impossible.

Husbands were swept past their wives, and children were borne along at a terrible speed to certain death before the eyes of their terrorized and frantic parents. It was said at the depot that it was impossible to estimate the number whose lives were lost in the flood. It will simply be a matter of conjecture for several days as to who was lost and who escaped.

The people of Johnstown were warned of the possibility of the bursting of the dam during the morning, but very few if any of the inhabitants took the warning seriously. Shortly after noon it gave way about five miles above Johnstown, and sweeping everything before it burst upon the town with terrible force.

Everything was carried before it, and not an instant's time was given to seek safety. Houses were demolished, swept from their foundations and carried in the flood to a culvert near the town. Here a mass of all manner of débris soon lodged, and by evening it had dammed the water back into the city over the tops of many of the still remaining chimneys.

The Dam Always a Menace.

Assistant Superintendent Trump, of the Pennsylvania, is at Conemaugh, but the officials at the depot had not been able to receive a line from him until as late as half-past two o'clock this morning. It was said also that it will be impossible to get a train through either one way or the other for at least two or three days. This applies also to the mails, as there is absolutely no way of getting mails through.

THE JOHNSTOWN HORROR.

"We were afraid of that lake," said a gentleman who had lived in Johnstown for years, "we were afraid of that lake seven years ago. No one could see the immense height to which that artificial dam had been built without fearing the tremendous power of the water behind it. I doubt if there was a man or woman in Johnstown who at some time or other had not feared and spoken of the terrible disaster that has now come.

"People wondered and asked why the dam was not strengthened, as it certainly had become weak, but nothing was done, and by and by they talked less and less about it as nothing happened, though now and then some would shake their heads as though conscious that the fearful day would come some time when their worst fears would be transcended by the horror of the actual occurrence.

Converted Into a Lake.

"Johnstown is in a hollow between two rivers, and that lake must have swept over the city at a depth of forty feet. It cannot be, it is impossible that such an awful thing could happen to a city of ten thousand inhabitants, and if it has, thousands have lost their lives, and men are to blame for it, for warnings have been uttered a thousand times and have received no attention."

The body of a Welsh woman, sixty years of age, was taken from the river near the suspension bridge, at ten o'clock this morning. Four other bodies were seen, but owing to the mass of wreckage which is coming down they could not be recovered, and passed down the Ohio River.

A citizens' meeting has been called to devise means to aid the sufferers. The Pennsylvania Railroad officials have already placed cars on Liberty street for the purpose of receiving provisions and clothing, and up to this hour many prominent merchants have made heavy donations.

Anxiety of the People.

The difficulty of obtaining definite information added tremendously to the excitement and apprehension of the people in Pittsburgh who had relatives and friends at the scene of the disaster.

Members of the South Fork Club, and among them some of the most eminent men in the Pittsburgh financial and mercantile world, were in or near Johnstown, and several of them were accompanied by their wives and families. There happened to be also quite a number of residents of Johnstown in Pittsburgh, and when the news of the horror was confirmed and the railroads bulletined the fact that no trains would go east last night the scene at Union Depot was profoundly pathetic and exciting. But two trains were sent out by the Pennsylvania road from the Union station at Pittsburgh.

A despatch states that the Cambria Iron Company's plant on the north side of the Conemaugh River at Johnstown is a complete wreck. Until this despatch was received it was not thought that this portion of the plant had been seriously injured. It was known

THE JOHNSTOWN HORROR. 49

that the portion of the plant located on the south bank of the river was washed away, and this was thought to be the extent of the damage to the property of that immense corporation. The plant is said to be valued at $5,000,000.

CHAPTER II.

Death and Desolation.

The terrible situation on the second day after the great disaster only intensifies the horror. As information becomes more full and accurate, it does not abate one tittle of the awful havoc. Rather it adds to it, and gives a thousand-fold terror to the dreadful calamity.

Not only do the scenes which are described appear all the more dreadful, as is natural, the nearer they are brought to the imagination, but it seems only too probable that the final reckoning in loss of life and material wealth will prove far more stupendous than has even yet been supposed.

The very greatness of the destruction prevents the possibility of an accurate estimate. Beneath the ghastly ruins of the once happy towns and villages along the pathway of the deluge, who shall say how many victims lie buried? Amid the rocks and woods that border the broad track of the waters, who shall say how many lie bruised and mangled and unrecognizable, wedged between boulders or massed amid débris and rubbish, or hidden beneath the heaped-up deposits of earth, and whether all of them shall ever be found and given the last touching rites?

Already the air of the little valley, which four days ago was smiling with all the health of nature and the contentment of industrious man, is waxing pestiferous with the awful odor of decaying human bodies. Buzzards, invited by their disgusting instinct, gather for a promised feast, and sit and glower on neighboring perches or else circle round and round in the blue empyrean over the location of unfriended corpses, known only to their keen sense of smell or vision.

But another kind of buzzard, more disgusting, more hideous, more vile, has hastened to this scene of woe and anguish and desolation to exult over it to his profit. Thugs and thieves in unclean hordes have mysteriously turned up at Johnstown and its vicinity, as hyenas in the desert seem to spring bodily out of the deadly sand whenever the corpse of a gallant warrior, abandoned by his kind, lies putrefying in the night.

There is a cry from the afflicted community for the policing of the devastated region, and there is no doubt it is greatly needed. Happily, Nemesis does not sleep this time in the face of such provocation as is given her by these atrociously inhuman human beings. It is a satisfaction to record that something more than a half dozen of them have been dealt with as promptly and as mercilessly as they deserve. For such as they there should be no code of pity.

There is an inexhaustible store of pathos and heroism in the tale of this disaster. Of course, in all of its awful details it never can be fitly written. One reason is that too many of the witnesses of its more fearful phases "sleep the sleep that knows not waking."

But there is a greater reason, and that is that there is a point in the intenser actuality of things at which all human language fails to do justice to it. Yet—as simply told as possible—there are many incidents of this great tragedy which nothing has ever surpassed or ever can surpass in impressiveness. It is a consolation, too, that human nature at such times does betray here and there a gleam of that side of it which gives forth a reflection of the ideal manhood or womanhood. Bits of heroism and of tender devotedness scattered throughout this dark, dismal picture of destruction and despair light it up with wonderful beauty, and while they bring tears to the eyes of the sternest reader, will serve as a grateful relief from the pervading hue of horror and blackness.

There is the very gravest need of vigorous relief measures in favor of the survivors of the flood. A spontaneous movement in that direction has been begun, but as yet lacks the efficiency only to be derived from a general and organized co-operation.

Complete Annihilation.

When Superintendent Pitcairn telegraphed from Johnstown to Pittsburgh Friday night that the town was annihilated he came very close to the facts of the case, although he had not seen the ill-fated city. To say that Johnstown is a wreck is but stating the facts of the case. Nothing like it was ever seen in this country. Where long rows of dwelling houses and business blocks stood forty-eight hours ago, ruin and desolation now reign supreme.

The losses, however, are as nothing compared to the frightful sacrifices of precious human lives. During Sunday Johnstown has been drenched with the tears of stricken mortals, and the air is filled with sobs that come from breaking hearts. There are scenes enacted here every hour and every minute that affect all beholders profoundly. When brave men die in battle, for country or for principle, their loss can be reconciled to the stern destinies of life. When homes are torn asunder in an instant, and the loved ones hurled from the arms of loving and devoted mothers, there is an element of sadness connected with the tragedy that touches every heart.

The loss of life is simply dreadful. The most conservative people declare that the number will reach 5000, while others confidently assert that 8000 or 10,000 have perished.

How Johnstown Looks after Flood and Fire Have Done Their Worst.

An eye-witness writing from Pittsburgh says:—We have just returned from a trip through what is left of Johnstown. The view from beyond is almost impossible to describe. To look upon it is a sight that neither war nor catastrophe can equal. House is piled upon house, not as we have seen in occasional floods of the the Western rivers, but the remains of two and four storied buildings piled upon the top of one another.

The ruins of what is known as the Club House are in perhaps the best condition of any in that portion of the town, but it is certainly damaged beyond possibility of repair. *On the upper floor five bodies are lying unidentified.* One of them, a woman of genteel birth, judging by her dress, is locked in one of the small rooms to prevent a possibility of spoiliation by wreckers, who are flocking to the spot from all directions and taking possession of everything they can get hold of

Here and there bodies can be seen sticking in the ruins. Some of the most prominent citizens are to be seen working with might and main to get at the remains of relatives whom they have located.

There is no doubt that, wild as the estimates of the loss of life and damage to property have been, it is even larger than there is any idea of.

Close on to 2,000 residences lie in kindling wood at the lower end of the town.

Freaks of the Flood.

An idea of the eccentricity of the flood may be gathered from the fact that houses that were situated at Woodvale and points above Johnstown are piled at the lower end of the town, while some massive houses have been lifted and carried from the lower end as far as the cemetery at the extreme upper portion of the town. All through the ruins are scattered the most costly furniture and store goods of all kinds.

Thieves are Busy.

I stood on the keyboard and strings of a piano while I watched a number of thieves break into the remnants of houses and pilfer them, while others again had got at a supply of fine groceries and had

THE JOHNSTOWN HORROR. 55

broken into a barrel of fine brandy, and were fairly steeping themselves in it. I met quite a number of Pittsburghers in the ruins looking for friends and relatives. If the skiffs which were expected from Pittsburgh were there they would be of vast assistance in reaching the ruins, which are separated by the stream of water descending from the hills. A great fear is felt that there will be some difficulty in restoring the stream to its proper channel. Its course now lies right along Main street, and it is about two hundred yards wide.

Something should be done to get the bodies of the dead decently taken care of. The ruins are reeking with the smell of decaying bodies. Right at the edge of the ruins the decaying body of a stout colored woman is lying like the remains of an animal, without any one to identify and take care of it.

Lynching the Ghouls.

A number of Hungarians collected about a number of bodies at Cambria which had been washed up and began rifling the trunks. After they had secured all the contents they turned their attention to the dead.

The ghastly spectacle presented by the distorted features of those who had lost their lives during the flood had no influence upon the ghouls, who acted more like wild beasts than human beings. They took every article from the clothing on the dead bodies, not leaving anything of value or anything that would serve to identify the remains.

After the miscreants had removed all their plunder

to dry ground a dispute arose over a division of the spoils. A pitched battle followed and for a time the situation was alarming. Knives and clubs were used freely. As a result several of the combatants were seriously wounded and left on the ground, their fellow countrymen not making any attempt to remove them from the field of strife.

JOHNSTOWN, PA., June 2, 11 A. M.
They have just hung a man over near the railroad to the telegraph pole for cutting the finger off of a dead woman in order to get a ring.

Vengeance, Swift and Sure.

The way of the transgressor in the desolated valley of the Conemaugh is hard indeed. Each hour reveals some new and horrible story of suffering and outrage, and every succeeding hour brings news of swift and merited punishment meted out to the fiends who have dared to desecrate the stiff and mangled corpses in the city of the dead, and torture the already half crazed victims of the cruelest of modern catastrophes.

As the roads to the lands round about are opened tales of almost indescribable horror come to light, and deeds of the vilest nature, perpetrated in the darkness of the night, are brought to light.

Followed by Avenging Farmers.

Just as the shadows began to fall upon the earth last evening a party of thirteen Hungarians were noticed stealthily picking their way along the banks of the Conemaugh toward Sang Hollow. Suspicious of their purpose, several farmers armed themselves and started in pursuit. Soon their most horrible fears were realized. The Hungarians were out for plunder.

Lying upon the shore they came upon the dead and mangled body of a woman upon whose person there were a number of trinkets and jewelry and two diamond rings. In their eagerness to secure the plunder, the Hungarians got into a squabble, during which one of the number severed the finger upon which were the rings, and started on a run with his fearful prize. The revolting nature of the deed so wrought upon the pursuing farmers, who by this time were close at hand, that they gave immediate chase. Some of the Hungarians showed fight, but being outnumbered were compelled to flee for their lives. Nine of the brutes escaped, but four were literally driven into the surging river and to their death. The inhuman monster whose atrocious act has been described was among the number of the involuntary suicides. Another incident of even greater moment has just been brought to notice.

Anxious to be a Murderer.

At half-past eight this morning an old railroader who had walked from Sang Hollow stepped up to a number of men who were congregated on the platform stations at Curranville and said:—"Gentlemen, had I a shotgun with me half an hour ago I would now be a murderer, yet with no fear of ever having to suffer for my crime.

"Two miles below here I watched three men going along the banks *stealing the jewels from the bodies of the dead wives and daughters of men who have been robbed of all they held dear on earth."*

He had no sooner finished the last sentence than five burly men, with looks of terrible determination written on their faces, were on their way to the scene of plunder, one with a coil of rope over his shoulder and another with a revolver in his hand. In twenty minutes, so it is stated, they had overtaken two of the wretches, who were then in the act of cutting pieces from the ears and fingers from the hands of the bodies of two dead women.

Brutes at Bay.

With revolver levelled at the scoundrels the leader of the posse shouted, "Throw up your hands or I'll blow your heads off!" With blanched faces and trembling forms they obeyed the order and begged for mercy. They were searched, and as their pockets were emptied of their ghastly finds the indignation of the crowd intensified, and when *a bloody finger of an infant, encircled with two tiny gold rings*, was found among the plunder in the leader's pocket, a cry went up "*Lynch them! Lynch them!*" *Without a moment's delay ropes were thrown around their necks and they were dangling to the limbs of a tree, in the branches of which an hour before were entangled the bodies of a dead father and son.*

After the expiration of a half hour the ropes were cut, and the bodies lowered and carried to a pile of rocks in the forest on the hill above. It is hinted that an Allegheny county official was one of the most prominent actors in this justifiable homicide.

Another case of attempted lynching was witnessed this evening near Kernville. The man was observed stealing valuable articles from the houses. He was seized by a mob, a rope was placed around his neck and he was jerked up into the air. The rope was tied to the tree and his would-be lynchers left him. Bystanders cut him down before he was dead. The other men did not interfere and he was allowed to go. The man was so badly scared that he could not give his name if he wanted to do so.

Two colored men were shot while robbing the dead bodies, by the Pittsburgh police, who are doing guard about the town.

Fiends in Human Form.

To one who saw bright, bustling Johnstown a week ago the sight of its present condition must cause a thrill of horror, no matter how callous he might be. I doubt if any incident of war or flood ever caused a more sickening sight. Wretchedness of the most pathetic kind met the gaze on every side.

Unlawfulness runs riot. If ever military aid was needed now is the time. *The town is perfectly overrun with thieves,* many of them from Pittsburgh. The Hungarians are the worst. They seem to operate in regular organized bands. In Cambria City this morning they entered a house, drove out the occupants at the point of revolvers and took possession. They can be constantly seen carrying large quantities of plunder to the hills.

The number of drunken men is remarkable. Whiskey seems marvelously plenty. Men are actually carrying it around in pails. Barrels of the stuff are constantly located among the drifts, and men are scrambling over each other and fighting like wild beasts in their mad search for it.

At the cemetery, at the upper end of the town, I saw a sight that rivals the inferno. A number of ghouls had found a lot of fine groceries, among them a barrel of brandy, with which they were fairly stuffing themselves. One huge fellow was standing on the strings of an upright piano singing a profane song, every little while breaking into a wild dance. A half dozen others were engaged in a hand-to-hand fight over the possession of some treasure stolen from a ruined house, and the crowd around the barrel were yelling like wild men.

The cry for help increases every hour. Something must be done to get the bodies decently taken care of. The ruins are reeking with the smell of decaying bodies. At the very edge of the ruins the body of a large colored woman, in an advanced state of decomposition, is lying like the body of an animal.

Watched Their Friends Die.

The fire in the drift above the bridge is still burning fiercely and will continue to do so for several days. The skulls of six people can be seen sticking up out of the ruins just above the east end of the bridge. Nothing but the blackened skulls can be seen. They are all together.

The sad scenes will never all be written. One lady

told me this morning of seeing her mother crushed to pieces just before her eyes and the mangled body carried off down the stream. William Yarner lost six children and saved a baby about eighteen months old. His wife died just three weeks ago. An aged German, his wife and five daughters floated down on their house to a point below Nineveh, where the house was wrecked. The five daughters were drowned, but the old man and his wife stuck in a tree and hung there for twenty-four hours before they could be taken off.

Died Kissing Her Babe.

One of the most pitiful sights of this terrible disaster came to my notice this afternoon, when the body of a young lady was taken out of the Conemaugh River. The woman was apparently quite young, though her features were terribly disfigured. Nearly all the clothing except the shoes was torn off the body. The corpse was that of a mother, for although cold in death the woman clasped a young male babe apparently not more than a year old tightly in her arms. The little one was huddled close up to its mother's face, who when she realized their terrible fate, had evidently raised the babe to her lips to imprint upon its little lips the last motherly kiss it was to receive in this world. The sight was a pathetic one and turned many a stout heart to tears.

Among the miraculous escapes to be recorded in connection with the great disaster is that of George J. Leas and his family. He resided on Iron street. When the rush of water came there were eight people on the roof. The little house swung around off its moorings and floated about for nearly half an hour before it came up against the bank of drift above the stone bridge. A three-year-old girl with sunny golden hair and dimpled cheeks prayed all the while that God would save them, and it seemed that God really answered the prayer of this innocent little girl and directed the house against the drift, enabling every one of the eight to get off. Mrs. Leas carried the little girl in her arms, and how she got off she doesn't know. Every house around them, she said, was crushed, and the people either killed or drowned.

Thugs at Their Work.

One of the most dreadful features of this catastrophe has been the miserable weakness displayed by the authorities of Johnstown and the surrounding boroughs. Johnstown needed them sadly for forty-eight hours. There is supposed to be a Burgess, but like most burgesses he is a shadowy and mythical personage. If there had been concerted and intelligent action the fire in the débris at the dam could have been extinguished within a short time after it started. Too many cooks spoiled this ghastly broth.

Even now if dynamite or some other explosive was intelligently applied the huge mass of wreckage which has up to the present time escaped the flame, and no doubt contains a number of bodies, could be saved from fire.

This, however, is a matter of small import compared with the immunity granted the outrageous and open graveyard robbery and disgusting thievery which have thriven bravely since Friday morning.

Foreigners and natives carrying huge sacks, and in some instances even being assisted by horses and carts, have been busily engaged hunting corpses and stealing such valuables as were to be found in the wreckage.

Dozens of barrels of strong liquor have been rescued by the Hungarian and Polish laborers from among the ruins of saloons and hotels and the contents of the same have been freely indulged in. This has led to an alarming debauchery, which is on the increase. All day the numbers of the drunken crowd have been augmented from time to time by fresh arrivals from the surrounding districts.

Those who have suffered from the tidal wave have become much embittered against the law breakers. There have been many small fights and several small riots in consequence. This has been regarded with apprehension by the State authorities, and Adjutant General Hastings has arrived at Johnstown to examine into the condition of affairs and to guard the desolated district with troops. The Eighteenth regiment, of Pittsburgh, has tendered its services to this work, but has received no reply to its tender.

General Hastings estimates that the loss of life is at least eight thousand.

An employee of J. L. Gill, of Latrobe, says he and thirty-five other men were in a three-story building in Johnstown last night. They had been getting out logs for the Johnstown Lumber Company. The man says that the building was swept away and all the men were drowned except Gill and his family.

Handling the Dead.

The recovery of bodies has taken up the time of thousands all day. The theory now is that most of those killed by the torrent were buried beneath the débris. To-day's work in the ruins in a large degree justifies this assumption. I saw six bodies taken out of one pile of rubbish not eight feet square.

The truth is that bodies are almost as plentiful as logs. The whirl of the waters puts the bodies under and the logs and boards on top. The rigidity of arms standing out at right angles to the bloated and bruised bodies show that death in ninety-nine out of a hundred cases took place amid the ruins—that is after the wreck of houses had closed over them.

Dr. D. G. Foster, who has been here all day, is of the opinion that most of the victims were killed by coming into violent contact with objects in the river and not by drowning. He found many fractured skulls and on most heads blows that would have rendered those receiving them instantly unconscious, and the water did the rest.

Not fewer than three hundred bodies have been taken from the river and rubbish to-day. It has been the labor of all classes of citizens, and marvellous work has been accomplished. The eastern end of Main street, through which the waters tore most madly and destructively, and in which they left their legacy of wrecked houses, fallen trees and dead bodies in a greater degree than in any other portion of the city, has been cleared and the remains of over fifty have been taken out.

All over town the searchers have been equally successful. As soon as a body is found it is placed on a litter and sent to the Morgue, where it is washed and

INTERIOR OF THE MORGUE.

placed on a board for several hours to await identification.

The Morgue is the Fourth-ward school house, and it has been surrounded all day by a crowd of several thousand people. At first the crowd were disposed to stop those bearing the stretchers, uncover the remains and view them, but this was found to be prolific not only of great delay, also scenes of agony that not even the bearers could endure.

Now a litter is guarded by a file of soldiers with fixed bayonets, and the people are forced aside until the Morgue is reached. It is astonishing to find how small a number of injured are in the city. Few survived. It was death or nothing with the demon of the flood.

Now that an adequate idea of what has befallen them has been reached, and the fact that a living has still to be made, that plants must be taken care of, that contracts must be filled, the business people of the city are giving their attention to the future. Vice President and Director James McMillan, of the Cambria Iron Company, says their loss has been well nigh incalculable. They are not daunted, but will to-morrow begin the work of clearing up the ruins of their mills preparatory to rebuilding and repairing their works. They will also immediately rebuild the Gautier Iron Works. This is the disposition of all.

"Our pockets are light," they say, "but if nothing happens all of us will be in business again." The central portion of Johnstown is as completely obliterated as if it had never had foundation. The river has made its bed upon the sites of hundreds of dwellings, and a vast area of sand, mud and gravel marks the old channel.

It is doubtful whether it will be possible even to reclaim what was once the business portion of the city. The river will have to be returned to its old bed in order to do this.

Among the lost is H. G. Rose, the District Attorney of Cambria county, whose body was among the first discovered.

Governor Foraker, of Ohio, this afternoon sent five hundred tents to this city. They will be pitched on the hillside to-morrow. They are sadly needed, as the buildings that are left are either too damp or too unsafe for occupancy.

Burying the Dead.

The work of burying the dead began this morning and has been kept up till late this evening. The bruising of the bodies by logs and trees and other débris and other exposure in the water have tended to hasten decomposition, which has set in in scores of cases, making interment instantly necessary.

Bodies are being buried as rapidly as they are identified. The work of Pittsburgh undertakers in examining the dead has rendered it possible to keep all those embalmed two or three days longer, but this is desirable only in cases where identification is dubious and no claimants appear at all.

To-day the cars sent out from Pittsburgh with provisions for the living were hastily cleared in order to contain the bodies of the dead intended for interment in suburban cemeteries and in graveyards handy to the city.

Formality is dispensed with. In some instances only the undertaker and his assistants are present, and in others only one or two members of the family of the dead.

The dead are more plentiful than the mourners.

Death has certainly dealt briefly with the stricken city. "Let the dead bury the dead" has been more nearly exemplified in this instance than in any other in this country's history. The magnitude of the horror increases with the hours. It is believed that not less than two thousand of the drowned found lodgment beneath the *omnium gatherum* in the triangle of ground that the Conemaugh cut out of the bank between the river and the Pennsylvania Railroad bridge.

The Greatest Funeral Pyre in History.

The victims were not upon it, but were parts of it. Whole houses were washed into the apex of the triangle. Hen coops, pigstys and stables were added to the mass. Then a stove ignited the mass and the work of cremation began. It was a literal breast of fire. The smoke arose in a huge funnel-shaped cloud, and at times it changed to the form of an hour glass. At night the flames united would light up this misty remnant of mortality. The effect upon the living, both ignorant and intelligent, was the same. That volume of smoke with its dual form, produced a feeling of awe in many that was superior in most cases to that felt in the awful moment of the storm's wrath on Friday.

Hundreds stood for hours regarding the smoke and wondering whether it foreboded another visitation more dire than its predecessor.

The people hereabouts this morning awoke to find that nothing was left but a mass of ashes, calcined human bones, stoves, old iron and other approximately indestructible matter, from which only a light blue vapor was arising. General Hastings took precautions to prevent the extension of the fire to another huge pile, a short distance away, and this will be rummaged to-day for bodies of flood victims.

The Pittsburgh undertakers have contributed more to facilitate the preparation of the dead for the graves than all others besides.

There was a disposition on the part of many foreigners and negroes to raid the houses, and do an all around thieving business, but the measures adopted by the police had a tendency to frighten them off in nearly every case.

One man was caught in the act of robbing the body of an old woman, but he protested that he had got nothing and was released. He immediately disappeared, and it was found afterward that he had taken $100 from the pocket of the corpse.

A half-breed negro yesterday and this morning was doing a thriving business in collecting hams, shoulders, chickens and even furniture. He had thieves in his employ, and while to some of them he was paying regular salaries, others were doing the work for a drink of whiskey. The authorities stopped this thing very suddenly, but not until a number of the people threatened to lynch the half breed. In one or two instance very narrow escapes from the rope were made.

Thousands of coffins and rough boxes have already arrived, and still the supply is short. They are brought in marked to some undertaker, who has a list of his dead, and as fast as the coffins come he writes the name of its intended tenant and tells the friends (when there are any) where to find it.

How a Funeral Takes Place.

Two of them go after it, and, carrying it between them to the Morgue or to their homes, place the body in it and take it to the burial grounds.

One unfortunate feature of the destruction is the fact that some one has been drowned from nearly every house in the city, and teams are procurable only with the greatest difficulty.

Dead horses are seen everywhere. In one stable two horses, fully harnessed, bridled and ready to be taken out, stand dead in their stable, stiff and upright. In a sand pile near the Pennsylvania Railroad depot a horse's hind feet, rump and tail are all that can be seen of him. He was caught in the rapidly running waters and had been driven into the sand.

The following telegram from Johnstown has been received at Pittsburg:

"For God's sake tell the sight-seers to keep away from Johnstown for the present. What we want is people to work, not to look on. "Citizen's Committe."

Three trains have already been sent out with crowded cargoes of sight-seers. At every station along the road excited crowds are waiting for an opportunity to get aboard.

That's what would have happened to the owners of South Fork if they had put in an appearance.

There is great indignation among the people of Johnstown at the wealthy Pittsburghers who own South Fork. They blame them severely for having maintained such a frightfully dangerous institution there. The feeling among the people was intense. If any of the owners of the dam had put in an appearance in Johnstown they would have been lynched.

The dam has been a constant menace to this valley ever since it has been in existence, and the feeling, which has been bitter enough on the occasion of every flood hitherto, after this horrible disaster is now at fever heat.

Without seeing the havoc created no idea can be given of the area of the desolation or the extent of the damage.

Only One Left to Mourn.

An utterly wretched woman stood by a muddy pool of water, trying to find some trace of a once happy home. She was half crazed with grief, and her eyes were red and swollen. As I stepped to her side she raised her pale and haggard face, crying:

"They are all gone. Oh God be merciful to them. My husband and my seven dear little children have been swept down with the flood and I am left alone. We were driven by the raging flood into the garret, but the waters followed us there. Inch by inch it kept rising until our heads were crushing against the roof. It was death to remain. So I raised a window and one by one placed my darlings on some drift wood, trusting to the Great Creator. As I liberated the last one, my sweet little boy, he looked at me and said:

"'Mamma, you always told me that the Lord would care for me; will he look after me now?'"

"I saw him drift away with his loving face turned toward me, and with a prayer on my lips for his deliverance he passed from sight forever. The next moment the roof crashed in and I floated outside to be rescued fifteen hours later from the roof of a house in Kernville. If I could only find one of my darlings, I could bow to the will of God, but they all are gone. I have lost everything on earth now but my life, and I will return to my old Virginia home and lay me down for my last great sleep."

A handsome woman, with hair as black as a raven's wing, walked through the depot, where a dozen or more bodies were awaiting burial. Passing from one to another, she finally lifted the paper covering from the face of a woman, young and with traces of beauty showing through the stains of muddy water. With a cry of anguish she reeled backward, to be caught by a rugged man who chanced to be passing. In a moment or so she had calmed herself sufficiently to take one more look at the features of her dead. She stood gazing at the unfortunate as if dumb. Finally turning away with another wild burst of grief she said:—

"And her beautiful hair all matted and her sweet face bruised and stained with mud and water."

THE JOHNSTOWN HORROR. 73

The dead woman was the sister of the mourner. The body was placed in a coffin a few minutes later and sent away to its narrow house.

These incidents are but fair samples of the scenes familiar to every turn in this stricken city.

THE AWFUL RUSH OF WATERS.

CHAPTER III.

The Horror Increases.

During the night thirty-three bodies were brought to one house. As yet the relief force is not perfectly organized and bodies are lying around on boards and doors. Within twenty feet of where this was written the dead body of a colored woman lies.

Provision has been made by the Relief Committee for the sufferers to send despatches to all parts of the country. The railroad company has a track through to the bridge. The first train arrived about half-past nine o'clock this morning. A man in a frail craft got caught in the rapids at the railroad bridge, and it looked as if he would increase the already terrible list of dead, but fortunately he caught on a rock, where he now is and is liable to remain all day.

The question on every person's lips is—Will the Cambria Iron Company rebuild? The wire mill is completely wrecked, but the walls of the rolling mill are still standing. If they do not resume it is a question whether the town will be rebuilt. The Hungarians were beginning to pillage the houses, and the arrival of police was most timely. Word had just been received that all the men employed by Peabody, the Pittsburgh contractor, have been saved.

The worst part of this disaster has not been told. Indeed, the most graphic description that can be written will not tell half the tale. No pen can describe nor tongue tell the vastness of this devastation.

I walked over the greater part of the wrecked town this morning, and one could not have pictured such a wreck, nor could one have imagined that an entire town of this size could be so completely swept away.

A. J. Haws, one of the prominent men of the town, was standing on the hillside this morning, taking a view of the wreck. He said:

"I never saw anything like this, nor do I believe any one else ever did. No idea can be had of the tremendous loss of property here. It amounts up into the millions. I am going to leave the place. I never will build here."

I heard the superintendents and managers of the Cambria Iron Works saying they doubted if the works will be rebuilt. This would mean the death blow to the place. Mr. Stackhouse, first vice-president of the iron works, is expected here to-day. Nothing can be done until a meeting of the company is held.

Preparations for Burial.

Adjutant General Hastings, who is in charge of the relief corps at the railroad station, has a force of carpenters at work making rough boxes in which to bury the dead. They will be buried on the hill, just above the town, on ground belonging to the Cambria Iron Company. The graves will be numbered. No one will be buried that has not been identified without a careful description being taken. General Hastings drove fifty-eight miles across the country in order to get here, and as soon as he came took charge. He has the whole town organized, and in connection with

PREPARATIONS FOR BURIAL.

L. S. Smith has commenced the building of bridges and clearing away the wrecks to get out the dead bodies.

General Hastings has a large force of men clearing private tracks of the Cambria Iron Company in order that the small engines can be put to work bringing up the dead that have been dragged out of the river at points below.

The bodies are being brought up and laid out in freight cars. Mr. Kittle, of Ebensburg, has been deputized to take charge of the valuables taken from the bodies and keep a registry of them, and also to note any marks of identification that may be found. A number of the bodies have been stripped of rings or bracelets and other valuables.

Over six hundred corpses have now been taken out on the south side of Stony Creek, the greater portion of which have been identified.

Send Us Coffins.

Preparations for their burial are being carried on as rapidly as possible, and "coffins, coffins," is the cry. No word has been received anywhere of any being shipped. Even rough boxes will be gladly received. Those that are being made, and in which many of the bodies are being buried, are of rough unplaned boards. One hundred dead bodies are laid out at the soap factory, while two hundred or more people are gathered there that are in great distress. Boats are wanted. People have the greatest difficulty in getting to the town.

Struggling for Order.

Another account from Johnstown on the second day after the disaster says:

The situation here has not changed, and yesterday's estimates of the loss of life do not seem to be exaggerated. Six hundred bodies are now lying in Johnstown, and a large number have already been buried. Four immense relief trains arrived last night, and the survivors are being well cared for.

Adjutant General Hastings, assisted by Mayor Sanger, has taken command at Johnstown and vicinity. Nothing is legal unless it bears the signature of the former. The town itself is guarded by Company H, Sixth regiment, Lieutenant Leggett in command. New members were sworn in by him, and they are making excellent soldiers.

Special police are numerous, and the regulations are so strict that even the smoking of a cigar is prohibited. General Hastings expresses the opinion that more troops are necessary.

Mr. Alex. Hart is in charge of the special police. He has lost his wife and family. Notwithstanding his great misfortune he is doing the work of a Hercules in his own way.

Firemen and Soldiers Arriving.

Chief Evans, of the Pittsburgh Fire Department, arrived this evening with engines and several hose carts, with a full complement of men. A large number of Pittsburgh physicians came on the same train.

A squad of Battery B, under command of Lieutenant Brown, the forerunners of the whole battery, arrived at the improvised telegraph office at half-past six o'clock. Lieutenant Brown went at once to Adjutant General Hastings and reported for duty.

A portion of the police force of Pittsburgh and Alleghany are on duty, and better order is maintained than prevailed yesterday. Communication has been restored between Cambria City and Johnstown by a foot bridge.

The work of repairing the tracks between Sang Hollow and Johnstown is going on rapidly, and trains will probably be running by to-morrow morning. Not less than fifteen thousand strangers are here.

The unruly element has been put down and order is now perfect. The Citizen's Committee are in charge and have matters well organized.

A proclamation has just been issued that all men who are able to work must report for work or leave the place. "We have too much to do to support idlers," says the Citizen's Committee, "And will not abuse the generous help that is being sent by doing so." From to-morrow all will be at work.

Money now is greatly needed to meet the heavy pay rolls that will be incurred for the next two weeks. W. C. Lewis, Chairman of the Finance Committee, is ready to receive the same.

Fall of the Wall of Water.

Mr. Crouse, proprietor of the South Fork Fishing Club Hotel, came to Johnstown this afternoon. He says:—

"When the dam of Conemaugh Lake broke the water seemed to leap, scarcely touching the ground. It bounded down the valley, crashing and roaring, carrying everything before it. For a mile its front seemed like a solid wall twenty feet high."

Freight Agent Dechert, when the great wall that

held the body of water began to crumble at the top sent a message begging the people of Johnstown for God's sake to take to the hills. He reports no serious accidents at South Fork.

Richard Davis ran to Prospect Hill when the water raised. As to Mr. Dechert's message, he says just such have been sent down at each flood since the lake was made. The warning so often proved useless that little attention was paid to it this time. "I cannot describe the mad rush," he said. "At first it looked like dust. That must have been the spray. I could see houses going down before it like a child's play blocks set on edge in a row. As it came nearer I could see houses totter for a moment, then rise and the next moment be crushed like egg shells against each other."

To Rise Phœnix-like.

James McMillin, vice-president of the Cambria Iron Works, was met this afternoon. In a conversation he said:

"I do not know what our loss is. I cannot even estimate, as I have not the faintest idea what it may be. The upper mill is totally wrecked—damaged beyond all possibility of repairs. The lower mill is damaged to such an extent that all machinery and buildings are useless.

"The mills will be rebuilt immediately. I have sent out orders that all men that can must report at the mill to-morrow to commence cleaning up. I do not think the building was insured against a flood. The great thing we want is to get the mill in operation again."

THE BRIDGE, WHERE A THOUSAND HOUSES, JAMBED TOGETHER, CAUGHT FIRE.

THE VALLEY OF DEATH.

A MOTHER AND CHILD PERISH TOGETHER.

ONLY A MINUTE'S WARNING.

ALL PERISHED IN THE FLOOD.

WRECK OF THE CHICAGO LIMITED EXPRESS.

SWEPT AWAY BY THE TORRENT.

LYNCHING AND DROWNING THIEVES.

DISTRIBUTING SUPPLIES TO THE DESTITUTE.

A CRAZED SOLDIER COMMITS SUICIDE.

MADE ORPHANS BY THE FLOOD.

A FATHER'S DESPAIR AT THE LOSS OF HIS FAMILY.

VALLEY OF THE CONEMAUGH NEAR JOHNSTOWN.

MEETING OF FRIENDS AND RELATIVES AFTER THE FLOOD.

MOTHER AND BABE CAST UP BY THE WATERS.

RELIEF FOR JOHNSTOWN—PENNSYLVANIA RAILROAD STATION, PHILADELPHIA.

THE MILITIA AT REST.

The Gautier Wire Works was completely destroyed. The buildings will be immediately rebuilt and put in operation as soon as possible. The loss at this point is complete. The land on which it stood is to-day as barren and desolate as if it were in the midst of the Sahara Desert.

The Cambria Iron Company loses its great supply stores. The damage to the stock alone will amount to $50,000.

The building was valued at $150,000, and is a total loss. The company offices which adjoins the store was a handsome structure. It was protected by the first building, but nevertheless is almost totally destroyed.

The Dartmouth Club, at which employees of the works boarded, was carried away in the flood. It contained many occupants at the time. None were saved.

Estimates of the losses of the Cambria Iron Company given are from $2,000,000 to $2,500,000. But little of this can be recovered.

History of the Works.

The Cambria Iron Works at Johnstown were built in 1853. It was the second largest plant of its kind in the country, and was completely swept away. Its capacity of finished steel per annum was 180,000 net tons of steel rails and 20,000 net tons of steel in other shapes. The mill turned out steel rails, spike bars, angles, flats, rounds, axles, billets and wire rods. There were nine Siemens and forty-two reverbatory heating furnaces, one seven ton and two 6,000 pound hammers and three trains of rolls.

The Bessemer Steel Works made their first blow July 10, 1871, and they contained nine gross ton converters, with an annual capacity of 200,000 net tons of ingots. In 1878 two fifteen gross tons Siemens open-hearth steel furnaces were built, with an annual capacity of 20,000 net tons of ingots.

The Cambria Iron Company also owns the Gautier Steel Works at Johnstown, which were erected in 1878.

The rolling mill produced annually 30,000 net tons of merchant bar steel of every size and for every purpose. The wire mill had a capacity alone of 30,000 tons of fence wire.

There are numerous bituminous coal mines near Johnstown, operated by the Cambria Iron Company, the Euclid Coal Company and private persons. There were three woolen mills, employing over three hundred hands and producing an annual product valued at $300,000.

Awful Work of the Flames.

Fifty acres of town swept clean. One thousand two hundred buildings destroyed. Eight thousand to ten thousand lives lost.

That is the record of the Johnstown calamity as it looked to me just before dark last night. Acres of the town were turned into cemeteries, and miles of the river bank were involuntary storage rooms for household goods.

From the half ruined parapet at the end of the stone railroad bridge, in Johnstown proper, one sees sights so gruesome that none but the soulless Hungarian and Italian laborers can command his emotions.

At my right is a fiery pit that is now believed to have been the funeral pyre of almost a thousand persons.

Streets Obliterated.

The fiercest rush of the current was straight across the lower, level part of Johnstown, where it entirely obliterated Cinder, Washington, Market, Main and Walnut streets. These streets were from a half to three-quarters of a mile in length, and were closely crowded along their entire course with dwellings and other buildings, and there is now no more trace of streets or houses than there is at low tide on the beach at Far Rockaway.

In the once well populated boroughs of Conemaugh and Woodvale there are to-night literally but two buildings left, one the shell of the Woodvale Woolen Mill and the other a sturdy brick dwelling.

The buildings which were swept from twenty out of the thirty acres of devastated Johnstown were crowded against the lower end of the big stone bridge in a mass 200 yards wide, 500 yards broad and from 60 to 100 feet deep. They were crushed and split out of shape and packed together like playing cards.

When you realize that in nearly every one of these buildings there were at least one human being, while in some there were as many as seventy-five, it is easy to comprehend how awful it was when this mass began to burn fiercely last night. It was known that a large number of persons were imprisoned in the débris, for they could be plainly seen by those on shore, but it was not until people stopped to think and to ask themselves questions, which startled them in a ghastly way, that the fact became plain that instead of a pitiful hundred or two of victims at least a thousand were in that roaring, crackling, loathsome, blazing mass upon the surface of the water and in the huge, inaccessible arches of the big bridge.

Charred Bodies.

Charred bodies could be seen here and there all through the glowing embers. There was no attempt to check the fire by the authorities, nor for that matter did they try to stop the robbing of the dead, nor any other glaring violation of law. The fire is spreading toward a large block of crushed buildings further up the stream. There is a broad stretch of angry water above and below, while over there, just opposite the end of the bridge, is the ruin of the great Cambria Iron Works, which have been damaged to the extent of over $1,000,000.

The Gautier Steel Works have been wiped away, and are represented by a loss of $1,000,000 and a big hole.

The Holbert House, owned by Renford Brothers, has entirely disappeared. It was a five story building, was the leading hotel of Johnstown, and contained a hundred rooms. Of the seventy-five guests who were in it when the flood came, only eight have been saved. Most of them were crushed by the fall of the walls and flooring.

THE JOHNSTOWN HORROR. 85

Hundreds of searching parties are looking in the muddy ponds and among the wreckage for bodies, and they are being gathered in ghastly heaps.

In one building among the bloated victims, I saw a young and well-dressed man and woman, still locked in each other's arms, a young mother with her babe pressed with delirious tenacity to her breast, and on a small pillow was a tiny babe a few hours old, which the doctors said must have been born in the water. It is said that 720 bodies have so far been recovered, or have been located.

The coroner of Westmoreland county is ordering coffins by the carload.

In the Raging Waters.

A dispatch from Derry says: In this city the poor people in the raging waters cried out for aid that never came. More than one brave man risked his life in trying to save those in the flood. Every hour details of some heroic action are brought to light. In many instances the victims displayed remarkable courage and gave their chances for rescue to friends with them. Sons stood back for mothers, and were lost while their parents were taken out. Many a son went down to a watery grave that a sister or a father might be saved. Such instances of sacrifice in the face of fearful danger are numerous.

The Force of the Waters.

One can estimate the force of the water when it is known that it carried locomotives down the mountain side and turned them upside down where they are now lying. Long trains of cars have been derailed and carried great distances from the railroads.

The first sight that greeted the men at nine this morning was the body of a beautiful woman lying crushed and mangled under the ponderous wheels of a gondola car. The clothing was torn to shreds. Dr. Berry said that he never saw such intense pain pictured on a face before.

Terrible Stories.

At this time of writing it is impossible to secure the names of any of the lost. Every person one meets along the road has some horrible tale of drowned and dead bodies recovered.

One thousand people or more were buried and crushed in the great fire. The flats below Conemaugh are full of cars with many dead bodies lying under them. At Sang Hollow a man named Duncan sat on the roof of a house and saw his father and mother die in the attic below him. The poor fellow was powerless to help them, and he stood there wringing his hands and tearing his hair.

A man was seen clinging to a tree, covered with blood. He was lost with the others.

Long after dark the flames of fire shot high above the burning mass of timber, lighting the vast flood of rushing waters on all sides.

The Dead.

Dead bodies are being picked up. The train master, E. Pitcairn, has been working manfully directing the rescuing of dead bodies at Nineveh. In a ten acre field seventy-five bodies were taken out within a half mile of each other. Of this number only five were men, the rest being women and children. Many beautiful young girls, refined in features and handsomely dressed, were found, and women and young mothers with their hair matted with roots and leaves are constantly being removed.

The wrecking crew which took out these bodies are confident that 150 bodies are lying buried in the sand and under the débris on those low-lying bottom lands. Some of the bodies were horribly mangled, and the features were twisted and contorted as if they had died in the most excrutiating agony. Others are found lying stretched out with calm faces.

Many a tear was dropped by the men as they worked away removing the bodies. An old lady with fine gray hair was picked up alive, although every bone in her body was broken. Judging from the number of women and children found in the swamps of Nineveh, the female portion of the population suffered the most.

A Fatal Tree.

Mr. O'Conner was at Sang Hollow when the flood began. He remained there through the afternoon and night, and he states that there was a fatal tree on the island against which a number of people were dashed and instantly killed. Their bodies were almost tied in a knot doubled over the tree by the force of the current. Mr. O'Conner says that the first man who came down had his brains knocked out against this obstruction. In fact, those who hit the tree met the same fate and were instantly killed under the pile of driftwood collected there. He could give no estimate of the number lost at this point, but says that it is certainly large.

Braves Death for His Family.

One of the most thrilling incidents of the disaster was the performance of A. J. Leonard, whose family reside in Morrellville, a short distance below this point. He was at work here, and hearing that his house had been swept away determined at all hazards to ascertain the fate of his family. The bridges having been carried away he constructed a temporary raft, and clinging to it as close as a cat to the side of a fence, he pushed his frail craft out in the raging torrent and started on a chase which, to all who were watching, seemed to mean an embrace in death.

Heedless of cries "For God's sake go back, you will be drowned," and "Don't attempt it," he persevered. As the raft struck the current he threw off his coat and in his shirt sleeves braved the stream. Down plunged the boards and down went Leonard, but as it rose he was seen still clinging. A mighty shout arose from the throats of the hundreds on the banks, who were now deeply interested, earnestly hoping he would successfully ford the stream.

Down again went his bark, but nothing, it seemed, could shake Leonard off. The craft shot up in the air apparently ten or twelve feet, and Leonard stuck to it tenaciously. Slowly but surely he worked his boat to the other side of the stream, and after what seemed an awful suspense he finally landed amid ringing cheers of men, women and children.

The last seen of him he was making his way down a mountain road in the direction of the spot where his house had lately stood. His family consisted of his wife and three children.

An Angel in the Mud.

The Pennsylvania Railroad Company's operators at Switch Corner, which is near Sang Hollow, tell thrilling stories of the scenes witnessed by them on Friday afternoon and evening. Said one of them:

"In order to give you an idea of how the tidal wave rose and fell, let me say that I kept a measure and timed the rise and fall of the water, and in forty-eight minutes it fell four and a half feet.

"I believe that when the water goes down about seventy-five children and fifty grown persons will be found among the weeds and bushes in the bend of the river just below the tower.

"There the current was very strong, and we saw dozens of people swept under the trees, and I don't believe that more than one in twenty came out on the other side."

"They found a little girl in white just now," said one of the other operators.

"Good God!" said the chief operator, "she isn't dead, is she!"

"Yes; they found her in a clump of willow bushes, kneeling on a board, just about the way we saw her when she went down the river." Turning to me he said:—

"That was the saddest thing we saw all day yesterday. Two men came down on a little raft, with a little girl kneeling between them, and her hands raised and praying. She came so close to us we could see her face, and that she was crying. She had on a white dress and looked like a little angel. She went under that cursed shoot in the willow bushes at the bend like all the rest, but we did hope she would get through alive."

"And so she was still kneeling," he said to his companion, who had brought the unwelcome news.

"She sat there," was the reply, "as if she were still praying, and there was a smile on her poor little face, though her mouth was full of mud."

All agreed in saying that at least one hundred people were drowned below Nineveh.

Direful Incidents.

The situation at Johnstown grows worse as fuller particulars are being received in Pittsburgh.

This morning it was reported that three thousand people were lost in the flood. In the afternoon this number was increased to six thousand, and at this writing despatches place the number at ten thousand.

It is the most frightful destruction of life that has ever been known in the United States.

Vampires at Hand.

It is stated that already a large gang of thieves and vampires have descended on and near the place. Their presumed purpose is to rob the dead and ransack the demolished buildings.

The Tenth regiment of the Pennsylvania National Guard has been ordered out to protect property.

A telegram from Bolivar says Lockport did not suffer much, but that sixty-five families were turned out of their homes. The school at that place is filled with mothers, fathers, daughters and children.

Noble Acts of Heroism.

Edward Dick, a young railroader living in the place, saw an old man floating down the river on a tree trunk whose agonized face and streaming gray hair excited his compassion. He plunged into the torrent, clothes and all, and brought the old man safely ashore. Scarcely had he done this when the upper story of a house floated by on which Mrs. Adams, of Cambria, and her two children were borne. He plunged in again, and while breaking through the tin roof of the house cut an artery in his left wrist, but, although weakened with loss of blood, succeeded in saving both mother and children.

George Shore, another Lockport swimmer, pulled out William Jones, of Cambria, who was almost exhausted and could not possibly have survived another twenty minutes in the water.

John Decker, who has some celebrity as a local pugilist, was also successful in saving a woman and boy, but was nearly killed in a third attempt to reach the middle of the river by being struck by a huge log.

The most miraculous fact about the people who

reached Bolivar alive was how they passed through the falls half way between Lockport and Bolivar. The seething waters rushed through that barrier of rock with a noise which drowned that of all the passing trains. Heavy trees were whirled high in the air out of the water, and houses which reached there whole were dashed to splinters against the rocks.

A Tale of Horror.

On the floor of William Mancarro's house, groaning with pain and grief, lay Patrick Madden, a furnace man of the Cambria Iron Company. He told of his terrible experience in a voice broken with emotion. He said: "When the Cambria Iron Company's bridge gave way I was in the house of a neighbor, Edward Garvey. We were caught through our own neglect, like a great many others, and a few minutes before the houses were struck Garvey remarked that he was a good swimmer, and could get away no matter how high the water rose. Ten minutes later I saw him and his son-in-law drowned.

"No human being could swim in that terrible torrent of débris. After the South Fork reservoir broke I was flung out of the building and saw, when I rose to the surface of the water, my wife hanging upon a piece of scantling. She let it go and was drowned almost within reach of my arm and I could not help or save her. I caught a log and floated with it five or six miles, but it was knocked from under me when I went over the dam. I then caught a bale of hay and was taken out by Mr. Morenrow.

A despatch from Greensburg says the day express, which left Pittsburgh at eight o'clock on Friday morning was lying at Johnstown in the evening at the time the awful rush of waters came down the mountains. We have been informed by one who was there that the coach next to the baggage car was struck by the raging flood, and with its human freight cut loose from the rest of the train and carried down the stream. All on board, it is feared, perished. Of the passengers who were left on the track, fifteen or more who endeavored to flee to the mountains were caught, it is thought, by the flood, and likewise carried to destruction. Samuel Bell, of Latrobe, was conductor on the train, and he describes the scene as the most appalling and heart-rending he ever witnessed.

A special despatch from Latrobe says:—"The special train which left the Union Station, Pittsburgh, at half-past one arrived at Nineveh Station, nine miles from Johnstown, last evening at five o'clock. The train was composed of four coaches and locomotive, and carried, at the lowest calculation, over nine hundred persons, including the members of the press. The passengers were packed in like sardines and many were compelled to hang out upon the platform. A large proportion of the passengers were curiosity seekers, while there was a large sprinkling of suspicious looking characters, who had every appearance of being crooks and wreckers, such as visit all like disasters for the sole purpose of plundering and committing kindred depredations.

94   THE JOHNSTOWN HORROR.

When the train reached Nineveh the report spread through it that a number of bodies had been fished out of the water and were awaiting identification at a neighboring planing mill. I stopped off to investigate the rumor, while the balance of the party journeyed on

TAKING DEAD BODIES FROM A ROOF.

toward Sang Hollow, the nearest approach to Johnstown by rail. I visited Mumaker's planing mills and found that the report was true.

All day long the rescuers had been at work, and at this writing (six o'clock) they have taken out seventy-eight dead bodies, the majority of whom are women and children. The bodies are horribly mutilated and covered with mud and blood. Fifteen of them are those of men. Their terribly mutilated condition makes identification for the present almost impossible. One of the bodies found was that of a woman, apparently about thirty-five years of age.

Every conveyance that could be used has been pressed into service. Latrobe is all agog with excitement over the great disaster. Almost every train takes out a load of roughs and thugs who are bent on mischief. They resemble the mob that came to Pittsburgh during the riots.

Measures of Relief.

Pittsburgh is in a wild state of excitement. A large mass meeting was held yesterday afternoon and in a short space of time $1,000 was subscribed for the sufferers.

The Pennsylvania company has been running trains every hour to the scene of the disaster or as near it as they can get. Provisions and a large volunteer relief corps have been sent up. The physicians have had an enthusiastic meeting at which one and all freely offered their services.

The latest project is to have the wounded and the survivors who fled to the hillsides from the angry rush of waters brought to Pittsburgh. The Exposition Society has offered the use of its splendid new building as a temporary hospital. All the hospitals in the city have also offered to care for the sufferers free of charge to the full limit of their capacity.

THE JOHNSTOWN HORROR.

Word has been received at Allegheny Junction, twenty-two miles above Pittsburgh, from Leechburg that a woman and two children were seen floating past there at five o'clock yesterday morning on top of some wreckage. They were alive, and their pitiful cries for help drew the attention of the people on the shore. Some men got a boat and endeavored to reach the sufferers.

As they rowed out in the stream the woman could be heard calling to them to save the children first.

The men made a gallant effort. It was all without avail, as the strong current and floating masses of débris prevented them from reaching the victims, and the latter floated on down the stream until their despairing cries could no longer be heard.

Mrs. Chambers, of Apollo, was swept away when her house was wrecked during the night. She had gone to bed when the flood came and she had not time to dress. Fortunately she managed to secure a hold on some wreckage which was being carried past her. She kept her hold until her cries were heard by some men a short distance above Leechburg. They got out a boat and succeeded in reaching her, and took her to a house near the bank of the river. When they got her there it was found that she was badly bruised and all her clothing had been torn off by the débris with which she had come in contact, leaving her entirely naked. She was also rescued at Natrona.

A Lucky Change of Residence.

Mr. F. J. Moore, of the Western Union office in this city, is giving thanks to-day for the fortunate escape of his wife and two children from the devastated city. As if by some foreknowledge of the impending disaster, Mr. Moore had arranged to have his family move yesterday from Johnstown and join him in this city. Their household goods were shipped on Thursday, and yesterday just in time to save themselves, the little party departed in the single train which made the trip between Johnstown and Pittsburgh. I called on Mrs. Moore at her husband's apartments, No. 4 Webster avenue, and found her completely prostrated by the news of the final catastrophe, coupled with the dangerous experience through which she and her little ones had passed.

"Oh, it was terrible," she said. "The reservoir had broken, and before we got out of the house the water filled the cellar, and on the way to the depot it was up to the carriage bed. Our train left at a quarter to two P. M., and at that hour the flood had commenced to rise with terrible rapidity. Houses and sheds were carried away, and two men were drowned almost under our very eyes. People gathered on the roofs to take refuge from the water which poured into the lower rooms of their dwellings, and many families took fright and became scattered beyond hope of being reunited. Just as the train pulled out I saw a woman crying bitterly. Her house had been flooded and she had escaped, leaving her husband behind, and her fears for his safety made her almost crazy. Our house was in the lower part of the town, and it makes me shudder to think what would have happened had we remained in it an hour longer. So far as I know we were the only passengers from Johnstown on the train, and therefore I suppose we are the only persons who got away in time to escape the culminating disaster."

Mrs. Moore's little son told me how he had seen the rats driven out of their holes by the flood and running along the tops of the fences. Mr. Moore endeavored to get to Johnstown yesterday, but was prevented by the suspension of traffic and says he is very glad of it.

What the Eye Hath Seen.

The scenes at Heanemyer's planing mill at Nineveh, where the dead bodies are lying, are never to be forgotten. The torn, bruised and mutilated bodies of the victims are lying in a row on the floor of the planing mill which looks more like the field of Bull Run after that disasterous battle than a work shop. The majority of the bodies are nude, their clothing having been torn off. All along the river bits of clothing—a tiny shoe, a baby dress, a mother's evening wrapper, a father's coat, and in fact every article of wearing apparel imaginable may be seen hanging to stumps of trees and scattered on the bank.

One of the most pitiful sights of this terrible disaster came to my notice this afternoon when the body of a young lady was taken out of the Conemaugh river. The woman was apparently quite young, though her features were terribly disfigured. Nearly all the clothing excepting the shoes was torn off the body. The corpse was that of a mother, for although cold in death she clasped a young male babe, apparently not more than a year old, tightly in her arms. The little one was huddled close up to the face of the mother, who when she realized their terrible fate had evidently raised it to her lips to imprint upon its lips the last kiss it was to receive in this world. The sight forced many a stout heart to shed tears. The limp bodies, with matted hair, some with holes in their heads, eyes knocked out and all bespattered with blood were a ghastly spectacle.

Story of The First Fugitives.

The first survivors of the Johnstown wreck who arrived in the city last night were Joseph and Henry Lauffer and Lew Dalmeyer, three well known Pittsburghers. They endured considerable hardship and had several narrow escapes with their lives. Their story of the disaster can best be told in their own language. Joe, the youngest of the Lauffer brothers, said :—

"My brother and I left on Thursday for Johnstown. The night we arrived there it rained continually, and on Friday morning it began to flood. I started for the Cambria store at a quarter past eight on Friday, and in fifteen minutes afterward I had to get out of the store in a wagon, the water was running so rapidly. We then arrived at the station and took the day express and went as tar as Conemaugh, where we had to stop. The limited, however got through, and just as we were about to start the bridge at South Fork gave way with a terrific crash, and we had to stay there. We then went to Johnstown. This was at a quarter to ten in the morning, when the flood was just beginning. The whole city of Johnstown was inundated and the people all moved up to the second floor.

Mountains of Water.

"Now this is where the trouble occurred. These poor unfortunates did not know the reservoir would burst, and there are no skiffs in Johnstown to escape in. When the South Fork basin gave way mountains of water twenty feet high came rushing down the Conemaugh River, carrying before them death and destruction. I shall never forget the harrowing scene. Just think of it! thousands of people, men, women and children, struggling and weeping and wailing as they were being carried suddenly away in the raging current. Houses were picked up as if they were but a feather, and their inmates were all carried away with them, while cries of 'God help me!' 'Save me!' 'I am drowning!' 'My child!' and the like were heard on all sides. Those who were lucky enough to escape went to the mountains, and there they beheld the poor unfortunates being crushed among the débris to death without any chance of being rescued. Here and there a body was seen to make a wild leap into the air and then sink to the bottom.

"At the stone bridge of the Pennsylvania company people were dashed to death against the piers. When the fire started there hundreds of bodies were burned. Many lookers-on up on the mountains, especially the women, fainted.

Mr. Lauffer's brother, Harry, then told his part of the tale, which was not less interesting. He said:—
"We had the most narrow escapes of anybody, and I tell you we don't want to be around when anything of that kind occurs again.

"The scenes at Johnstown have not in the least been exaggerated, and indeed the worst is to be heard. When we got to Conemaugh and just as we were about to start the bridge gave way. This left the day express, the accommodation, a special train and a freight train at the station. Above was the South Fork water basin, and all of the trains were well filled. We were discussing the situation when suddenly, without any warning, the whistles of every engine began to shriek, and in the noise could be heard the warning of the first engineer, 'My God! Rush to the mountains, the reservoir has burst.' Then, with a thundering like peal came the mad rush of waters. No sooner had the cry been heard than those who could with a wild leap rushed from the train and up the mountains. To tell this story takes some time, but the moments in which the horrible scene was enacted were few. Then came the tornado of water, leaping and rushing with tremendous force. The waves had angry crests of white and their roar was something deafening. In one terrible swath they caught the four trains and lifted three of them right off the track, as if they were only a cork. There they floated in the river. Think of it, three large locomotives and finely varnished Pullmans floating around, and above all the hundreds of poor unfortunates who were unable to escape from the car swiftly drifting toward death. Just as we were about to leap from the car I saw a mother, with a smiling, blue eyed baby in her arms. I snatched it from her and leaped from the train just as it was lifted off of the track. The mother and child were saved, but if one more minute had elapsed we all would have perished.

Beyond the Power of Words.

"During all of this time the waters kept rushing down the Conemaugh and through the beautiful town of Johnstown, picking up everything and sparing nothing.

The mountains by this time were black with people, and the moans and sighs from those below brought tears to the eyes of the most stony hearted. There in that terrible rampage were brothers, sisters, wives and husbands, and from the mountain could be seen the panic stricken marks in the faces of those who were struggling between life and death. I really am unable to do justice to the scene, and its details are almost be yond my power to relate. Then came the burning of the débris near the Pennsylvania Railroad bridge The scene was too sickening to endure. We left the spot and journeyed across country and delivered many notes, letters, etc., that were intrusted to us.

We rode thirty-one miles in a buckboard, then walked six miles, reached Blairsville and journeyed again on foot to what is called the "Bow," and from thence we arrived home. On our way we met Mr. F.

THE JOHNSTOWN HORROR. 108

Thompson, a friend of ours, who resides in Nineveh, and he stated that rescuing parties were busy all day at Annom. One hundred and seventy-five bodies were recovered at that place. An old couple about sixty years of age were rescued from a tree, on which they came floating down the stream. They were clasped in each other's arms.

President Harrison's private secretary, Elijah Halford, and wife, were on the train which was swept away, but escaped and were in the mountains when I left.

Among the lost are Colonel John P. Linton and his wife and children. Colonel Linton was prominent in the Grand Army of the Republic and in the Knights of Pythias and other orders. He was formerly Auditor General of Pennsylvania.

NINEVEH STATION, WHERE TWO HUNDRED BODIES VERE FOUND.

CHAPTER IV.

Multiplication of Terrors.

The handsome brick High School Building is damaged to such an extent that it will have to be rebuilt. The water attained the height of the window sills of the second floor. Its upper stories formed a refuge for many persons. All Saturday afternoon two little girls could be seen at the windows frantically calling for aid. They had spent all night and the day in the building, cut off from all aid. Without food and drinking water their condition was lametable. Late in the evening the children were removed to higher ground and properly cared for.

A number of persons had been taken from this building earlier in the day, but in the excitement the children were forgotten. Their names could not be obtained.

Death in Many Forms.

Morrell Institute, a beautiful building and the old homestead of the Morrell family, is totally ruined. The water has weakened the walls and foundations to such an extent that there is danger of its collapsing. Many families took refuge in this building and were saved. Now that the waters have receded there is danger from falling walls. All day long the crashing of walls could be heard across the river. Before daybreak this morning the sounds could not but make one shudder at the very thought of the horrible deaths that awaited many who had escaped the devastating flood.

Library Hall was another of the fine buildings of the many in the city that is destroyed. Of the Episcopal church not a vestige remains. Where it once stood, there is now a placid lake. The parsonage is swept away, and the rector of the church, Rev. Mr. Diller, was drowned.

Buried Under Falling Buildings.

The church was one of the first buildings to fall. It carried with it several of the surrounding houses. Many of them were occupied. The victims were swept into the comparatively still waters at the bridge, and there met death either by fire or water.

James M. Walters, an attorney, spent the night in Alma Hall and relates a thrilling story. One of the most curious occurrences of the whole disaster was how Mr. Walters got to the hall. He has his office on the second floor. His home is at No. 135 Walnut street. He says he was in the house with his family when the waters struck it. All was carried away. Mr. Walter's family drifted on a roof in another direction. He passed down several streets and alleys until he came to the hall. His dwelling struck that edifice and he was thrown into his own office.

Long, Dark Night of Terror.

About two hundred persons had taken refuge in the hall, and were on the second, third and fourth stories. The men held a meeting and drew up some rules, which all were bound to respect. Mr. Walters was chosen president. Rev. Mr. Beale was put in charge of the first floor, A. M. Hart of the second floor, Doctor Matthews of the fourth floor. No lights were allowed, and the whole night was spent in darkness. The sick were cared for. The weaker women and children had the best accommodations that could be had, while the others had to wait. The scenes were most agonizing. Heartrending shrieks, sobs and moans pierced the gloomy darkness. The crying of children mingled with the suppressed sobs of the women. Under the guardianship of the men all took more hope. No one slept during all the long dark night. Many knelt for hours in prayer, their supplications mingling with the roar of the waters and the shrieks of the dying in the surrounding houses. In all this misery two women gave premature birth to children.

Here is a Hero.

Dr. Matthews is a hero. Several of his ribs were crushed by a falling timber and his pains were most severe, yet through all he attended the sick. When two women in a house across the street shouted for help he with two other brave young men climbed across the drift and ministered to their wants. No one died during the night, but women and children surrendered their lives on the succeeding day as a result of terror and fatigue. Miss Rose Young, one of the young ladies in the hall, was frightfully cut and bruised. Mrs. Young had a leg broken. All of Mr. Walter's family were saved.

While the loss of property about Brookville, the lumber centre of Pennsylvania, by the great flood has been enormous, variously estimated at from $250,000 to $500,000, not a single life has been lost. At least there have been none reported so far, and I have travelled over the line from Red Bank, on the Valley road, to Dubois, on the low grade division. Every creek is swollen to many times its natural size. A great deal of the low-lying farm lands and roads in places have water enough over them to float an ordinary steamboat.

Leaving Pittsburgh Saturday morning on the valley road, we ran past millions and millions of feet of lumber. From the city to the junction opposite Freeport the river was almost choked with débris of broken and shattered houses. In places the river was fairly black with floating masses of lath, shingles, roofs, floors and other lumber that had formerly been houses. The sight was appalling and spoke louder than any pen can describe.

At Red Bank the river was filled with a different kind of lumber, including huge saw logs ready for cutting. From the estimates of an old lumber man who was on the train I was told that between the stations named we passed at least ten million feet of lumber, which means a loss of fully $100,000 to the owners. A big portion of this came out of the Clarion river, the estimated money loss from that section alone being anywhere from $500,000 to $750,000.

All along the Allegheny river were gathered people trying to catch the logs, risking their lives, for the logs swept down the river in a current that was running fully ten miles an hour. The work was very hazardous. The catchers are allowed by law six and a quarter cents for each log captured, and the river was almost lined with people trying to save the property.

At Red Bank, which we left at noon, there were at least six feet of water expected from Oil City, and with it, according to the reports from up the river, was an immense amount of lumber. Leaving the valley road at Red Bank we went up the low grade division to Bryant, where immense sawmills, the largest in the vicinity are located. The current was rushing along at a rate anywhere from twelve to fifteen miles an hour, tossing the huge logs around like so many toothpicks and carrying everything before them. So great was the current and mass of logs that the big iron bridge at Reynoldsville, sixteen miles above Brookville, was swept away, as were two wagon bridges and several small foot bridges.

Hundreds Homeless and Suffering.

Many houses here and there along Red Bank Creek were turned upside down, some of them floating clear away, while the more secure ones were flooded with water clear into the second floors. Many of the smaller cottages and shanties were covered, leaving only the peaks of the roofs sticking out to show the spots that families had but a few hours before called home. All along the railroad track was piled the few household effects, furniture, bedding, tables and clothes which the poor owners had saved before they were forced out on the high ground. These same people had gone to bed last evening thinking themselves safe from the high water, only to be wakened about midnight by the noise of the rushing floods and the huge saw logs bumping against their homes. The very narrow escapes that some of them made while getting their families into places of safety would fill many pages of this book.

Floating to Safety on Saw Logs.

One man had to mount the different members of his family on logs. The mother and children alike sat astride of them, and then, with the father on the other end, were poled across to the high ground.

Another man, whose house was in a worse place, swam ashore and, throwing a rope back to the mother, who was surrounded on the porch of the house by the children, yelled for her to tie one end to the little ones so he could pull them over the fast running water. This operation was continued until the entire family was rescued.

Willing workers from the neighborhood were not long in getting huge bonfires started, and with the aid of these and dry clothing brought in haste by people whose homes stood on higher ground the family were soon warmed.

The same willing hands hastily constructed sheds, and with immense bonfires the people were kept warm till daylight. Others, more fortunate, were able to save enough from their houses to make themselves comfortable for a short season of camping. One poor family I noticed had saved enough carpet to make a tent out of, and under this temporary shelter the mother was doing her best to prepare a meal and attend to her other household duties.

Sheltered by Friendly Neighbors.

In Brookville a great many houses were submerged, but no lives were lost. While the people were driven from their homes, they were more fortunate than the people of Bryants, because they could at once find shelter under the roofs of the neighbors' houses.

All of the saw mills, the chief industry of the town, were closed down. Some because the water was over the first floor, and others because their entire working force were on the creek trying to construct temporary booms, by which they expected to save at least a portion of the property from being swept away. One man rigged a boom with the aid of a cable 1,600 feet long and thick enough to hold the heaviest steamer. About fifty logs were chained together for further protection. This arrangement for a time checked the mass of logs, but just when everybody was thinking it would stop the output a small dam gave way, bringing down with it another half million feet of lumber. When this struck the temporary boom it parted, as if the huge cable was a piece of thread, and the logs shot past.

Just at Bryants, however, a gorge formed shortly after two o'clock Friday afternoon, and within a remarkably short time there was a pile of logs wedged

THE JOHNSTOWN HORROR.

in that stretched back fully a quarter of a mile and the top of which was more than ten feet high. This of course changed the course of the stream a little, but the natural gorge had saved enough logs to amount to more than $100,000 in money.

The following comments by one of our journals sum up the situation after receiving the dreadful news of the three preceding days:

The Great Calamity.

The appalling catastrophy which has spread such awful havoc through the teeming valley of the Conemaugh almost surpasses belief and fairly staggers imagination. Without yet measuring its dire extent, enough is known to rank it as the greatest calamity of the natural elements which this country has ever witnessed. Nothing in our history short of the deadly blight of battle has approached this frightful cataclysm, and no battle, though destroying more life, has ever left such a ghastly trail of horror and devastation. It seems more like one of those terrible convulsions of nature from which we have hitherto been happily spared, but which at rare intervals have swallowed up whole communities in remote South American or oriental lands.

Ingenious and masterful as the human intellect is in guiding and controlling the ordinary forces of nature, how impotent and insignificant it appears in the presence of such a transcendent disaster! It is well nigh inconceivable that a great section throbbing with populous towns, and resonant with the hum of industry, should be wiped out in the twinkling of an eye by a mighty, raging torrent, more consuming than fire and more violent than the earthquake. The suddenness of the blow and the impossibility of communicating with the scene add to the terror of the event. The sickening spectacle of ruin and death which will be revealed when the veil of darkness is lifted is left to conjecture. The imagination can scarcely picture the dread realities, and it would be difficult to overdraw the awful features of a calamity which has every element of horror.

The River and Lake.

Nature is so framed at the fated point for such a disaster that man was called upon for unceasing vigilance. The Conemaugh makes its channel through a narrow valley between high ranges. Numerous streams drain the surrounding mountains into its current. Along its course swarm frequent hamlets busy with the wealth dug from the seams of the earth. The chief of these towns, the seat of an immense industry, lies in a little basin where the gap broadens to take in a converging stream and then immediately narrows again, no outlet save the constricted waterway. High above stands a great lake which is held in check only by an artificial barrier, and which, if once unchained, must pour its resistless torrent through this narrow gorge like a besom of destruction overwhelming everything before it. There were all the elements of an unparalleled disaster. Years of immunity had given a feeling of security for all time without some extra ordinary and unexpected occasion. But the occasion appeared when in unforseen force the rains descended and the floods came, and to-day desolation reigns.

A Direful Calamity.

It is impossible yet to measure the extent of the calamity. But the destruction of life and property must be something that it is appalling to think of, and the sorrow and suffering to follow are incalculable. A solemn obligation devolves upon the people of the whole country. We can not remedy the past but we can alleviate the present and the future. Thousands of families are homeless and destitute; thousands are without means of support; perchance, thousands are bereft of the strong arms upon which they have relied. There is an instant, earnest demand for help. Let there be immediate, energetic, generous action. Let us do our part to relieve the anguish and mitigate the suffering of a community upon whom has fallen the most terrible visitation in all our history.

An Historic Catastrophe.

When an American Charles Reade wishes in the future to weave into the woof of his novel the account of some great public calamity he will portray the misfortune which overwhelmed the towns and villages lying in the valley of the Conemaugh River. The bursting of a reservoir, and the ensuing scenes of death and destruction, which are so vividly described in "Put Yourself in His Place," were not the creatures of Mr. Reade's imagination, but actual occurrences. The novelist obtained facts and incidents for one of the most striking chapters in all of his works from the events which followed the breaking of the Dale Dyke embankment at Sheffield, England, in March, 1864, when 238 lives were lost and property valued at millions was destroyed.

It will need even more vivid and vigorous descriptive powers than Mr. Reade possessed to adequately delineate the scene of destruction and death now presented in Johnstown and the adjacent villages. The Sheffield calamity, disastrous as it proved, to be, was a small affair when compared with this latest reservoir accident. The Mill River reservoir disaster of May, 1874, with its 200 lives lost and $1,500,000 of property destroyed, almost sinks into insignificance beside it. The only recorded calamity of the kind which anywhere approaches it occurred in Estrecho de Rientes, in Spain, in April, 1802, when a dam burst and drowned 600 persons and swept $7,000,000 worth of property away. But above all these calamities in sad pre-eminence will stand the Conemaugh disaster.

But dark as the picture is, it will doubtless be relieved by many acts of heroism. The world will wait to learn if there was not present at Conemaugh some Myron Day, whose ride on his bareback steed before the advancing wall of water that burst from Mill River Dam in 1874, shouting to the unsuspecting people as he rode: "The reservoir is breaking! The flood is coming! Fly! Fly for your lives," was the one mitigating circumstance in that scene of woe and destruction. When the full story of the Conemaugh calamity is told it will, doubtless, be found that there were many deeds of heroism performed, many noble sacrifices made and many an act as brave as any performed on the field of battle. Already we are told of husbands and mothers who preferred to share a watery grave with their wives and children sooner than accept safety alone.

Such a calamity, while it makes the heart sick with its story of death and suffering, always serves to bring out the better and higher qualities in men and women, and to illustrate how closely all mankind are bound together by ties of sympathy and compassion. This fact will be made evident now by the open-handed liberality which will quickly flow in to relieve the suffering, and, as far as possible, to repair the loss caused by this historic calamity.

CHAPTER V.
The Awful Work of Death.

The record of June 3rd continues as follows: The horror of the situation does not lessen. The latest estimate of the number of dead is an official one by Adjutant General Hastings, and it places the number between 12,000 and 15,000.

The uncovering of hundreds of bodies by the recession of the waters has already filled the air with pestilential odors. The worst is feared for the surviving population, who must breathe this poisoned atmosphere. Sharp measures prompted by sheer necessity have resulted in an almost complete subsidence of cowardly efforts to profit by the results of the disaster. Thieves have slunk into places of darkness and are no longer to be seen at their unholy work.

All thoughts are now fixed upon the hideous revelation that awaits the light of day, when the waters shall have entirely quitted the ruins that now lie beneath them, and shall have exposed the thousands upon thousands of corpses that are massed there.

A sad and gloomy sky, almost as sad and gloomy as the human faces under it, shrouded Johnstown to-day. Rain fell all day and added to the miseries of the wretched people. The great plain where the best part of Johnstown used to stand was half covered with water. The few sidewalks in the part that escaped the flood were inches thick with black, sticky mud, through which tramped a steady procession of poor women who are left utterly destitute. The tents where the people are housed who cannot find other shelter were cold and cheerless.

A Great Tomb.

The town seemed like a great tomb. The people of Johnstown have supped so full of horrors that they go about in a sort of a daze and only half conscious of their griefs. Every hour, as one goes through the streets, he hears neighbors greeting each other and then inquiring without show of feeling how many each had lost in his family. To-day I heard a gray haired man hail another across the street with this question.

"I lost five; all are gone but Mary and I," was the reply.

"I am worse off than that," said the first old gentleman. "I have only my grandson left. Seven of us gone."

And so they passed on without apparent excitement. They and everyone else had heard so much of these melancholy conversations that somehow the calamity had lost its significance to them. They treat it exactly as if the dead persons had gone away and were coming back in a week.

The Ghastly Search.

The melancholy task of searching the ruins for more bodies went on to-day in the soaking rain. There were little crowds of morbid curiosity hunters around each knot of workingmen, but they were not residents of Johnstown. All their curiosity in that direction was satiated long ago. Even those who come in from neighboring towns with the idea of a day's strange and ghastly experiences did not care to be near after they had seen one body exhumed. There were hundreds and thousands of these visitors from the country to-day. The effect of the dreadful things they saw and heard was to drive most of them to drink. By noon the streets were beginning to be full of boisterous and noisy countrymen, who were trying to counteract the strain on their nerves with unnatural excitement. Then the chief of police, foreseeing the unseemly sights that were likely to disgrace the streets, drove out and kept out all the visitors who had not some good reason for their presence. After that and far into the evening all the country roads were filled with drunken stragglers, who were trying to forget what they had seen.

One thing that makes the work of searching for the bodies very slow is the strange way that great masses of objects were rolled into intricate masses of rubbish.

Horrible Masses.

As the flood came down the valley of the South Fork it obliterated the suburb of Woodvale, where not a house was left, nor a trace of one. The material they had contained rolled on down the valley, over and over, grinding it up to pulp and finally leaving it against an unusually firm foundation or in the bed of an eddy. The masses contain human bodies, but it is slow work to pick them to pieces. In the side of one of them I saw the remnants of a carriage, the body of a harnessed horse, a baby cradle and a doll, a tress of woman's

THE REMAINS OF CAMBRIA CITY.

hair, a rocking horse, and a piece of beefsteak still hanging on a hook.

The city is now very much better patrolled than it has been at any time since the flood occurred. Many members of the police force of Pittsburgh came in and offered their services. One of them showed his spirit during the first hour by striking a man, whom he saw opening a trunk among the rubbish, a tremendous blow over the head which knocked him senseless. Several big trunks and safes lie in full sight on the desolate plain in the lower part of the town, but no one dared to touch them after that.

The German Catholic Church at Cambria City, a short distance west of Johnstown, is almost a complete wreck. Rather a singular coincidence in connection with the destruction of the above is that the Immaculate Conception, that stood in the northwest corner of the lecture rooms, stands just as it was when last seen. The figure, which is wax, was not even scratched, and the clothes, which are made of white silk and deep duchess lace, were spotless. This seems strange, when the raging water destroyed everything else in the building. Hundreds of persons visited the place during the day.

Ten Bodies an Hour.

Bodies are now being brought in at lower Cambria at the rate of ten per hour.

A man named Dougherty tells a thrilling story of a ride down the river on a log. When the waters struck the roof of the house on which he had taken shelter he jumped astride a telegraph pole, riding a distance of some twenty-three miles, from Johnstown to Bolivar, before he was rescued.

Many inquiries have been made as to why the militia did not respond when ordered out by Adjutant General Hastings. "In the first place it is beyond the

General's authority to order troops to a scene of this kind unless the Governor first issues a proclamation, then it becomes his duty to issue orders." The General said he was notified that the Pittsburgh troops, consisting of the Fourteenth and Eighteenth regiments, had tendered their services, and no doubt would have been of great service. The General consulted with the Chief Burgess of Johnstown and Sheriff of Cambria county in regard to calling the troops to the scene, but both officials strenuously objected, as they claimed the people would object to anything of this kind. As a proof of this not a breach of peace was committed last night in Johnstown and vicinity.

It has not been generally believed that the district in the neighborhood of Kernville would be so extremely prolific of corpses as it has proven to be. I visited that part of the town where both the river and Stony Creek have done their worst. I found that within the past twenty-four hours almost one thousand bodies had been recovered or were in sight. The place is one great repository of the dead.

The Total May Never be Known.

The developments of every hour make it more and more apparent that the exact number of lives lost in the Johnstown horror will never be known. All estimates made to this time are conservative, and when all is known will doubtless be found to have been too small. Over one thousand bodies have been found since sunrise to-day, and the most skeptical concede that the remains of thousands more rest beneath the débris above the Johnstown bridge. The population of Johnstown, the surrounding towns and the portion of the valley affected by the flood is, or was, from 50,000 to 55,000. Numerous leading citizens of Johnstown, who survived the flood, have been interviewed, and the concensus of opinion was that fully thirty per cent. of the residents of Johnstown and Cambria had been victims of the continued disasters of fire and water. If this be true, the total loss of life in the entire valley cannot be less than seven or eight thousand and possibly much greater. Of the thousands who were devoured by the flames and whose ashes rest beneath the smoking débris above Johnstown bridge, no definite information can ever be obtained.

Hundreds Carried Miles Away.

As little will be learned of hundreds that sank beneath the current and were borne swiftly down the Conemaugh only to be deposited hundreds of miles below on the banks and in the driftwood of the raging Ohio. Probably one-third of the dead will never be recovered, and it will take a list of the missing weeks hence to enable even a close estimate to be made of the number of lives that were lost. That this estimate can never be accurate will be understood when it is remembered that in many instances whole families and their relatives were swept away, and found a common grave beneath the wild waste of waters. The total destruction of the city leaves no data to even demonstrate that the names of these unfortunates ever found place on the pages of eternity's history.

"All indications point to the fact that the death list will reach over five thousand names, and in my opinion the missing will reach eight thousand in number," declared General D. H. Hastings to-night.

At present there are said to have been twenty-two hundred bodies recovered. The great difficulties experienced in getting a correct list is the great number of morgues. There is no central bureau of information, and to communicate with the different dead houses is the work of hours. The journey from the Pennsylvania Railroad morgue to the one in the Fourth ward school house in Johnstown occupies at least one hour. This renders it impossible to reach all of them in one day, particularly as some of the morgues are situated at points inaccessible from Johnstown. At six o'clock in the evening the 630th body had been recovered at the Cambria depository for corpses.

None Left to Care for the Dead.

Kernville is in a deplorable condition. The living are unable to take care of the dead. The majority of the inhabitants of the town were drowned. A lean-to of boards has been erected on the only street remaining in the town. This is the headquarters for the committee that controls the dead. As quickly as the dead are brought to this point they are placed in boxes and then taken to the cemetery and buried.

A supply store has opened in the town. A milkman who was overcharging for milk narrowly escaped lynching. The infuriated men appropriated all his milk and distributed it among the poor and then drove him out of the town. The body of the Hungarian who was lynched in an orchard was removed by his friends during the night.

There is but one street left in the town. About one hundred and fifty-five houses are standing where once there stood a thousand. None of the large buildings in what was once a thriving little borough have escaped. One thousand people is a low estimate of the number of lives lost from this town, but few of the bodies have been recovered. It is directly above the ruins and the bodies have floated down into them, where they burned. A walk through the town revealed a desolate sight. Only about twenty-five able-bodied men have survived and are able to render any assistance. Men and women can be seen with black eyes, bruised faces and cut heads.

Useless Calls for Help.

The appearance of some of the ladies is heart-rending. They were injured in the flood, and since that have not slept. Their faces have turned a sickly yellow and dark rings surround the eyes. Many have succumbed to nervous prostration. For two days but little assistance could be rendered them. The wounded remained uncared for in some of the houses cut off by the water, and died from their injuries alone. Some were alive on Sunday, and their shout could be heard by the people on the shore.

A man is now in a temporary jail in what is left of the town. He was caught stealing a gold watch. A shot was fired at him but he was not wounded. The only thing that saved him from lynching was the smallness of the crowd. His sentence will be the heaviest that can be given him.

Services in the chapel from which the bodies were buried consisted merely of a prayer by one of the survors. No minister was present. Each coffin had a descriptive card on it, and on the graves a similar card was placed, so that bodies can be removed later by friends.

There are about thirty Catholic priests and nuns here. The sisters are devoting themselves to the cure of the sick and injured in the hospitals, while the priests are doing anything and everything and making themselves generally useful. Bishop Phelan, who reached here on Sunday evening, returned to Pittsburgh on the three o'clock train yesterday afternoon. He has organized the Catholic forces in this neighborhood, and all are devoting themselves to hard work assiduously.

Mr. Derlin, who heeded the warning as to the danger of the dam, had hurried his wife and two children to the hills, but returned himself to save some things from his house. While in the building the flood struck it and swept it away, jamming it among a lot of other houses and hurling them all around with a regular churning motion. Mr. Derlin was in a fix, but went to his top story, clambered to the roof and escaped from there to solid structures and then to the ground. His property was entirely ruined, but he thinks himself fortunate in saving his family.

Where Woodvale once stood there is now a sea of mud, broken but rarely by a pile of wreckage. I waded through mud and water up the valley to-day over the site of the former village. As has been often stated, nothing is standing but the old woollen mills. The place is swept bare of all other buildings but the ruins of the Gautier wire mill. The boilers of this great works were carried one hundred yards from their foundations. Pieces of engines, rolls and other machinery were swept far away from where they once stood. The wreck of a hose carriage is sticking up out of the mud. It belonged to the crack company of Johnstown. The engine house is swept away and the cellar is filled with mud, so that the site is obliterated.

A German watchman was on guard at the mill when the waters came. He ran for the hillside and succeeded in escaping. He tells a graphic story of the appearance of the water as it swept down the valley. He declares that the first wave was as high as the third story of a house.

The place is deserted. No effort is being made to clean off the streets. The mire has formed the grave for many a poor victim. Arms and legs are protruding from the mud and it makes the most sickening of pictures.

General Hastings' Report.

In answer to questions from Governor Beaver, Adjutant-General Hastings has telegraphed the following:

"Good order prevailed throughout the city and

vicinity last night. Police arrangements are excellent. Not one arrest made. No need of sending troops. The Mayor of Johnstown and the Sheriff of Cambria county, with whom I am in constant communication, request that no troops be sent. I concur in their judgment. There is a great outside clamor for troops. Do not send tents. Have nine hundred here, which are sufficient. I advise you to make a call on the general public for money and other assistance."

"About two thousand bodies have been rescued and the work of embalming and burying the dead is going on with regularity. There is plenty of medical assistance. We have a bountiful supply of food and clothing to-day, and the fullest telegraphic facilities are afforded and all inquiries are promptly answered.

"Have you any instructions or inquiries? The most conservative estimates here place the number of lives lost at fully 5,000. The prevailing impression is that the loss will reach from 8,000 to 10,000. There are many widows and orphans and a great many wounded—impossible to give an estimate. Property destroyed will reach $25,000,000. The popular estimate will reach $40,000,000 to $50,000,000.

"I will issue a proclamation to-night to the people of the country and to all who sympathize with suffering to give aid to our deeply afflicted people. Tell them to be of good cheer, that the sympathies of all our people, irrespective of section, are with them, and wherever the news of their calamity has been carried responses of sympathy and aid are coming in. A single subscription from England just received is for $1,000."

Grand View Cemetery has three hundred buried in it. All met death in the flood. They have thirty-five men digging graves. Seven hundred dead bodies in the hospital on Bedford street, Conneaut. One hundred dead bodies in the school-house hospital, Adam street, Conneaut. Three hundred bodies found to-day in the sand banks along Stony Creek, vicinity of the Baltimore and Ohio; 182 bodies at Nineveh.

ON A MISSION OF MERCY.

CHAPTER VI.
Shadows of Despair.

Another graphic account of the fearful calamity is furnished by an eye-witness: The dark disaster of the day with its attendant terrors thrilled the world and drew two continents closer together in the bonds of sympathy that bind humanity to man. The midnight terrors of Ashtabula and Chatsworth evoked tears of pity from every fireside in Christendom, but the true story of Johnstown, when all is known, will stand solitary and alone as the acme of man's affliction by the potent forces to which humanity is ever subject.

The menacing clouds still hover darkly over the valley of death, and the muttering thunder that ever and anon reverberates faintly in the distance seems the sardonic chuckle of the demon of destruction as he pursues his way to other lands and other homes.

The Waters Receding.

But the modern deluge has done its worst for Johnstown. The waters are rapidly subsiding, but the angry torrents still eddy around Ararat, and the winged messenger of peace has not yet appeared to tell the pathetic tale of those who escaped the devastation.

It is not a hackneyed utterance to say that no pen can adequately depict the horrors of this twin disaster —holocaust and deluge. The deep emotions that well from the heart of every spectator find most eloquent expression in silence—the silence that bespeaks recognition of man's subserviency to the elements and impotence to avert catastrophe. The insignificance of human life is only fully realized by those who witness such scenes as Johnstown, Chatsworth and Ashtabula, and to those whose memory retains the picture of horror the dread experience cannot fail to be a fitting lesson.

A Dreary Morning.

This morning opened dark and dreary. Great drops of rain fell occasionally and another storm seems imminent. Every one feels thankful though that the weather still remains cold, and that the gradual putrefaction of the hundreds of bodies that still line the streams and lie hidden under the miles of driftwood and débris is not unduly hastened.

The peculiar stench of decaying human flesh is plainly perceptible to the senses as one ascends the bank of Stony Creek for a half mile along the smouldering ruins of the wreck, and the most skeptical now conceive the worst and realize that hundreds—aye, perhaps thousands—of bodies lie charred and blackened beneath this great funeral pyre. Searchers wander wearily over this smoking mass, and as occasionally a sudden shout comes over the waters, the patient watchers on the hill realize that another ghastly discovery has been added to that long list of revelations that chill every heart and draw tears to the eyes of pessimists.

From the banks many charred remains of victims of flames and flood are plainly visible to the naked eye, as the retreating waters reluctantly give up their dead. Beneath almost every log or blackened beam a glistening skull or the blanched remnants of ribs or limbs mark all that remains of life's hopes and dreams.

Since ten o'clock last night the fire engines have been busy. Water has been constantly playing on the burning ruins. At times the fire seems almost extinguished, but fitful flames suddenly break out afresh in some new quarter, and again the water and flames wage fierce combat.

The Count is Still Lacking.

As yet there is no telling how many lives have been lost. Adjutant General Hastings, who has charge of everything, stated this morning that he supposed there were at least two thousand people under the burning débris, but the only way to find out how many lives were lost was to take a census of the people now living and subtract that from the census before the flood. Said he, "In my opinion there are any way from twelve thousand to fifteen thousand lost."

Up to this morning people living here who lost whole families or parts of families hardly seemed to realize what a dreadful calamity had befallen them. To-day, however, they are beginning to understand the situation. Agony is stamped on the faces of every one, and it is truly a city of mourning.

The point of observation is on the hillside, midway between the woolen mills of Woodvale and Johnstown proper, which I reached to-day after a journey through the portions of the city from which the waters, receding fast, are revealing scenes of unparalleled horror. From the point on the hillside referred to an excellent view of the site of the town can be obtained. Here it can be seen that from the line of the Pennsylvania Railroad, which winds along the base of Prospect Hill, to a point at which St. John's Catholic Church formerly stood, and from the stone bridge to Conemaugh, on the Conemaugh River, but twelve houses by actual count remain, and they are in such a condition as to be practically useless. To any one familiar with the geography of the iron city of Cambria county this will convey a vivid idea of a swarth averaging one-half mile in width and three miles in length. In all the length and breadth of the most peaceful and costly portion of Johnstown not a shingle remains except those adhering to the buildings mentioned.

Houses Upside Down.

But do not think for an instant that this comprehends in full the awfulness of the scene. What has just been mentioned is a large waste of territory swept as clean as if by a gigantic broom. In the other direction some few of the houses still remain, but they are upside down, piled on top of each other, and in many ways so torn asunder that not a single one of them is available for any purpose whatever. It is in this district that the loss of life has been heartrending. Bodies are being dug up in every direction.

On the main street, from which the waters have receded sufficiently to render access and work possible, bodies are being exhumed. They are as thick as potatoes in a field. Those in charge seem to have the utmost difficulty in securing the removal of bodies after they have been found.

The bodies are lying among the mass of wrecked buildings as thick as flies. The fire in the drift above the bridge is under control and is being rapidly smothered by the Pittsburgh firemen in charge of the work. About seven o'clock this morning a crowd of Battery B boys discovered a family of five people in the smoking and burned ruins above the bridge. They took out father, mother and three children, all terribly burned and mutilated. The little girl had an arm torn off.

Finding the Dead.

The work of rescuing the bodies from the mud and débris has only fairly begun, and yet each move in that direction reveals more fully the horrible extent of the calamity. It is estimated that already 1,800 corpses have been found in all parts of the valley and given some little attention. Many of them were so mangled as to be beyond identification.

A regularly organized force of men has been at work most of the day upon the mass of débris about the stone bridge. Early in the forenoon ten bodies were found close together. There was nothing to identify them, as they were burnt almost to a crisp. Several of them must have belonged to one household, as they were taken from under the blackened timbers of a single roof.

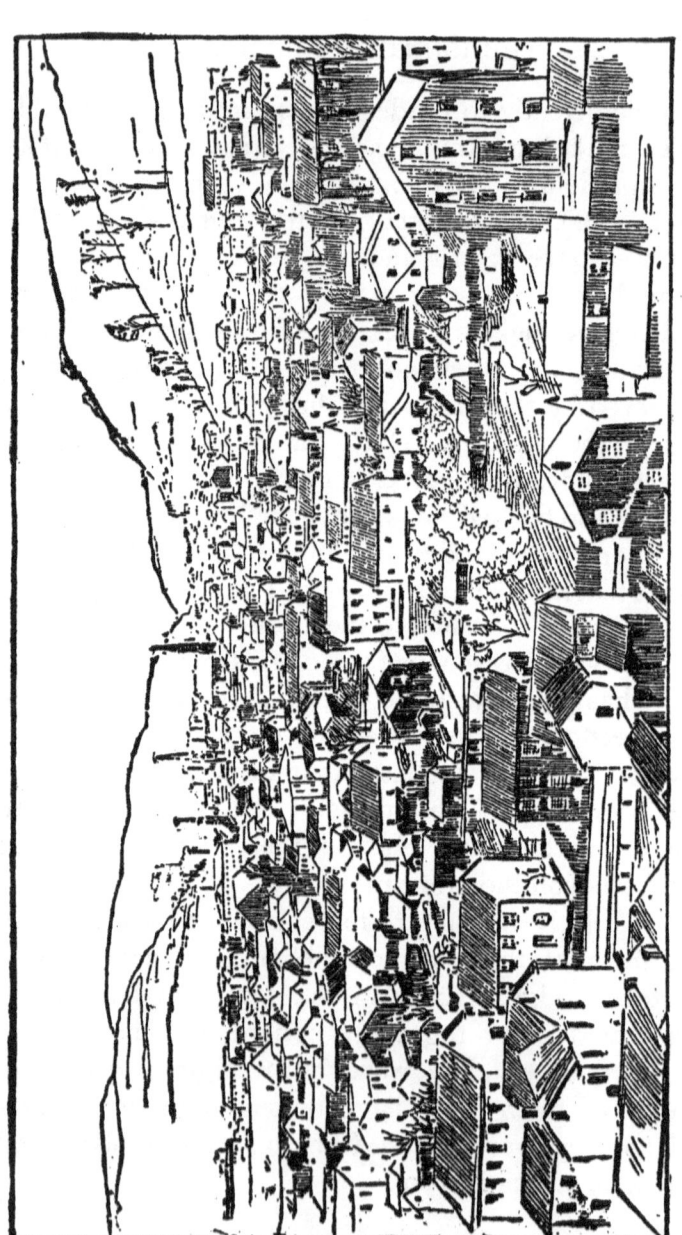

THE VILLAGE OF JOHNSTOWN BEFORE THE FLOOD.

Soon after a man, woman and child were taken from the ruins. The child was clasped in the arms of the woman, and the trio were evidently husband, wife and child.

It is a most distressing sight to see the relatives of people supposed to be lost standing around and watching every body as it is pulled out, and acting more like maniacs than sensible people.

As the work progressed the number of the ghastly finds increased. The various parties of workmen turned out from ten to fifteen bodies and fragments of bodies an hour all day long.

Many of the corpses found had valuables still clasped in their hands. One woman taken from the mill this morning had several diamond rings and earrings, a roll of government bonds and some money clasped in her hands. She was a widow, and was very wealthy. Her body has been embalmed and is at the house of relatives.

Suicide Brought Relief.

From under the large brick school-house 124 bodies were taken last night and to-day, and in every corner and place the bodies are being found and buried as fast as possible. The necessity for speedy burial is becoming manifest, and the stench is sickening. A number of bodies have been found with a bullet hole in them, showing conclusively that in their maddening fright suicide was resorted to by many.

Work was commenced during the day on the south side of the town. It is supposed that five hundred or six hundred bodies will be found in that locality.

About twelve o'clock ten bodies were taken out of the wreck near the Cambria Library. On account of the bruised and mangled condition, some having faces crushed in, it was impossible to identify them. It is supposed they were guests at the Hurlbert House, which is completely demolished.

Eight bodies were recovered near the Methodist Church at eleven o'clock. It is said that fully one hundred and fifty bodies were found last evening in a sort of pocket below the Pennsylvania Railroad signal tower at Sang Hollow, where it was expected there would be a big find.

Kernville One Vast Morgue.

Over one thousand bodies have been taken from the river, dragged from the sluggish pools of mud or dug out of the sand about Kernville during the day. Three hundred of them were spread out upon the dry sand along the river's bank at one time this afternoon. The sight is one that cannot be described, and is one of the most distressing ever witnessed. A crowd of at least five hundred were gathered around, endeavoring to find the bodies of some friends or relatives. There were no coffins there at the time and the bodies had to be laid on the ground. However, five hundred coffins are on the way here, and the undertakers have sent for five hundred additional ones. Kernville from now on will be the place where most of the bodies will be found. The water has fallen so much that it is possible to get at the bodies. However, all the bodies have to be dug out of the sand, and it causes no end of work.

It is thought that most of the bodies that will be found at Kernville are under a large pile of débris, about an acre in length. This is where most of the buildings drifted, and it is natural to suppose that the bodies floated with them. A rain is now falling, but this does not interfere with the work. Most of the rescuing party have been up for two days, yet they work with a determination that is wonderful.

Nineveh, the City of the Dead.

Nineveh is literally a city of the dead. The entire place is filled with corpses. At the depot eighty-seven coffins were piled up and boxed. On the streets coffin boxes covered the sidewalks. Improvised undertaking shops have embalmed and placed in their shrouds 198 persons. The dead were strewn about the town in all conceivable places where their bodies would be protected from the thoughtless feet of the living.

Most of the bodies embalmed last night had been taken out of the river in the morning by the people at Nineveh, who worked incessantly night and day searching the river. The bodies when found were placed in a four-horse wagon, frequently twelve at a time, and driven away. Of the bodies taken out near Moorhead fully three-fourths are women and the rest children. But few men are found there. In one row at the planing mill to-day were eighteen children's bodies awaiting embalming. Next to them was a woman whose head had been crushed in so as to destroy her features. On her hand were three diamond rings.

Dr. Graff, of the State Board of Health, stationed at Nineveh, states that up till ten o'clock this morning they had embalmed about two hundred bodies, and by noon to-day would about double that number, as they were fishing bodies out of the river at this point at the rate of one every five minutes. In the driftwood and débris bodies are being exhumed, and an additional force of undertakers has been despatched to this place.

In a Charnel House.

At the public school-house the scene beggars description. Boards have been laid from desk to desk, and as fast as the hands of a large body of men and women can put the remains in recognizable shape they are laid out for possible identification and removed as quickly as possible. Seventy-five still remain, although many have been taken away, and they are being brought in every moment. It is something horrifying to see one portion of the huge school taken up by corpses, each with a clean white sheet covering it, and on the other side of the room a promiscuous heap of bodies in all sorts of shapes and conditions, looking for all the world like decaying tree trunks. Among the number identified are two beautiful young ladies named respectively Mrs. Richardson, who was a teacher in the kindergarten school, and Miss Lottie Yost, whose sister I afterwards noticed at one of the corners near by, weeping as if her very heart was broken. Not a single acquaintance did she count in all of the great throng who passed her by, although many tendered sincere sympathy, which was accentuated by their own losses.

Lost and Found.

At the station of Johnstown proper this morning the following names were added to the list of bodies found and identified: Charles Marshall, one of the engineers Cambria Company. A touching incident in connection with his death is that he had been married but a short time and his widow is heartbroken.

Order at any Cost.

Ex-Sheriff C. L. Dick, who was at one time Burgess of Johnstown, has charge of a large number of special deputies guarding the river at various points. He and a posse of his men caught seven Hungarians robbing dead bodies in Kernville early this morning, and threw them all into the river and drowned them. He says he has made up his mind to stand no more nonsense with this class of persons, and he has given orders to his men to drown, shoot or hang any man caught stealing from the dead. He said the dead bodies of the Huns can be found in the creek.

Sheriff Dick, or "Chall" as he is familiarly called, is a tall, slim man, and is well known in Pittsburgh, principally to sportsmen. He is a first-class wing shot, and during the past year he has won several live bird matches. He is slow to anger, but when forced into a fight his courage is unfailing.

Shooting Looters on the Wing.

Dick wears corduroy breeches, a large hat, a cartridge belt, and is armed with a Winchester rifle. He is a crack shot and has taken charge of the deputies in the wrecked portion of the city. Yesterday afternoon he discovered two men and a woman cutting the finger from a dead woman to get her rings. The Winchester rifle cracked twice in quick succession, and the right arm of each man dropped, helplessly shattered by a bullet. The woman was not harmed, but she was so badly frightened that she will not rob corpses again. Some five robbers altogether were shot during the afternoon, and two of them were killed.

The lynchings in the Johnstown district so far number from sixteen to twenty.

Treasure Lying Loose.

Notwithstanding this, and the way that the town is most thoroughly under martial law, the pilfering still goes on. The wreck is a gold mine for pilferers. A Hungarian woman fished out a trunk down in Cambria City yesterday, and on breaking it open found $7,500 in it. Another woman found a jewel box containing several rings and a gold watch. In one house in Johnstown there is $1,700 in money, but it is impossible to get at it.

Hanged and Riddled with Bullets.

Quite an exciting scene took place in the borough of Johnstown last night. A Hungarian was discovered by two men in the act of blowing up the safe in the First National Bank Building with dynamite. A cry was raised, and in a few minutes a crowd had collected and the cry of "Lynch him!" was raised, and

THE JOHNSTOWN HORROR. 141

in less time than it takes to tell it the man was strung up to a tree in what was once about the central portion of Johnstown. Not content with this the Vigilance Committee riddled the man's body full of bullets. He remained hanging to the tree for several hours, when some person cut him down and buried him with the other dead.

The stealing by Hungarians at Cambria City and points along the railroad has almost ceased. The report of several lynchings and the drowning of two Italians while being pursued by citizens yesterday, put an end to the pilfering for a time.

While Deputy Sheriff Rose was patrolling the river bank he found two Hungarians attempting to rob several bodies, and at once gave chase. The men started for the woods when he pulled out a pistol and shot twice, wounding both men badly. From the latest reports the men are still living, but they are in a critical condition.

Cutting Off a Head for a Necklace.

It is reported that two Hungarians found the body of a lady between Woodvale and Conemaugh who had a valuable necklace on. The devils dragged her out of the water and severed her head from her body to get the necklace. At eleven o'clock to-day the woods were being scoured for the men who are supposed to be guilty of the crime.

Pickets Set, Strangers Excluded.

Up till noon to-day General Hastings has had his headquarters on the east side of the river, but this morning he came over to the burning débris, followed by about one hundred and twenty-five men carrying coffins. He started to work immediately, and has ordered men from Philadelphia, Harrisburg, and all eastern towns to do laboring work.

The Citizen's Committee are making desperate efforts to preserve peace, and the Hungarians at Cambria City are being kept in their houses by men with clubs, who will not permit them to go outside. There seems considerable race prejudice at Cambria City, and trouble may follow, as both the English and Hungarians are getting worked up to a considerable extent.

The Sheriff has taken charge of Johnstown and armed men are this morning patrolling the city. The people who have been properly in the limits are permitted to enter the city if they are known, but otherwise it is impossible to get into the town. The regulation seems harsh, but it is a necessity.

Troops Sent Home.

Battery B, of Pittsburgh, arrived in the city this morning under command of Lieutenant Sheppard, who went to the quarters of Adjutant-General Hastings in the railroad watch tower. The General had just got up, and as the officer approached the General said:—

"Who sent you here?"

"I was sent here by the Chamber of Commerce," replied the Lieutenant.

"Well, I want to state that there are only four people who can order you out, viz.:—The Governor,

Adjutant-General, Major General and the Commander of the Second Brigade. You have committed a serious breach of discipline, and my advice to you is to get back to Pittsburgh as soon as possible, or you may be mustered out of service. I am surprised that you should attempt such an act without any authority whatever."

This seemed to settle the matter, and the battery started back to Pittsburgh. In justice to Lieutenant Sheppard it might be stated that he was told that an order was issued by the Governor. General Hastings stated afterwards that the sending down of the soldiers was like waving a red flag, and it would only tend to create trouble. He said everything was quiet here, and it was an insult to the citizens of Johnstown to send soldiers here at present.

Extortioners Held in Check.

A riot was almost caused by the exorbitant prices that were charged for food. One storekeeper in Millville borough was charging $5 a sack for flour and seventy-five cents for sandwiches on Sunday. This caused considerable complaint and the citizens grew desperate. They promptly took by force all the contents of the store. As a result this morning all the stores have been put under charge of the police. An inventory was taken and the proprietor was paid the market price for his stock.

A strong guard is kept at the office of the Cambria Iron Company. Saturday was pay day at the works, and $80,000 is in the safe. This became known, and the officials are afraid that an attempt would be made to rob the place.

Sheriff Dick and a posse of his men got into a riot this afternoon with a crowd of Hungarians at Cambria City. The Hungarians got the better of him, and he called on a squad of Battery B boys, who charged with drawn sabres, and soon had the crowd on the run.

Men Hard at Work.

Order is slowly arising out of chaos. The survivors are slowly realizing what is the best course to pursue. The great cry is for men. Men who will work and not stand idly by and do nothing but gaze at the ruins. The following order was posted on a telegraph pole in Johnstown to-day:—

"Notice—During the day men who have been idle have been begged to aid us in clearing the town, and many have not refused to work. We are now so organized that employment can be found for every man who wants to work, and men offered work who refuse to take the same and who are able to work must leave Johnstown for the present. We cannot afford to feed men who will not work. All work will be paid for. Strangers and idlers who refuse to work will be ejected from Johnstown.

"By order of Citizens' Committee."

Turning Away the Idlers.

Officers were stationed at every avenue and railroad that enters the town. All suspicious looking characters are stopped. But one question is asked.

It is, "Will you work?" If an affirmative answer is given a man escorts him to the employment bureau, where he is put to work. If not, he is turned back. The committee has driven one or two men out of the town. There is a lot of idle vagabond negroes in Johnstown who will not work. It is likely that a committee will escort them out of town. They have caused the most trouble during the past terrible days.

It is a fact, although a disagreeable one to say, that not a few of the relief committees who came to this city, came only out of curiosity and positively refused to do any work, but would hang around the cars eating food. The leaders of the committee then had to do all the work. They deserve much credit.

Begging for Help.

An old man sat on a chair placed on a box at the intersection of two streets in Johnstown and begged for men. "For God's sake," he said, "can we not find men. Will not some of you men help? Look at these men who have not slept for three days and are dropping with fatigue. We will pay well. For God's sake help us." Tears rolled down his cheeks as he spoke. Then he would threaten the group of idlers standing by and again plead with them. Every man it seems wants to be a policeman.

CHAPTER VII.

Burial of the Victims.

Hundreds have been laid away in shallow trenches without forms, ceremonies or mourners. All day long the work of burial has been going on. There was no time for religious ceremonies or mourning and many a mangled form was coffined with no sign of mourning save the honest sympathy of the brave men who handled them. As fast as the wagons that are gathering up the corpses along the stream arrive with their ghastly loads they are emptied and return again to the banks of the merciless Conemaugh to find other victims among the driftwood in the underbrush, or half buried in the mud. The coffins are now beginning to arrive, and on many streets on the hillside they are stacked as high as the second and third story windows.

At Kernville the people are not so fortunate. It would seem that every man is his own coffin maker, and many a man can be seen here and there claiming the boards of what remains of his house in which perhaps he has found the remains of a loved one, and busily patching them together with nails and hoops or any available thing to hold the body.

When the corpses are found they are taken to the nearest dead house and are carefully washed. They are then laid out in rows to await identification.

Cards are pinned to their breasts as soon as they are identified, and their names will be marked on the headboards at the graves.

Wholesale Funerals.

There were many rude funerals in the upper part of the town. The coffins were conveyed to the cemeteries in wagons, each one carrying two, three or more.

At Long View Cemetery and at one or two other points long trenches have been dug to receive the coffins. The trenches are only about three feet deep, it being thought unnecessary to bury deeper, as almost all the bodies will be removed by friends. Nearly three hundred bodies were buried thus to-day.

There will be no public ceremony, no funeral dirge, and but few weeping mourners. The people are too much impressed with the necessity of immediate and constant work to think of personal grief.

The twenty-six bodies taken to the hose house in Minersville were buried shortly after ten o'clock yesterday morning. Of the twenty-six, thirteen were identified. Eight women, a baby and four men were buried without having been identified.

All day yesterday men were engaged in burying the dead. They ran short of coffins, and in order to dispose of the rapidly decomposing bodies they built rough boxes out of the floating lumber that was caught. In this way they buried temporarily over fifty bodies in the cemetery just above the town.

Putrefaction of dead bodies threatens the health of

the whole region. Now that the waters are fast shrinking back from the horrid work of their own doing and are uncovering thousands of putrid and ill-smelling corpses the fearful danger of pestilence is espied, stalking in the wake of more violent destruction.

The air is already reeking with infectious filth, and the alarm is widespread among the desolated and overwrought population.

Cremation Best.

Incident to this phase of the situation the chief sensation of the morning was the united remonstrance of the physicians against the extinguishment of the burning wreck of the demolished town which is piled up against the bridge. They maintain, with a philosophy that to anxious searchers seems heartless, that hundreds, if not thousands, of lifeless and decaying bodies lie beneath this mass of burning ruins.

"It would be better," they say, " to permit Nature's greatest scavenger—the flames—to pursue his work unmolested than to expose to further decay the horde of putrefying bodies that lie beneath this débris. There can be but one result. Days will elapse before the rubbish can be sufficiently removed to permit the recovery of these bodies, and long before that every corpse will be a putrid mass, giving forth those frightful emanations of decaying human flesh that in a crowded community like this can have but one result —the dreadful typhus. Every battlefield has demonstrated the necessity of the hasty interment of decaying bodies, and the stench that already arises is a fore-

THE JOHNSTOWN HORROR. 149

runner of impending danger. Burn the wreck, burn the wreck."

Sorrow Rejects Safety.

A loud cry of indignation arose from the lips of the vast multitude and the warnings of science were lost in the eager demands of those that sought the remains of the near and dear. The hose was again turned upon the hissing mass, and rapidly the flames yielded to the supremacy of water.

It is almost impossible to conceive the extent of these smoking ruins. An area of eight or ten acres above the dam is covered to a depth of forty feet with shattered houses, borne from the resident centre of Johnstown. In each of these houses, it is estimated, there were from one to twenty or twenty-five people. This is accepted as data upon which to estimate the number that perished on this spot, and if the data be correct the bodies that lie beneath these ruins must run well up into the thousands.

Members of the State Board of Health arrived in Nineveh this morning and determined to proceed at once to dredge the river, to clean it of the dead and prevent the spreading of disease. To this end they have wired the State Department to furnish them with the proper appliances.

Drinking Poisoned Water.

From other points in this and connecting valleys the same fear of pestilence is expressed. The cities of Pittsburgh and Allegheny, which have a population of three hundred and fifty thousand and drink the waters of the Allegheny River, down which corpses and débris from Johnstown must flow unless stopped above, are in danger of an epidemic. The water is to-day thick with mud, and bodies have been found as far south of here as Beaver, a distance of thirty miles below Pittsburgh. To go this distance the bodies followed the Conemaugh from Johnstown to the Kiskiminetas, at Blairsville, joining the Allegheny at Freeport, and the Ohio here, the entire distance from this point being about one hundred and fifty miles.

"This is a very serious matter," said a prominent Pittsburgh physician who is here to me to-day, "and one that demands the immediate attention of the Board of Health officials. The flood of water that swept through Johnstown has cleaned out hundreds of cesspools. These and the barnyards' manure and the dirt from henneries and swamps that were swept by the waters have all been carried down into the Allegheny River. In addition to this there are the bodies of persons drowned. Some of these will, in all likelihood, be secreted among the débris and never be found. Hundreds of carcasses of animals of various kinds are also in the river.

Typhus Dreaded.

"These will decay, throwing out an animal poison. This filth and poisonous matter is being carried into the Allegheny, and will be pumped up into the reservoir and distributed throughout the city. The result is a cause for serious apprehension. Take, for example, the town of Hazleton, Pa. There the filth from some outhouse was carried into the reservoir and distributed through the town. The result was a typhoid fever epidemic and hundreds of people lost their lives. The water that we are drinking to-day is something fearful to behold."

The municipal authorities of Pittsburgh have issued a notice embodying the above facts.

Sanitary Work.

A message was received by the Relief Committee this morning confirming the report that for the health of the cities of Pittsburgh and Allegheny it is absolutely necessary that steps be taken immediately to remove the bodies and drift from the river, and begging the committee to take early action. The contract for clearing the river was awarded to Captain Jutte, and he will start up the Allegheny this afternoon as far as Freeport, and then work down. His instructions are to clear the river thoroughly of anything that might in any way affect the water supply.

Helping Hands.

The work of relief at the scene of the great disaster is going on rapidly. The Alliance (Ohio) Relief Committee arrived here this morning on a special train with five carloads of provisions. The party is composed of the most prominent iron and steel merchants of Alliance.

They have just returned from a tour of the ruined town. They have been up to Stony Creek, a distance of five miles and up the Conemaugh River toward South Fork, a distance of two miles.

In describing their trip, one of their number said:—
"I tell you the half has never been told. It is impos-

DISTRIBUTING SUPPLIES FROM THE RELIEF TRAIN.

sible to tell the terrible tale. I thought I had seen horrible sights, and I served five years in the War of the Rebellion, but in all my life it has never been my lot to look upon such ghastly sights as I have witnessed to-day.

"While making the circuit of the ruined places we saw 103 bodies taken out of the débris along the bank of the river and Stony Creek. Of this number, we identified six of the victims as our friends."

SCENE ON SOUTH CLINTON STREET.

CHAPTER VIII.

Johnstown and Its Industries.

At this point of our narrative a sketch of Johnstown, where the most frightful havoc of the flood occurred, will interest the reader.

The following description and history of the Cambria Iron Company's Works, at Johnstown, is taken from a report prepared by the State Bureau of Industrial Statistics:

The great works operated by the Cambria Iron Company originated in a few widely separated charcoal furnaces, which were built by pioneer iron workers in the early years of this century. It was chartered under the general law authorizing the incorporation of iron manufacturing companies, in the year 1852. The purpose was to operate four old-fashioned charcoal furnaces, located in and about Johnstown, some of which had been erected many years before. Johnstown was then a village of 1300 inhabitants. The Pennsylvania Railroad had only been extended thus far in 1852, and the early iron manufacturers rightly foresaw a great future for the industry at this point.

Immense Furnaces.

Coal, iron and limestone were abundant, and the new railroad would enable them to find ready markets for their products. In 1853 the construction of four coke furnaces was commenced, and it was two years before the first was completed, while some progress was made on the other three. England was then shipping rails into this country under a low duty, and the iron industry, then in its infancy, was struggling for existence.

The furnaces at Johnstown labored under greater difficulties in the years between 1852 and 1861 than can be appreciated at this late day. Had it not been for a few patriotic citizens in Philadelphia, who loaned their credit and means to the failing company, the city of Johnstown would possibly never have been built. Notwithstanding the protecting care of the Philadelphia merchants, the company in Johnstown was unable to continue in business, and suspended in 1854. Among its heaviest creditors in Philadelphia were Oliver Martin and Martin, Morrell & Co. More money was subscribed, but the establishment failed again in 1855. D. J. Morrell, however, formed a new company with new credit.

Recovery From a Great Fire.

The year of 1856, the first after the lease was made, was one of great financial depression, and the following year was worse. To render the situation still more gloomy a fire broke out in June, 1857, and in three hours the large mill was a mass of ruins. Men stood in double ranks passing water from the Conemaugh river, 300 yards distant, with which to fight the flames. So great was the energy, determination and financial ability of the new company that in one week after the fire the furnaces and rolls were once more in operation under a temporary structure. At this early stage in the manufacturing the management found it advisable to abandon the original and widely separated charcoal furnaces and depend on newly constructed coke furnaces. As soon as practicable after the fire a permanent brick mill was erected, and the company was once more fully equipped. When the war came and with it the Morrill tariff of 1861 a broader field was opened up. Industry and activity in business became general; new life was infused into every enterprise. In 1862 the lease by which the company had been successfully operated for seven years expired, and by a reorganization the present company was formed.

Advent of Steel Rails.

A new era in the manufacture of iron and steel was now about to dawn upon the American people. In this year 1870 there were 49,757 tons of steel produced in the United States, while in 1880 the production was 1,058,314 tons. Open hearth steel, crucible steel and blister steel, prior to this, had been the principal products, but were manufactured by processes too slow and too expensive to take the place of iron. The durability of steel over iron, particularly for rails, had long been known, but its cost of production prevented its use. In 1857 one steel rail was sent to Derby, England, and laid down on the Midland Railroad, at a place where the travel was so great that iron rails then in use had to be renewed sometimes as

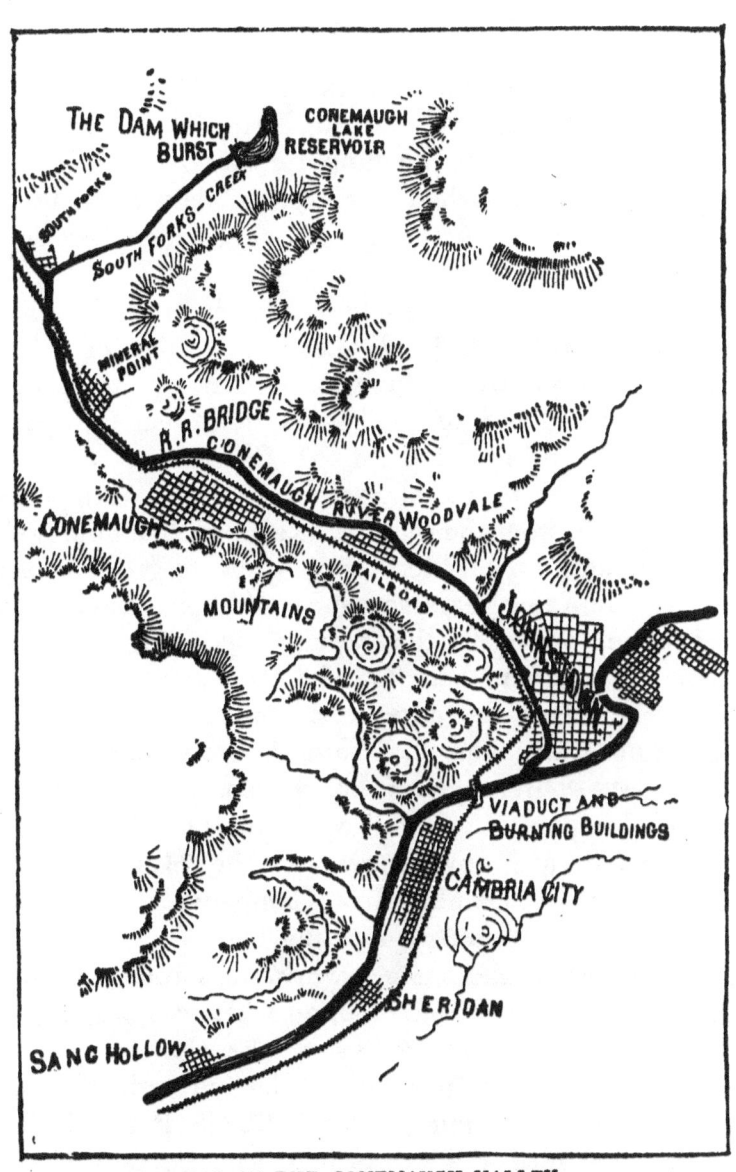

MAP OF THE CONEMAUGH VALLEY.

often as once in three months. In June, 1873, after sixteen years of use, the rail, being well worn, was taken out. During its time 1,250,000 trains, not to speak of the detached engines, etc., had passed over it. This was the first steel rail, now called Bessemer rail, ever used.

About ten years ago the Cambria Iron Company arranged with Dr. J. H. Gautier & Sons, of Jersey City, to organize a limited partnership association under the name of "The Gautier Steel Company, Limited," to manufacture, at Johnstown, wire and various other forms of merchant steel. Within less than a mile from the main works extensive mills were erected and the business soon grew to great proportions. In a few years so much additional capital was required, owing to the rapidly increasing business, that Dr. Gautier, then far advanced in life, wished to be relieved of the cares and duties incident to the growing trade, and the Cambria Iron Company became the purchaser of his works. "The Gautier Steel Company, Limited," went out of existence and the works are now known as the "Gautier Steel Department of Cambria Iron Company."

Description of the Works.

The blast furnaces, steel works and rolling mills of the company are situated upon what was originally a river flat, where the valley of the Conemaugh expanded somewhat just below the borough of Johnstown, and now forming part of Millville Borough. The arrangement of the works has been necessarily governed by the fact that they have gradually expanded from the original rolling-mill and four old style blast furnaces to their present character and capacity of which some idea may be obtained by the condensed description given below.

The Johnstown furnaces, Nos. 1, 2, 3 and 4, form one complete plant, with stacks seventy-five feet high, sixteen feet diameter of bosh. Steam is generated in forty boilers, fired by furnace gas, for eight vertical direct-acting blowing engines. Nos. 5 and 6 blast furnaces form together a second plant with stacks seventy-five feet high, nineteen feet diameter of bosh. No. 5 has iron hot blast stoves and No. 6 has four Whitwell fire-brick hot blast stoves. The furnaces have together six blowing engines exactly like those at Nos. 1, 2, 3 and 4 furnaces. The engines are supplied with steam by thirty-two cylinder boilers.

Marvelous Machinery.

The Bessemer plant was the sixth started in the United States (July, 1871). The main building is 102 feet in width by 165 feet in length. The cupolas are six in number. Blast is supplied from eight Baker rotary pressure blowers driven by engines sixteen inches by twenty-four inches, at 110 revolutions per minute. The cupolas are located on either side of the main trough, into which they are tapped, and down which the melted metal is directed into a ten-ton ladle set on a hydraulic weighing platform, where it is stored until the converters are ready to receive it. There are two vessels of eight and a half tons capacity each, the products being distributed by a hydraulic ladle crane. The vessels are blown by three engines. The Bessemer works are supplied with steam by a battery of twenty-one tubular boilers.

The best average, although not the very highest work done in the Bessemer department is 103 heats of eight and a half tons each for twenty-four hours. The best weekly record reached 1,847 tons of ingots, the best monthly record of 20,304 tons, and the best daily output, 900 tons ingots. All grades of steel are made in the converters from the softest wire and bridge stock to spring steel. All the special stock, that is other than rails, is carefully analyzed by heats, and the physical properties are determined by a tension test.

Ponderous Steam-Hammers.

The open hearth building, 120 feet in width by 155 feet in length, contains three Pernot revolving hearth furnaces of fifteen tons capacity each, supplied with natural gas. A separate pit with a hydraulic ladle crane of twenty tons capacity is located in front of each pan. In a portion of the mill building, originally used as a puddle mill, is located the bolt and nut works, wherein are made track bolts and machine bolts. This department is equipped with bolt-heading and nut making machines, cutting, tapping and facing machines, and produces about one thousand kegs of finished track bolts, of 200 pounds each, per month, besides machine bolts. Near this, also, are located the axle and forging shops, in the old puddle mill building. The axle shop has three steam hammers to forge and ten machines to cut off, centre and turn axles. The capacity of this shop is 100 finished steel axles per day. All axles are toughened and annealed by a patented process, giving the strongest axle possible. In the forging plant, located in the same building, there is an 18,000 pound Bement hammer, and a ten-ton traveling crane to convey forgings from the furnaces to the hammer. There are two furnaces for heating large ingots and blooms for forgings.

A ventilating fan supplies fresh air to the mills through pipes located overhead, and having outlets near the heating furnaces. One hundred thousand cubic feet of fresh air per minute is distributed throughout the mills. The mill has in addition to its boilers, over the heating-furnaces, a brick and iron building, located near the rail mill, 205 feet long and 45 feet wide, containing twenty-four tubular boilers, aggregating about 2000 horse-power.

Tons of Barbed Wire.

The "Gautier Steel Department" consists of a brick building 200 feet by 500 feet, where the wire is annealed, drawn and finished; a brick warehouse 373 feet by 43 feet; many shops, offices, etc.; the barb wire mill, 50 feet by 256 feet, where the celebrated Cambria Link barb wire is made; and the main merchant mill, 725 feet by 250 feet. These mills produce wire, shafting, springs, plowshare, rake and harrow teeth and other kinds of agricultural implement steel. In 1887 they produced 50,000 tons of this material, which was marketed mainly in the Western states.

Grouped with the principal mills are the foundries, pattern and other shops, drafting offices, time offices, etc., all structures being of a firm and substantial character. The company operates about thirty-five miles of railroad tracks, employing in this service twenty-four locomotives, and it owns 1500 cars.

In the fall of 1886 natural gas was introduced into the works

Building up Johnstown.

Anxious to secure employment for the daughters and widows of the employees of the company who were willing to work, its management erected a woolen mill which now employs about 300 persons. Amusements were not neglected, and the people of Johnstown are indebted to the company for the erection of an opera house, where dramatic entertainments are given.

The company owns 700 houses, which are rented exclusively to employees. The handsome library erected by the company and presented to the town was stocked with nearly 7000 volumes. The Cambria Hospital is also under the control of the beneficial association of the works. The Cambria Clubhouse is a very neat pressed brick building on the corner of Main and Federal streets. It was first operated in 1881, and is used exclusively for the entertainment of the guests of the company and such of their employees as can be accommodated. The store building occupied by Wood, Morrell & Co., limited, is a four-story brick structure on Washington street, with three large store rooms on the first floor, the remainder of the building being used for various forms of merchandise.

Including the surrounding boroughs, Kernville, Morrellville and Cambria City, all of which are built up solidly to Johnstown proper, the population is about 30,000. The Cambria Iron Company employs, in Johnstown, about 7500 people, which would certainly indicate a population of not less than 20,000 depending upon the company for a livelihood.

A large proportion of the population of Johnstown are citizens of foreign birth, or their immediate descendants. Those of German, Irish, Welsh and English birth or extraction predominate, with a few Swedes and Frenchmen. As a rule the working people and their families are well dressed and orderly; in this they are above the average. Most of the older workmen of the company, owing largely to its liberal policy, own their houses, and many of them have houses for rent.

CHAPTER IX.

View of the Wreck.

Each visitor to the scene of the great disaster witnessed sights and received impressions different from all others. The following graphic account will thrill every reader:

The most exaggerative imagination cannot too strongly picture the awful harvest of death, the wreck which accompanied that terrible deluge last Friday afternoon. I succeeded in crossing from the north side of the Little Conemaugh, a short distance above the point, to the sandy muddy desert strewn with remnants of the buildings and personal property of those who know not their loss.

It is almost an impossibility to gain access to the region, and it was accomplished only after much difficulty in crossing the swiftly running stream.

Standing at a point in this abode of thousands of dead the work of the great flood can be more adequately measured than from any one place in the devastated region. Here I first realized the appalling loss of life and the terrible destruction of property.

It was about ten o'clock when the waters of Stony Creek rose, overflowed their banks and what is known as the "flats," which includes the entire business portion of the city of Johnstown. The Little Conemaugh was running high at the same time, and it had also overreached the limit of its banks. The water of both streams soon submerged the lower portion of the town. Up to this time there was no intimation that a terrible disaster was imminent. The water poured into the cellars of the houses in the lower districts and rose several inches in the streets, but as that had occurred before the people took no alarm.

Shortly after twelve o'clock the first drowning occurred. This was not because of the deluge, it was simply the carelessness of the victim, who was a driver for the Cambria Iron Company, in stepping into a cellar which had been filled with water. The water continued to rise, and at twelve o'clock had reached that part of the city about a block from the point between Stony Creek and the Little Conemaugh.

Topography of the Place.

The topography of Johnstown is almost precisely like that of Pittsburgh, only in a diminished degree. Stony Creek comes in from the mountains on the northeast, and the Little Conemaugh comes in from the northwest, forming the Conemaugh at Johnstown, precisely as the Allegheny and Monongahela form the Ohio at Pittsburgh. On the west side of Stony Creek are mountains rising to a great height, and almost perpendicularly from the water. On the north side of the Conemaugh River mountains equally as high as those on Stony Creek confine that river to its course. The hills in Johnstown start nearly a half mile from the business section of the city. This leaves a territory between the two rivers of about four hundred acres. This was covered by costly buildings, factories and other important manufactories.

When the waters of South Fork and Little Conemaugh broke over their banks into that portion of the city known as the "flats," the business community turned its attention to putting endangered merchandise in a place of safety.

First Alarm.

In the homes of the people the women began gathering household articles of any kind that may have been in the cellar. Little attention was paid to the water beyond this.

Looking from the "flats" at Johnstown toward and following the Pennsylvania Railroad tracks, which wind along the Little Conemaugh, the village of Woodville stands, or did stand, within sight of the "flats," and is really a continuation of the city at this point.

The mountains on the south side of the Little Conemaugh rise here and form a narrow valley where Woodville was located. Next joining this, without any perceptible break in the houses, was the town of East Conemaugh. The extreme eastern limit of East Conemaugh is about a mile and a half from Johnstown "flats."

A Narrow Chasm.

The valley narrows as it reaches eastward, and in a narrow chasm three miles from Johnstown "flats" is the little settlement of Mineral Point. A few of the houses have found a place on the mountain side, out of harm's way, and so they still stand.

At East Conemaugh there is located a roundhouse of the Pennsylvania Railroad, for the housing of locomotives used to assist trains over the mountains. The inhabitants of this place were all employees of the Pennsylvania and the Gautier Steel Works, of the Cambria Iron Company. The inhabitants numbered about 1,500 people. Like East Conemaugh, 2,000 or 2,500 people, who lived at Woodville, were employees of the same corporation and the woolen mills located there.

Just below Woodville the mountains upon the south bank of the Conemaugh disappear and form the commencement of the Johnstown "flats." The Gautier Steel Works of the Cambria Iron Company are located at this point, on the south bank. The Pennsylvania Railroad traverses the opposite bank, and makes a long curve from this point up to East Conemaugh.

Timely Warning to Escape.

At what is known as the point where Stony Creek and the Little Conemaugh form the Conemaugh the mountains followed by Stony Creek take an abrupt turn northward, and the waters of the Little Conemaugh flow into the Conemaugh at right angles with these mountains.

A few hundred feet below this point the Pennsylvania Railroad bridge crosses the Conemaugh River. The bridge is a massive stone structure. From the east end of the bridge there is a heavy fill of from thirty to forty feet high to Johnstown Station, a distance of a quarter of a mile.

Within a few feet of the station a wagon bridge crosses the Little Conemaugh, five hundred feet above the point connecting the "flats" and the country upon the north side of the river.

The Cambria Iron Company's Bessemer department lies along the north bank of the Conemaugh, commencing at the fill, and extends for over two miles down the Conemaugh River upon its northern bank.

Below the Cambria Iron Company's property is Millville Borough, and on the hill back of Millville Borough is Minersville properly—the Second ward of Millville Borough.

The First ward of Millville was washed away completely.

While the damage from a pecuniary sense was large, the loss of life was quite small, inasmuch as the people had timely warning to escape.

Below the Pennsylvania Railroad Bridge at Johnstown, upon the south bank of the Conemaugh, was the large settlement of Cambria. It had a population of some five thousand people. At Cambria the mountain retreats for several hundred feet, leaving a level of two or three hundred acres in extent. Just below the bridge the Conemaugh River makes a wide curve around this level. About eight or nine hundred houses stood upon this level.

Below Cambria stands Morrellville, a place about equal in size to Cambria.

From this description of the location of Johnstown and neighboring settlements the course of the waters may be better understood when described. It was about ten minutes to three o'clock Friday afternoon when Mr. West, of the local office of the Pennsylvania Railroad at Johnstown, received a dispatch from the South Fork station, advising him to notify the inhabitants that the big dam in the South Fork, above the city, was about to break. He at once despatched couriers to various parts of the city, and a small section was notified of the impending danger. The messenger was answered with,

"We will wait until we see the water."

Others called "Chestnuts!" and not one in fifty of the people who received the warning gave heed to it.

The Debris of Three Towns.

With the waters standing several inches deep in the streets of the "flats" of the city the deluge from South Fork Lake, burst the dam and rushed full upon Johnstown shortly after five o'clock on Friday afternoon the last day of May.

First it swept the houses from Mineral Point down into East Conemaugh. When the flood reached East Conemaugh the town was wiped out. This mass of débris was borne on to Johnstown, reinforced by the material of three towns.

The Gautier steel department of the Cambria Iron Company was the first property attacked in the city proper Huge rolls, furnaces and all the machinery in the great mills, costing $6,000,000, were swept away in a moment, and to-day there is not the slightest evidence that the mill ever stood there.

Swept From the Roofs.

Westward from this point the flood swept over the flats. The houses, as soon as the water reached them, were lifted from their foundation and hurled against their neighbors'. The people who at the first crash of their property managed to reach the roof or some other floating material were carried on until their frail support was driven against the next obstruction, when they went down in the crash together.

The portion of the "flats" submerged is bounded by Clinton street to the Little Conemaugh River, to the point at Stony Creek, then back to Clinton street by way of Bedford.

This region has an area of one mile square, shaped like a heart, and in this district there are not more than a dozen buildings that are not total wrecks.

Ten per cent. of this district is so covered with mud, stones, rocks and other material, where costly buildings once stood, that it will require excavating from eight to twenty feet to reach the streets of the city.

Remnants of the City.

Of the houses standing there is the Methodist church, the club house, James McMillen's residence, the Morrell mansion, Dr. Lohman's house and the First ward school building.

The Fourth ward school house and the Cambria

Iron Works' general office building are the only buildings standing on the north side of the river from the Pennsylvania Railroad bridge to the limits of the "flats."

The Pennsylvania Railroad, from its station in Johnstown City nearly to Wilmore, a distance of seven miles, had a magnificent road bed of solid rock. From East Conemaugh to the point in Johnstown opposite the Gautier Steel Works, this road bed, ballast and all are gone. Only a few rails may occasionally be seen in the river below.

Freaks of the Flood.

When the crash came in Johnstown the houses were crushed as easily by the huge mass as so many buildings of sand, making much the same sound as if a pencil were drawn over the slats of a shutter. Houses were torn from their foundations and torn to pieces before their occupants realized their danger. Hundreds of these people were crushed to death, while others were rescued by heroic men; but the lives of the majority were prolonged a few minutes, when they met a more horrible death further down the stream.

There is a narrow strip extending from the club house to the point which, in some singular manner, escaped the mass of filling that was distributed on the flats. This strip is about 200 feep wide, 300 long and from 3 to 20 feet deep. What queer turn the flood took to thus spare this section, when the surrounding territory was covered with mud, stones and other material, is a mystery. It is, however, one of the remarkable turns of the flood.

The German Catholic Church is standing, but is in an exceedingly shaky condition and may fall at any minute. This and Dr. Lohman's residence are the only buildings on the plot standing between Main street, Clinton street, Railroad street and the Little Conemaugh.

The destruction of life in this district was too awful to contemplate. It is estimated that not more than one thousand people escaped with their lives, and it is believed that there were fully five thousand persons remaining in the district when the flood came down. The flood wiped out the "flat" with the exception of the buildings noted. The water was twenty feet high here and hurled acres upon acres of houses against the Pennsylvania Railroad bridge which held it and dammed the water up until it was forty feet high. The mass accumulated until the weight became so great that it broke through the fill east of the bridge and the débris started out of the temporary reservoir with an awful rush.

It was something near five o'clock when the fill broke. The water rushed across the Cambria flats and swept every house away with the exception of a portion of a brewery. There is nothing else standing in this district which resembles a house.

The Johnstown Post Office Building, with all the office money and stamps, was carried away in the flood. The Postmaster himself escaped with great difficulty.

The dam broke in the centre at three o'clock on

Friday afternoon, and at four o'clock it was dry. That great body of water passed out in one hour. Park & Van Buren, who are building a new draining system at the lake, tried to avert the disaster by digging a sluiceway on one side to ease the pressure on the dam. They had about forty men at work and did all they could, but without avail. The water passed over the dam about a foot above its top, beginning at about half-past two. Whatever happened in the way of a cloud burst took place during the night. There had been but little rain up to dark. When the workmen woke in the morning the lake was very full and was rising at the rate of a foot an hour. It kept on rising until at two o'clock it first began breaking over the dam and undermining it. Men were sent three or four times during the day to warn people below of their danger.

The Break Two Hundred Feet Wide.

When the final break came, at three o'clock, there was a sound like tremendous and continued peals of thunder; rocks, trees and earth were shot up into mid-air in great columns, and then the wave started down the ravine. A farmer, who escaped, said that the water did not come down like a wave, but jumped on his house and beat it to fragments in an instant. He was safe upon the hillside, but his wife and two children were killed. At the present time the lake looks like a cross between the crater of a volcano and a huge mud puddle with stumps of trees and rocks scattered over it. There is a small stream of muddy water running through the centre of the lake site. The dam was seventy feet high and the break is about two hundred feet wide, and there is but a small portion of the dam left on either side. No damage was done to any of the buildings belonging to the club. The whole south fork is swept, with not a tree standing. There are but one or two small streams showing here and there in the lake. A great many of the workmen carried off baskets full of fish caught in the mud.

Three Millions Indemnity.

It is reported that the Sportsman's Association, which owned the South Fork dam, was required to file an indemnity bond of $3,000,000 before their charter was issued. When the bill granting them these privileges was before the Legislature the representatives from Cambria and Blair counties vigorously opposed its passage and only gave way, it is said, upon condition that such an indemnifying bond was filed. This bond was to be filed with the prothonotary of Cambria county.

Father Boyle, of Ebensburg, said the records at the county seat had no trace of such a bond. He found the record of the charter, but nothing about the bond. As the association is known to be composed of very wealthy people, there is much talk here of their being compelled to pay at least a part of the damages.

The Rain Did It.

It begins to dawn on us that the catastrophe was brought about not merely by the bursting of the dam of the old canal reservoir, but by a rainfall exceeding in depth and area all previously recorded phenomena of the kind. The whole drainage basin of the Kiskiminetas, and more particularly that of the Conemaugh, was affected. An area of probably more than 600 square miles poured its precipitation through the narrow valley in which Johnstown and associate villages are located. It is easy to see how, with a rainfall similar to that which caused the Butcher Run disaster of a few years ago, fully from thirty to fifty times as much water became destructive. The whole of the water of the lake would pass Suspension Bridge at Pittsburgh inside of from seven to ten minutes, while the gorge at Johnstown, narrowed by the activity of mines for generations past, was clearly insufficient to allow a free course for Stony Creek alone, which is a stream heading away up in Somerset county, twenty-five or thirty miles south of Johnstown. That the rainfall of the entire Allegheny Mountain system was unprecedented is clearly demonstrated to any one who has watched the Allegheny and Monongahela rivers for the past three days, and this view may serve to correct the impression in the public mind that would localize the causes of the widespread disaster to the bursting of any single dam.

Danger Was Anticipated.

Charles Parke, of Philadelphia, the civil engineer in the employ of the South Fork Fishing Club, in company with George C. Wilson, ex-United States District Attorney, and several other members of the club, reached Johnstown and brought with them the first batch of authoritative news from Conemaugh Lake, the bursting of which, it is universally conceded, caused the disaster.

Mr. Parke was at first averse to talking, and seemed more interested in informing his friends in the Quaker City that he was still in the land of the living. On being pressed he denied most emphatically that the dam had burst, and proceeded to explain that he first commenced to anticipate danger on Friday morning, when the water in the lake commenced to rise at a rapid rate. Immediately he turned his force of twenty-five Italians to opening an extra waste sluiceway in addition to the one that had always answered before.

The five members of the club on hand all worked like horses, but their efforts were in vain, and at three o'clock the supporting wall gave way with a sound that seemed like distant thunder and the work was done.

The Governor's Appeal.

HARRISBURG, Pa., June 3, 1886.—The Governor issued the following:—

"COMMONWEALTH OF PENNSYLVANIA,
"EXECUTIVE CHAMBER,
"HARRISBURG, Pa., June 3, 1889.

"TO THE PEOPLE OF THE UNITED STATES:—

"The Executive of the Commonwealth of Pennsylvania has refrained hitherto from making any appeal to the people for their benefactions, in order that he might receive definite and reliable information from the centres of disaster during the late floods, which have been unprecedented in the history of the State or nation. Communication by wire has been established with Johnstown to-day. The civil authorities are in control, the Adjutant General of the State co-operating with them; order has been restored and is likely to continue. Newspaper reports as to the loss of life and property have not been exaggerated.

"The valley of the Conemaugh, which is peculiar, has been swept from one end to the other as with the besom of destruction. It contained a population of forty thousand to fifty thousand people, living for the most part along the banks of a small river confined within narrow limits. The most conservative estimates place the loss of life at 5,000 human beings, and of property at twenty-five millions. [The reader will understand that this and previous estimates were the first and were far too small.] Whole towns have been utterly destroyed. Not a vestige remains. In the more substantial towns the better buildings, to a certain extent, remain, but in a damaged condition. Those who are least able to bear it have suffered the loss of everything.

"The most pressing needs, so far as food is concerned, have been supplied. Shoes and clothing of all sorts for men, women and children are greatly needed. Money is also urgently required to remove the débris, bury the dead, and care temporarily for the widows and orphans and for the homeless generally. Other localities have suffered to some extent in the same way, but not in the same degree.

"Late advices seem to indicate that there is great loss of life and destruction of property along the west branch of the Susquehanna and in localities from which we can get no definite information. What does come, however, is of the most appalling character, and it is expected that the details will add new horrors to the situation.

Generous Responses.

"The responses from within and without the State have been most generous and cheering. North and South, East and West, from the United States and from England, there comes the same hearty, generous response of sympathy and help. The President, Governors of States, Mayors of cities, and individuals and communities, private and municipal corporations, seem to vie with each other in their expressions of sympathy and in their contributions of substantial aid. But, gratifying as these responses are, there is no danger of their exceeding the necessities of the situation.

Organized Distribution.

"A careful organization has been made upon the ground for the distribution of whatever assistance is furnished. The Adjutant General of the State is there as the representative of the State authorities and giving personal attention, in connection with the Chief Burgess of Johnstown and a committee of relief to the distribution of the help which is furnished.

"A large force will be employed at once to remove the débris and bury the dead, so as to avoid disease and epidemic.

"The people of the Commonwealth and others whose unselfish generosity is hereby heartily appreciated and acknowledged may be assured that their contributions will be made to bring their benefactions to the immediate and direct relief of those for whose benefit they are intended.

"JAMES A. BEAVER.

"By the Governor, CHARLES W. STONE, Secretary of the Commonwealth."

Alive to the Situation.

The Masonic Relief Committee which went from Pittsburgh to Johnstown telegraphed President Harrison, urging the appointment of a national commission to take charge of sanitary affairs at the scene of the disaster. It was urged that the presence of so many decaying corpses would breed a pestilence there, besides polluting the water of the streams affecting all the country between Pittsburgh and New Orleans.

The disasters in Pennsylvania were the subject of a conference at the White House between the President, General Noble, the Secretary of the Interior, and Surgeon General Hamilton. The particular topic which engaged their attention was the possibility of the pollution of the water-supply of towns along the Conemaugh river by the many dead bodies floating down the stream.

The President was desirous that this new source of danger should be cut off, if any measures which could be taken by the government could accomplish it. It was suggested that the decomposition of so much human flesh and the settling of the decomposing fragments into the bed of the stream might make the water so foul as to breed disease and scatter death in a new form among the surviving dwellers in the valley.

Not Afraid of a Plague.

Surgeon General Hamilton expressed the opinion that the danger was not so great as might be supposed. There would be no pollution from those bodies taken from the river before decomposition set in, and the force of the freshet would tend to clear the river bed of any impurities in it rather than make new deposits. The argument which had the most weight, however, with the President was the efficiency of the local authorities. Pennsylvania has a State Board of Health and is a State with ample means at her disposal, both in money and men, and if there is any danger of this sort her local officials were able to deal with it. This was practically the decision of the conference. The gentlemen will meet again, if necessary, and stand ready to render every assistance which the situation calls for, but they will leave the control of the matter with the Commonwealth of Pennsylvania until it appears that she is unable to cope with it.

Governor Beaver to the President.

The following telegram was received by President Harrison from Governor Beaver, who made his way from York to Harrisburg :—

"Harrisburg, Pa., June 3, 1889.
"To the President, Washington:—

"The Sheriff of Cambria county says everything is quiet and that he can control the situation without the aid of troops. The people are fairly housed and good order prevails. The supply of food so far is equal to the demand, but supplies of food and clothing are still greatly needed.

"Conservative estimates place the loss of life at from five thousand to ten thousand, and loss of property at from $25,000,000 to $40,000,000. The people are at work heroically, and will have a large force tomorrow clearing away the débris.

"The sympathies of the world are freely expressed. One telegram from England gives $1,000. I will issue a general appeal to the public to-night. Help comes from all quarters. Its universality greatly encourages our people. I will communicate with you promptly if anything unusual occurs.

"James A. Beaver."

CHAPTER X.

Thrilling Experiences.

JOHNSTOWN, Pa., June 3, 1889.—Innumerable tales of thrilling individual experiences, each one more horrible than the others, are told.

Frank McDonald, a conductor on the Somerset branch of the Baltimore and Ohio, was at the Pennsylvania Railroad depot in this place when the flood came. He says that when he first saw the flood it was thirty feet high and gradually rose to at least forty feet.

"There is no doubt that the South Fork Dam was the cause of the disaster," said Mr. McDonald. "Fifteen minutes before the flood came Decker, the Pennsylvania Railroad agent read me a telegram that he had just received saying that the South Fork Dam had broken. As soon as he heard this the people in station, numbering six hundred, made a rush for a hill. I certainly think I saw one thousand bodies go over the bridge. The first house that came down struck the bridge and at once took fire, and as fast as the others came down they were consumed.

Saw a Thousand Persons Burn.

"I believe I am safe in saying that I saw one thousand bodies burn. It reminded me of a lot of flies on fly paper struggling to get away, with no hope and no chance to save them.

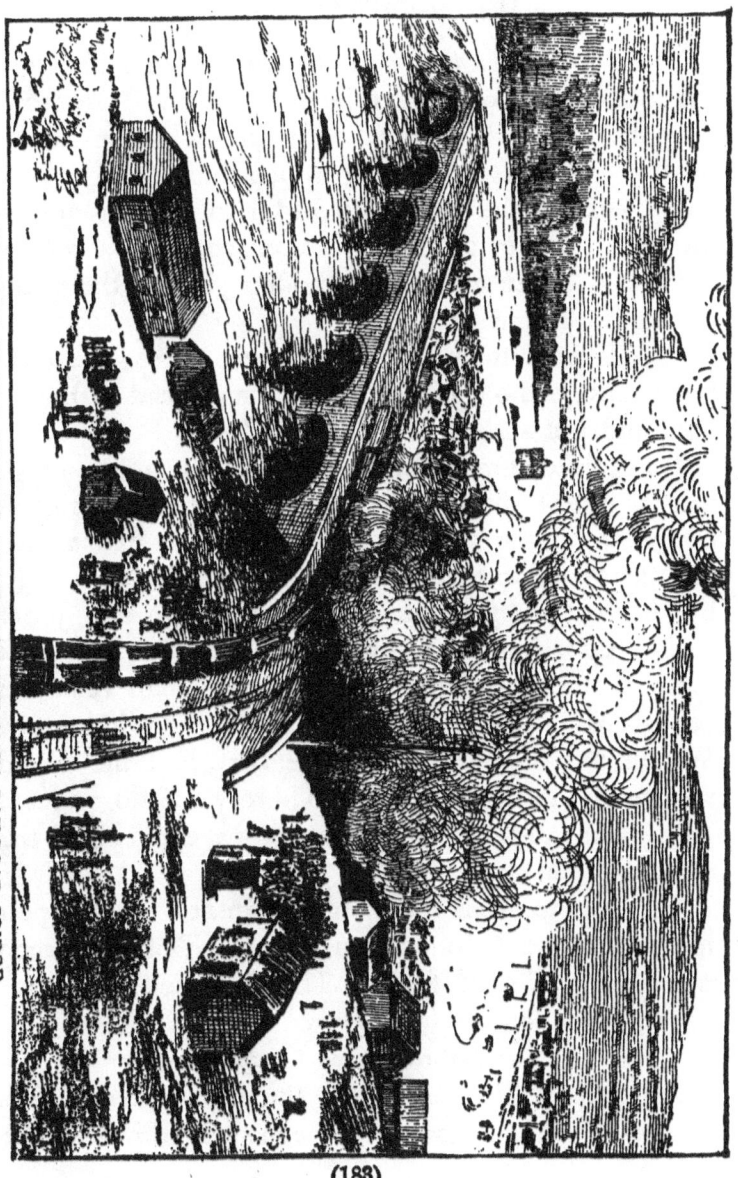
THE WRECKED HOUSES BURNING AT THE PENNSYLVANIA RAILROAD BRIDGE.

"I have no idea that had the bridge been blown up the loss of life would have been any less. They would have floated a little further with the same certain death. Then, again, it was impossible for any one to have reached the bridge in order to blow it out, for the waters came so fast that no one could have done it.

"I saw fifteen to eighteen bodies go over the bridge at the same time.

"I offered a man $20 to row me across the river, but could get no one to go, and finally had to build a boat and get across that way."

It required some exercise of acrobatic agility to get into or out of the town. A slide, a series of frightful tosses from side to side, a run and you had crossed the narrow rope bridge which spanned the chasm dug by the waters between the stone bridge and Johnstown. Crossing the bridge was an exciting task. Yet many women accomplished it rather than remain in Johnstown. The bridge pitched like a ship in a storm. Within two inches of your feet rushed the muddy waters of the Conemaugh. There were no ropes to guide one and creeping was more convenient than walking.

One had to cross the Conemaugh at a second point in order to reach Johnstown proper. This was accomplished by a skiff ferry. The ferryman clung to a rope and pulled the load over.

Confusion Worse Confounded.

It is impossible to describe the appearance of Main street. Whole houses have been swept down this one street and become lodged. The wreck is piled as high as the second story windows. The reporter could step from the wreck into the auditorium of the Opera House. The ruins consists of parts of houses, trees, saw logs, reels from the wire factory. Many houses have their side walls and roofs torn up, and you can walk directly into what had been second story bedrooms, or go in by way of the top. Further up town a raft of logs lodged in the street and did great damage.

The best way to get an idea of the wreck is to take a number of children's blocks, place them closely together and draw your hand through them.

At the commencement of the wreckage, which is at the opening of the valley of the Conemaugh, one can look up the valley for miles and not see a house. Nothing stands but an old woolen mill.

As Seen by an Eye-Witness.

Charles Luther is the name of the boy who stood on an adjacent elevation and saw the whole flood. He said he heard a grinding noise far up the valley, and looking up he could see a dark line moving slowly toward him. He saw that it was made up of houses. On they came like the hand of a giant clearing off his tables. High in the air would be tossed a log or beam, which fell back with a crash. Down the valley it moved sedately and across the little mountain city. For ten minutes nothing but moving houses were seen, and then the waters came with a roar and a rush. This lasted for two hours, and then it began to flow more steadily.

The pillaging of the houses in Johnstown is something awful to contemplate and describe. It makes one feel almost ashamed to call himself a man and know that others who bear the same name have converted themselves into human vultures, preying on the dead. Men are carrying shotguns and revolvers, and woe betide the stranger who looks even suspiciously at any article. Goods of great value were being sold in town to-day for a drink of whiskey.

A supply store has been established in the Fourth ward in Johnstown. A line of men, women and children, extending for a square, waited patiently to have their wants supplied.

An Improvised Morgue.

The school house has been converted into a morgue, and the dead are being buried from this place. A hospital has been opened near by and is full of patients. One of the victims was removed from a piece of wreckage in which he had been imprisoned three days. His leg was broken and his face badly bruised. He was delirious when rescued.

In some places it is said the railroad tracks were scooped out to a depth of twenty feet. A train of cars, all loaded, were run on the Conemaugh bridge. They with the bridge, now lie in the wreckage at this point. The Pennsylvania Railroad loses thirty-five engines and many cars.

Fire Still Raging.

The cling-cling-clang of the engines has a homelike sound. The fire has spread steadily all day and the upper part of the drift is burning to-night. The fire engine is stationed on the river bank and a line of hose laid far up the track to the coal mine. The flames to-night are higher than ever before, and by its

FIREMEN ON DUTY AT THE BRIDGE.

right long lines of the curious can be seen along the banks.

The natural gas has been shut off, owing to the many leaks in Johnstown. No fire is allowed in the city. The walls of many houses are falling. Their crash can be heard across the river, where the newspaper men are located. In the walk through the town to day the word "danger," could be noticed, painted by the rescuers on the walls.

Cremated.

One of the Catholic churches in the town was burned on Saturday. A house drifted down against it and set it on fire. A funeral was being held at the church at the time of the flood. The congregation deserted the church and the body was burned with the building. Two large trees passed entirely through a brick Catholic church located near the centre of the town. The building still stands, but is a total wreck.

Colonel Norman M. Smith, of Pittsburgh, while returning from Johnstown after a visit to Adjutant General Hastings, was knocked from the temporary bridge into the river and carried down stream a couple of hundred yards before he was able to swim ashore. He was not hurt.

A Lucky Escape.

O. J. Palmer, travelling salesman for a Pittsburgh meat house, was on the ill-fated day express, one car of which was washed away. He narrowly escaped drowning, and tells a horrible tale of his experience on that occasion. The engineer, the fireman and himself, when they saw the flood coming, got upon the top of the car, and when the coach was carried away they caught the driftwood, and fortunately it was carried near the shore and they escaped to the hills. Mr.

Palmer walked a distance of twenty miles around the flooded district to a nearby railroad station on this side.

Freaks of the Disaster.

A novel scene was witnessed yesterday near Johnstown borough. Some women who managed to escape from the town proper had to wear men's clothes, as their own had been torn off by the flood.

The force of the flood can be estimated by the fact that it carried three cars a mile and a half and the tender of an engine weighing twelve tons was carried fourteen miles down the river. A team of horses which was standing on Main street just before the flood was found a mile and a quarter below the town yesterday.

The damage to the Cambria Iron Works was not so great as at first reported. The ends of the blooming mill and open hearth furnace buildings were crushed in by the force of the flood. The water rushed through the mill and tore a great pile of machinery from its fastenings and caused other damage. The Bessemer steel mill is almost a ruin. The rolling and wire mills and the six blast furnaces were not much damaged. This morning the company put a large force of men at work and are making strenuous efforts to have at least a portion of the plant in operation within a few weeks. This has given encouragement to the stricken people of Johnstown, and they now seem to have some hope, although so many of their loved ones have met their death. The mill yard, with its numerous railroad tracks, is nothing but a waste. Large piles of pig metal were scattered in every direction. All the loose débris is being gathered into heaps and burned.

Hurled to a Place of Safety.

A pitiful sight was that of an old, gray haired man named Norn. He was walking around among the mass of débris, looking for his family. He had just sat down to eat his supper when the crash came, and the whole family, consisting of wife and eight children, were buried beneath the collapsed house. He was carried down the river to the railroad bridge on a plank. Just at the bridge a cross-tie struck him with such force that he was shot clear upon the pier and was safe. But he is a mass of bruises and cuts from head to foot. He refused to go to the hospital until he found the bodies of his loved ones.

Heroism in Bright Relief.

A Paul Revere lies somewhere among the dead. Who he is is now known, and his ride will be famous in history. Mounted on a grand, big bay horse, he came riding down the pike which passes through Conemaugh to Johnstown, like some angel of wrath of old, shouting his warning: "Run for your lives to the hills! Run to the hills!"

A Cloud of Ruin.

The people crowded out of their houses along the thickly settled streets awestruck and wondering. No one knew the man; and some thought he was a maniac and laughed. On and on, at a deadly pace, he rode, and shrilly rang out his awful cry. In a few moments, however, there came a cloud of ruin down the broad streets, down the narrow alleys, grinding, twisting, hurling, overturning, crashing—annihilating the weak and the strong. It was the charge of the flood, wearing its coronet of ruin and devastation, which grew at every instant of its progress. Forty feet high, some say, thirty according to others, was this sea, and it travelled with a swiftness like that which lay in the heels of Mercury.

On and on raced the rider, on and on rushed the wave. Dozens of people took heed of the warning and ran up to the hills.

Poor, faithful rider, it was an unequal contest. Just as he turned to cross the railroad bridge the mighty wall fell upon him, and horse, rider and bridge all went out into chaos together.

A few feet further on several cars of the Pennsylvania Railroad train from Pittsburgh were caught up and hurried into the caldron, and the heart of the town was reached.

The hero had turned neither to right nor left for himself, but rode on to death for his townsmen. He was overwhelmed by the current at the bridge and drowned. A party of searchers found the body of this man and his horse. He was still in the saddle. In a short time the man was identified as Daniel Periton, son of a merchant of Johnstown, a young man of remarkable courage. He is no longer the unknown hero, for the name of Daniel Periton will live in fame

A Devoted Operator.

Mrs. Ogle, the manager of the Western Union, who died at her post, will go down in history as a heroine of the highest order. Notwithstanding the repeated notifications which she received to get out of reach of the approaching danger, she stood by the instruments with unflinching loyalty and undaunted courage, sending words of warning to those in danger in the valley below. When every station in the path of the coming torrent had been warned she wired her companion at South Fork, "This is my last message," and as such it shall always be remembered as her last words on earth, for at that very moment the torrent engulfed her and bore her from her post on earth to her post of honor in the great beyond.

Another Hero.

A telegraph operator at the railroad station above Mineral Point, which is just in the gorge a short distance below the dam, and the last telegraph station above Conemaugh, had seen the waters rising, and had heard of the first break in the dam. Two hours before the final break came he sent a message to his wife at Mineral Point to prepare for the flood. It read: "Dress the three children in their best Sunday clothes. Gather together what valuables you can easily carry and leave the house. Go to the stable on the hillside. Stay there until the water reaches it;

apparently ten or twelve feet, and Leonard stuck to it tenaciously. Slowly but surely he worked his boat to the other side of the stream, and after what seemed an awful suspense he finally landed amid ringing cheers of men, women and children.

The last seen of him he was making his way down a mountain road in the direction of the spot where his house had lately stood. His family consisted of his wife and three children.

A Thrilling Escape.

Henry D. Thomas, a well-known dry goods merchant, tells the following story: "I was caught right between a plank and a stone wall and was held in that position for a long time. The water came rushing down and forced the plank against my chest. I felt as if it were going through me, when suddenly the plank gave way, and I fell into the water. I grabbed the plank quickly and in some unaccountable way managed to get the forepart of my body on it, and in that way I was carried down the stream. All around me were people struggling and drowning, while bodies floated like corks on the water. Some were crying for help, others were praying aloud for mercy and a few were singing as if to keep up their courage.

A large raft which went by bore a whole family, and they were singing, "Nearer my God to Thee." In the midst of their song the raft struck a large tree and went to splinters. There were one or two wild cries and then silence. The horror of that time is with me day and night. It would have driven a weak-minded person crazy.

"The true condition of things that night can never be adequately described in words. The water came down through a narrow gorge, which in places was hardly two hundred feet wide. The broken dam was at an elevation of about five hundred feet above Johnstown. The railroad bridge across the Conemaugh River is at the lower side of Johnstown, and the river is joined there by another mountain stream from the northeast. It was here that the débris collected and caught fire, and I doubt if it will ever be known how many perished there. The water came down with the speed of a locomotive. The people there are absolutely paralyzed—so much so that they speak of their losses in a most indifferent way. I heard two men in conversation. One said: 'Well, I lost a wife and three children.' 'That's nothing,' said the other; 'I lost a wife and six children.'

The Sudden Break.

A man named Maguire was met on his way from South Fork to Johnstown. He said he was standing on the edge of the lake when the walls burst. The waters were rising all day and were on a level with a pile of dirt which he said was above the walls of the dam. All of a sudden it burst with a report like a cannon and the water started down the mountain side, sweeping before it the trees as if they were chips. Bowlders were rolled down as if they were marbles. The roar was deafening. The lake was emptied in an hour then run to the mountain. The dam is breaking. The flood is coming. Lose no time."

His wife showed the message to her friends, but they laughed at her. They even persuaded her to not heed her husband's command. The wife went home and about her work. Meanwhile the telegraph operator was busy with his ticker. Down to Conemaugh he wired the warning. He also sent it on to Johnstown, then he ticked on, giving each minute bulletins of the break. As the water came down he sent message after message, telling its progress. Finally came the flood. He saw houses and bodies swept past him. His last message was: "The water is all around me; I cannot stay longer, and, for God's sake, all fly." Then he jumped out of his tower window and ran up the mountain just in time to save himself. A whole town came past as he turned and looked. Great masses of houses plunged up. He saw people on roofs yelling and crying, and then saw collisions of houses, which caused the buildings to crush and crumble like paper.

Racing with Death.

All the time he felt that his family were safe. But it was not so with them. When the roar of approaching water came the people of Mineral Point thought of their warning. The wife gathered her children and started to run. As she went she forgot her husband's advice to go to the mountain and fled down the street to the lowlands. Suddenly she remembered she had left the key of her home in the door. She took the children and ran back. As she neared the house the water came and forced them up between the two houses. The only outlet was toward the mountain, and she ran that way with her children. The water chased her, but she and the children managed to clamber up far enough to escape. Thus it was that an accident saved their lives. Only three houses and a school-house were saved at Mineral Point.

A Dangerous Venture.

One of the most thrilling incidents of the disaster was the performance of A. J. Leonard, whose family reside in Morrellville. He was at work, and hearing that his house had been swept away determined at all hazards to ascertain the fate of his family. The bridges having been carried away he constructed a temporary raft, and clinging to it as close as a cat to the side of a fence, he pushed his frail craft out into the raging torrent and started on a chase which, to all who were watching, seemed to mean an embrace in death.

Heedless of cries "For God's sake go back, you will be drowned." "Don't attempt it," he persevered. As the raft struck the current he pulled off his coat and in his shirt sleeves braved the stream. Down plunged the boards and down went Leonard, but as it arose he was seen still clinging. A mighty shout arose from the throats of the hundreds on the banks, who were now deeply interested, earnestly hoping he would successfully ford the stream.

Down again went his bark, but nothing, it seemed, could shake Leonard off. The craft shot up in the air

At the time there were about forty men at work up there, building a new draining system at the lake for Messrs. Parke and Van Buren. They did all they could to try and avert the disaster by digging a sluiceway on one side to ease the pressure on the dam, but their efforts were fruitless.

"It was about half-past two o'clock when the water reached the top of the dam. At first it was just a narrow white stream trickling down the face of the dam, soon its proportions began to grow with alarming rapidity, and in an extremely short space of time a volume of water a foot in thickness was passing over the top of the dam.

"There had been little rain up to dark. Whatever happened in the way of a cloud burst took place during the night. When the workmen woke in the morning the lake was very full and was rising at the rate of a foot an hour.

"When at two o'clock the water began to flow over the dam, the work of undermining began. Men were sent three or four times during the day

To Warn the People

below of their danger. At three o'clock there was a sound like tremendous and continued peals of thunder. The earth seemed to shake and vibrate beneath our feet.

"There was a rush of wind, the trees swayed to and fro, the air was full of fine spray or mist : then looking down just in front of the dam we saw trees, rocks and earth shot up into mid-air in great columns. It seemed as though some great unseen force was at work wantonly destroying everything; then the great wave, foaming, boiling and hissing, dashing clouds of spray hundreds of feet in height as it came against some obstruction in the way of its mad rush, clearing everything away before it, started on its terrible death-dealing mission down the fatal valley."

Engineer Henry's Awful Race.

Engineer Henry, of the second section of the express train, No. 8, which was caught at Conemaugh, tells a thrilling story. His train was caught in the midst of the wave and were the only cars that were not destroyed. "It was an awful sight," he said. "I have often seen pictures of flood scenes, and I thought they were exaggerations, but what I witnessed last Friday changes my former belief. To see that immense volume of water, fully fifty feet high, rushing madly down the valley, sweeping everything before it, was a thrilling sight. It is engraved indelibly on my memory. Even now I can see that mad torrent carrying death and destruction before it.

"The second section of No. 8, on which I was, was due at Johnstown about 10.15 in the morning. We arrived there safely, and were told to follow the first section. When we arrived at Conemaugh the first section and the mail were there. Washouts further up the mountain prevented our going, so we could do nothing but sit around and discuss the situation. The creek at Conemaugh was swollen high, almost overflowing. The heavens were pouring rain, but this did not prevent nearly all the inhabitants of the town from gathering along its banks. They watched

The Waters Go Dashing

by and wondered whether the creek could get much higher. But a few inches more and it would overflow its banks. There seemed to be a feeling of uneasiness among the people. They seemed to fear that something awful was going to happen. Their suspicions were strengthened by the fact that warning had come down the valley for the people to be on the lookout. The rains had swelled everything to the bursting point. The day passed slowly, however.

Noon came and went, and still nothing happened. We could not proceed, nor could we go back, as the tracks about a mile below Conemaugh had been washed away, so there was nothing for us to do but to wait and see what would come next.

Some time after 3 o'clock Friday afternoon I went into the train despatcher's office to learn the latest news. I had not been there long when I heard a fierce whistling from an engine away up the mountain. Rushing out I found dozens of men standing around. Fear had blanched every cheek. The loud and continued whistling had made every one feel that something serious was going to happen. In a few moments I could hear a train rattling down the mountain. About five hundred yards above Conemaugh the tracks make a slight curve and we could not see beyond this. The suspense was something awful. We did not know what was coming, but no one could get rid of the thought that something was wrong at the dam.

"Our suspense was not very long, however. Nearer and nearer the train came, the thundering sound still accompanying it. There seemed to be something behind the train, as there was a dull, rumbling sound which I knew did not come from the train. Nearer and nearer it came; a moment more and it would reach the curve. The next instant there burst upon our eyes a sight that made every heart stand still. Rushing around the curve, snorting and tearing, came an engine and several gravel cars. The train appeared to be putting forth every effort to go faster. Nearer it came, belching forth smoke and whistling long and loud. But

The Most Terrible Sight

was to follow. Twenty feet behind came surging along a mad rush of water fully fifty feet high. Like the train, it seemed to be putting forth every effort to push along faster. Such an awful race we never before witnessed. For an instant the people seemed paralyzed with horror. They knew not what to do, but in a moment they realized that a second's delay meant death to them. With one accord they rushed to the high lands a few hundred feet away. Most of them succeeded in reaching that place and were safe.

"I thought of the passengers in my train. The second section of No. 8 had three sleepers. In these three cars were about thirty people, who rushed through the train crying to the others 'Save your-

AN ENGINEER'S TERRIFIC RACE IN THE VALLEY OF DEATH

selves!' Then came a scene of the wildest confusion. Ladies and children shrieked and the men seemed terror-stricken. I succeeded in helping some ladies and children off the train and up to the highlands. Running back, I caught up two children and ran for my life to a higher place. Thank God, I was quicker than the flood! I deposited my load in safety on the high land just as it swept past us.

"For nearly an hour we stood watching the mad flood go rushing by. The water was full of debris. When the flood caught Conemaugh it dashed against the little town with a mighty crash. The water did not lift the houses up and carry them off, but crushed them one against the other and broke them up like so many egg shells. Before the flood came there was a pretty little town. When the waters passed on there was nothing but

Few Broken Boards

to mark the central portion of the city. It was swept as clean as a newly brushed floor. When the flood passed onward down the valley I went over to my train. It had been moved back about twenty yards, but it was not damaged. About fifty persons had remained in the train and they were safe. Of the three trains ours was the luckiest. The engines of both the others had been swept off the track and one or two cars in each train had met the same fate.

What saved our train was the fact that just at the curve which I mentioned the valley spread out. The valley is six or seven hundred yards broad where our train was standing. This, of course, let the floods pass out. It was only twenty feet high when it struck our train, which was about in the middle of the valley.

This fact, together with the elevation of the track, was all that saved us. We stayed that night in the houses in Conemaugh that had not been destroyed. The next morning I started down the valley and by 4 o'clock in the afternoon had reached Conemaugh furnace, eight miles west of Johnstown. Then I got a team and came home.

In my tramp down the valley I saw some awful sights. On the tree branches hung shreds of clothing torn from the unfortunates as they were whirled along in the terrible rush of the torrent. Dead bodies were lying by scores along the banks of the creeks. One woman I helped drag from the mud had tightly clutched in her hand a paper. We tore it out of her hand and found it to be a badly water-soaked photograph. It was probably a picture of the drowned woman."

Over the Bridge.

Frank McDonald, a railroad conductor, says: "I certainly think I saw 1,000 bodies go over the bridge. The first house that came down struck the bridge and at once took fire, and as fast as they came down they were consumed. I believe I am safe in saying I saw 1,000 bodies burn. It reminded me of a lot of flies on fly-paper struggling to get away, with no hope and no chance to save them. I have no idea that had the bridge been blown up the loss of life would have been any less. They woud have floated a little further with the same certain death. Then, again, it was impossible for any one to have reached the bridge in order to blow it up, for the waters came so fast that no one could have done it. I saw fifteen to eighteen bodies go over the bridge. At the same time I offered a man twenty dollars to row me across the river, but could get no one to go, and I finally had to build a boat and get across that way."

Nothing seems to have withstood the merciless sweep of the mighty on-rush of pent-up Conemaugh. As for the houses of the town a thousand of them lie piled up in a smouldering mass to the right of Conemaugh bridge.

At the present moment, away down in its terrible depths, this mass of torn and twisted timbers and dead humanity is slowly burning, and the light curling smoke that rises as high almost as the mountain, and the sickening smell that comes from the centre of this fearful funeral pile tell that the unseen fire is feeding on other fuel than the rafters and roofs that once sheltered the population of Johnstown.

A Ghastly Scene.

The mind is filled with horror at the supreme desolation that pervades the whole scene. It is small wonder that the pen cannot in the hands of the most skillful even pretend to convey one-hundredth part of what is seen and heard every hour in the day in this fearful place. At the present moment firemen and others are out on that ghastly aggregation of woodwork and human kind jammed against the unyielding mass of arched masonry.

Round them curls the white smoke from the smouldering interior of the heaped up houses of Johnstown. Every now and then the gleam of an axe and a group of stooping forms tell that another ghastly find has been made, and a whisper goes round among the hundreds of watchers that other bodies are being brought to light.

How many hundreds or thousands there are who found death by fire at this awful spot will never be known, and the people are already giving up hopes of ever reaching the knowledge of how their loved and lost ones met their doom, whether in the fierce, angry embrace of the waters of Conemaugh, or in the deadly grip of the fire fiend, who claimed the homes of Johnstown for his own above the fatal bridge.

Every hour it becomes more and more apparent that the exact number of lives lost will never be known. Up to the present time the disposition has been to under rather than overestimate the number of lives sacrificed.

A Mother Rescued by Her Daughter.

A daughter of John Duncan, superintendent of the Johnstown Street Car Company, had an awful struggle in rescuing her mother and baby sister. Mrs. Duncan and family had taken refuge on a roof, when a large log came floating down the river, striking the house with immense force, knocking Mrs. Duncan and daughter into the fast running river. Seeing what had happened, Alvania, her fifteen-year-old daughter, leaped into the water, and after a hard struggle landed both on the roof of the house.

The members of the Cambria Club tell of their battle for life in the following manner: They were about to sit down to dinner when they heard the crash, and knowing what had occurred they started for the attic just as the flood was upon them. When the members were assured of their safety they at once commenced saving others by grasping them as they floated by on tree tops, houses, etc. In this manner they saved seventy persons from death.

The Clock Stopped at 5.20.

One of the queerest sight in the centre of the town is a three-story brick residence standing with one wall, the others having disappeared completely, leaving the floors supported by the partitions. In one of the upper rooms can be seen a mantel with a lambrequin on it and a clock stopped at twenty minutes after five. In front of the clock is a lady's fan, though from the marks on the wall-paper the water has been over all these things.

In the upper part of the town, where the back water from the flood went into the valley with diminished force, there are many strange scenes. There the houses were toppled over one after another in a row, and left where they lay. One of them was turned completely over and stands with its roof on the foundations of another house and its base in the air. The owner came back, and getting into his house through the windows walked about on his ceiling. Out of this house a woman and her two children escaped safely and were but little hurt, although they were stood on their heads in the whirl. Every house has its own story. From one a woman shut up in her garret escaped by chopping a hole in the roof. From another a Hungarian named Grevins leaped to the shore as it went whirling past and fell twenty-five feet upon a pile of metal and escaped with a broken leg. Another is said to have come all the way from very near the start of the flood and to have circled around with the back water and finally landed on the flats at the city site, where it is still pointed out.

CHAPTER XI.

New Tales of Horror.

The accounts contained in the foregoing chapters bring this appalling story of death down to June 4th. We continue the narrative as given from day to day by eye-witnesses, as this is the only method by which a full and accurate description of Johnstown's unspeakable horror can be obtained.

On the morning of June 5th one of the leading journals contained the following announcements, printed in large type, and preceding its vivid account of the terrible situation at Johnstown.

Death, ruin, plague! Threatened outbreak of disease in the fate stricken valley. Awful effluvia from corpses! Swift and decisive means must be taken to clear away the masses of putrefying matter that underlie the wreck of what was once a town. Proposed use of explosives. Crowds of refugees are already attacked by pneumonia and the germs of typhus pervade both air and water. Victims yet unnumbered. Dreadful discoveries hourly made! Heaps of the drowned, the mangled and the burned are found in pockets between rocks and under packed accumulations of sand! Pennsylvania regiments ordered to the scene to keep ward over an afflicted and heart-broken people. Blame where it belongs.

The ears of the inhabitants were dulled to fear by warnings many times repeated—forty-two years ago the dam broke—vivid stories of witnesses of the great tragedy—the owners of the lake must bear a gigantic burden of remorse—sufferings of survivors!

These were the terrible headings in a single issue of a newspaper.

A registry of the living who were residents of Johnstown prior to the flood was begun to-day. Out of a total population of 39,400 the names of only 10,600 have been recorded. This may give an approximate idea of the number of those who lost their lives.

Gaunt Menace of Pestilence.

The most important near fact of to-day is the increasing danger of pestilence.

As the work of disengaging the bodies of the dead progresses the horrible peril becomes more and more apparent. There is need of the speediest possible measures to offset the gravity of the sanitary situation.

From every part of the stricken valley the same cry of alarm arises, for at every point where the dead are being discovered, as the waters continue to abate, the same peril exists.

The use of explosives, especially dynamite, has been discussed. There is some opposition to it, but it may yet be resorted to. The great mass of ruins at the Pennsylvania Railroad bridge, which is still smoking and smouldering, is a ghastly mine of human flesh and bones in all sorts of hideous shapes, and unless desperate means are employed, cannot be cleared away in weeks to come.

Still, vigorous work in that direction is being per-

READING THE HORRIBLE NEWS.

formed, and explosives will be used in a limited degree to further it. This great work may be divided into two parts—the clearing away of the mass of débris lodged against the Pennsylvania Railroad bridge, and the examination and removal of the many wrecked buildings which mark the site of Johnstown.

Order Out of Chaos.

Slowly something like order is beginning to appear in the chaos of destruction. Enough militia came to-day to put the town under strict martial law. Four hundred men of the Fourteenth regiment, of Pittsburgh, are here. There will be no more tramping over the ruins by ungoverned mobs. There will be no more fears of rioting.

The supplies of food are constantly growing. The much needed money is beginning to come in, though not at all needless relief committees are beginning to go out. Better quarters for the sufferers are being provided. Better arrangements for systematic relief are made. Something of the deep gloom has been dispelled, though Johnstown is still the saddest spot on earth.

The systematic attempt to clear up the ruins at the gorge and get out the bodies imprisoned there began to-day. The expectations of ghastly discoveries were more than realized. Scores of burned and mangled bodies were removed.

Freaks of the Torrent.

The great waste where the city stood looked a little different to-day. Some attempt was made to clear up the rubbish, and fires were burning in a dozen places to get rid of it. Tents for the soldiers and some of the sufferers were put up in the smooth stretch of sand where a great, five story hardware store used to stand. The dead animals that were here and there in the débris were removed, to the benefit of the towns-people's health.

Curious things come to light where the rubbish was cleared away. The solid cobblestone pavement had been scooped up by the force of the water and in some places swept so far away that there was not a sign of it. Behind a house that was resting on one corner was found a wickerwork baby carriage full of mud, but not injured or scratched in the least nor yet buried in the mud, but looking as if it had been rolled there and left. Very close to it was a piece of railroad iron that must have been carried half a mile, bent as if it were but common wire. Exactly on the site of a large grocery store was a box of soap and a bundle of clothespins, while of all the brick and stone, of which the store was built, and all the heavy furniture it contained there was not the slightest trace.

Many articles of wearing apparel were found here, but no bodies could be discovered in the whole stretch of the plain, from which it is inferred that most of the deaths occurred at the gorge or else the flood swept them far away.

Reminders of a Broken Home.

One of the few buildings that are left in this part of town is the fine house of Mr. Geranheiser, of the Cambria Iron Company. It presents a queer spectacle—that is common here but has not often been seen before. The flood reached almost to the second floor and was strong enough to cut away about half the house, leaving the rest standing. The whole interior of the place can be seen just as the frightened inmates left it. The carpets are torn up from the first floor, but the pictures are still hanging on the walls and an open piano stands against the wall full of mud; a Brussels carpet being half way out of the second story on the side where the wreck was and showing exactly how high the water came. There was a centre table in the room and an open book on it. Chairs stood about the room and the pictures were on the walls, and half of the room was gone miles away.

Seven Acres of Wreckage.

Just below the bare plain where the business block of Johnstown stood, and above the stone arch bridge on which the Pennsylvania Railroad crossed the river, are seven acres of the wreckage of the flood. The horrors that have been enacted in that spot, the horrors that are seen there every hour, who can attempt to describe? Under and amid that mass of conglomerate rubbish are the remains of at least one thousand persons who died the most frightful of deaths.

This is the place where the fire broke out within twenty minutes after the flood. It has burned ever since. The stone arch bridge acted as a dam to the flood, and five towns were crushing each other against it. A thousand houses came down on the great wave of water, and were held there a solid mass in the jaws of a Cyclopean vise.

A kitchen stove upset. The mass took fire. A

thousand people were imprisoned in these houses. A thousand more were on the roofs. For most of them there was no escape. The fire swept on from house to house. The prisoners saw it coming and shrieked and screamed with terror, and ran up and down their narrow quarters in an agony of fear.

Sights to Freeze Their Blood.

Thousands of people stood upon the river bank and saw and heard it all and still were powerless to help. They saw people kneeling in the flames and praying. They saw families gathered together with their arms around each other and waiting for death. They saw people going mad and tearing their hair and laughing. They saw men plunge into the narrow crevices between the houses and seek death in the water rather than wait its coming in the flames. Some saw their friends and some their wives and children perishing before them, and some in the awful agony of the hour went mad themselves and ran shrieking to the hillsides, and stronger men laid down on the ground and wept.

All that night and all the next day, and far into the morning of Monday, these dreadful shrieks resounded from that place of doom. The fire burned on, aided by the fire underneath, added to by fresh fuel coming down the river. All that time the people stood helpless on the bank and heard those heartrending sounds. What could they do? They could not fight the fire. Every fire engine in the town lay in that mass of rubbish smashed to bits. For hours they had to wait until they could get telegraph word to surrounding towns, and hours more until the fire engines arrived at noon on Monday.

Wrecks of Five Iron Bridges.

The shrieks ceased early in the morning. Men had began to search the ruins and had taken out the few that still lived. The fire engines began to play on the still smouldering fire. Other workmen began to remove the bodies. The fire had swept over the whole mass from shore to shore and burned it to the water. A great field of crushed and charred timbers was all that was left. The flood had gorged this in so tightly that it made a solid bridge above the water. A tremendous, irresistible force had ground and churned and macerated the débris until it was a confused, solid, almost welded, conglomerate, stretching from shore to shore, jammed high up against the stone bridge and extending up the river a quarter of a mile, perhaps half as wide. In this tangled heap and crush of matter were the twisted wrecks of five iron bridges, smashed locomotives, splintered dwellings and all their contents; human beings and domestic animals, hay and factory machinery; the rich contents of stores and brick walls ground to powder—all the products of human industry, all the elements of human interests, twisted, turned, broken in a mighty mill and all thrown together.

A Sickening Spectacle.

I walked over this extraordinary mass this morning and saw the fragments of thousands of articles. In one place the roofs of forty frame houses were packed in together just as you would place forty bended cards one on top of another. The iron rods of a bridge were twisted into a perfect spiral six times around one of the girders. Just beneath it was a woman's trunk, broken up and half filled with sand, with silk dresses and a veil streaming out of it. From under the trunk men were lifting the body of its owner, perhaps, so burned, so horribly mutilated, so torn from limb to limb, that even the workmen, who have seen so many of these frightful sights that they have begun to get used to them, turned away sick at heart.

I saw in one place a wrecked grocery store—bins of coffee and tea, flour, spices and nuts, parts of the counter and safe mingled together. Near it was the pantry of the house, still partly intact, the plates and saucers regularly piled up, a waiter and a teapot, but not a sign of the woodwork, not a recognizable outline of a house. In another place a halter, with a part of a horse's head tied to a bit of a manger, and a mass of hay and straw about, but no other signs of the stable in which the horse was burned. Two cindered towels, a cake of soap in a dish, and a bit of carpet were taken to indicate the location of a hotel. I saw a child's skull in a bed of ashes, but no sign of a body.

Recognized by Fragments.

In another place was a human foot and crumbling indications of a boot, but no signs of a body. A hay rick, half ashes, stood near the centre of the gorge. Workmen who dug about it to-day found a chicken coop, and in it two chickens, not only alive but clucking happily when they were released. A woman's hat, half burned; a reticule, with a part of a hand still clinging to it; two shoes and part of a dress told the story of one unfortunate's death. Close at hand a commercial traveller had perished. There was his broken valise, still full of samples, fragments of his shoes and some pieces of his clothing.

Scenes like these were occurring all over the charred field where men were working with pick and axe and lifting out the poor, shattered remains of human beings, nearly always past recognition or identification, except by guesswork, or the locality where they were found. Articles of domestic use scattered through the rubbish helped to tell who some of the bodies were. Part of a set of dinner plates told one man where in the intangible mass his house was. In one place was a photograph album with one picture recognizable. From this the body of a child near by was identified. A man who had spent a day and all night looking for the body of his wife, was directed to her remains by part of a trunk lid.

Dead Bodies Caressed.

Poor old John Jordan, of Conemaugh! Many a tear ran over swarthy cheeks for him to-day. All his family, his wife and children, had been swept from his sight in the flood. He wandered over the gorge yesterday looking for them, and last night the police could not bring him away. At daylight he found his wife's sewing machine and called the workmen to help him. First they found a little boy's jacket that he recognized and then they came upon the rest of them all buried together, the mother's burned arms still clinging to the little children. Then the white headed old man sat down in the ashes and caressed the dead bodies and talked to them just as if they were alive until some one came and led him quietly away. Without a protest he went to the shore and sat down on a rock and talked to himself, and then got up and disappeared on the hills.

To Blow Up the Gorge.

Was this the only such scene the day saw? There were scores like it. People worked in ruins all day to find their relatives and then went home with horrible uncertainty. People found what they were looking for and fainted at the sight. People looked and cried aloud and came and stood on the banks all day, afraid to look and still afraid to go away. The burned bodies are not the only ones in the gorge. Under the timbers and held down in the water there must be hundreds that escaped the fire, but were drowned. To get at these the gorge is to be blown up with dynamite. The sanitary reasons for such a step are becoming hourly more apparent. It is the belief of the physicians that a pestilence will be added to the other horrors of the place if such a thing is not done. All day the bodies have been brought to shore. Those that were not recognized were carried on stretchers to the Morgue. One hundred and twenty of the identified bodies were carried over the bridge in one procession.

THE JOHNSTOWN HORROR. 219

Relief work for the suffering goes on at the headquarters of the Relief Committee on that little, muddy, rubbish-filled street which escaped destruction at the edge of the flood.

The building is a wretched shanty, once a Hungarian boarding-house, and a long line of miserable women stretches out in front of it all day waiting for relief. They are the unfortunate who have lost everything in the flood.

Quarters for five thousand of these people are provided in tents on the hillside. For provisions they are dependent on the charity of the country. Bread and meat are served out to them on the committee's order.

They are the most mournful and pitiable sight. There was not one in the line who had not lost some one dear to her. Most of them were the wives of merchants or laborers who went down in the disaster. They were the sole survivors of their families. Very few had any more clothes than they wore when their houses were washed away. They stood there for hours in the rain yesterday without any protection, soaked with the drizzle, squalid and utterly forlorn—a sight to move a heart of stone.

Silent Sufferers.

They did not talk to one another as women generally do even when they are not acquainted. They got no words of sympathy from any one, and they gave none. Not a word was spoken along the whole line. They simply stood and waited. In truth, there is nothing about the survivors of the disaster that strikes one so forcibly as their evident inability to comprehend their misfortune and the absence of sympathetic expressions among them. It is not because they are naturally stolid, but the whole thing is so vast and bears upon them so heavily they cannot grasp it.

People in California know much more about the disaster than any resident of Johnstown knows; more information about it can be gotten from towns-people forty miles away than from those who saw it. The people here are not at all lacking in sympathy or kindliness of heart, but what words of sympathy would have any meaning in such a tremendous catastrophe? Every person of Johnstown has lost a relative or a friend, and so has every other resident he meets. They seem to see instinctively that condolence would be meaningless.

Famine Happily Averted.

On the west side of the lower town one or two little streets are left from the flood. They are crowded all the time with the survivors. As I have gone among them I have heard nothing but such conversations as this, which is literally reproduced:—

"Hello, Will! Where's Jim?"

"He's lost."

"Is that so! Goodby."

Another was:—

"Good morning, Mr. Holden; did you save Mrs. Holden?"

"No; she went with the house. You lost your two boys, didn't you?"

"Yes. Good morning."

Two women met on the narrow rope bridge which spans the creek. As they passed one said:—

"How about Aunt Mary?"

"Oh, she's lost; so is Cousin Hattie."

It gives an outside listener a strange sensation to hear people talk thus with about as little emotion as they would talk about the weather. But the people of Johnstown had so much to do with death that they think about nothing else. I will undertake to say that half the people have not the slightest idea what day of the week or month this is.

A Rope Bridge of Sighs.

To get from one part of the town to another it is necessary to cross the river or creek which is now flowing over the sites of business blocks. Of course every vestige of a bridge was swept far away, and to take their places two ropes have been hung from high timbers built upon the sandy island that was the city's site. On these ropes narrow boards are tied. The whole structure is not more than four feet wide, and it hangs trembling over the water in a way that makes nervous people shudder. Over this frail thing hundreds of people crowd every hour, and why there has not been another disaster is something no one can understand.

The river is rising steadily, and all the afternoon the middle of the bridge sagged down into the water, but the people kept on struggling across. Many of them carried coffins containing bodies from the Morgue.

There are no express wagons, no hearses—scarcely any vehicles of any kind in the town—and all the coffins have to be carried on the shoulders of the men.

Coffins are a dreadfully common sight. It is impossible to move a dozen steps in any direction without meeting one or very likely a procession of of them. One hundred of them were piled up in front of the Morgue this morning. Twice as many more were on the platform of the Pennsylvania station. Carloads of coffins were being unloaded from freight cars below town and carried along the roads. Almost every house has a coffin in it. Every boat that crosses the river carries one, and rows of them stood by the bank to receive the bodies.

Merely a Mud Plain.

There is a narrow fringe of houses on each side of the empty plain, which escaped because they were built on higher ground. Fine brick blocks and paved streets filled the business part of the town, which was about a mile long and half a mile wide. Where these blocks stood mud is in some places six feet deep. Over and through it all is scattered an extraordinary collection of rubbish—boilers, car wheels, fragments of locomotives, household furniture, dead animals, clothing, sewing machines, goods from stores, safes, passenger and street cars, some half buried in the sand, some all exposed, helter-skelter.

It is simply impossible to realize the tremendous force exercised by the flood, though the imagination is assisted by the presence of heavy iron beams twisted and bent, railroad locomotives swept miles away, rails torn up, the rocks and banks slashed away, and brick walls carried away, leaving no traces of their foundations. The few stone houses that resisted the shock were completely stripped of all their contents and filled four feet deep with sand and powdered débris.

A Glimpse from a Window.

As I write this, seated within a curious circular affair, which was once a mould for sewer pipe, are two operators busy with clicking instruments. The floor is a foot deep with clay. There are no doors. There are no windows which boast of glass or covering of any kind. The lookout embraces the bulk of the devastated districts. Just below the windows are the steep river banks, covered with a miscellaneous mass thrown up by the flood. The big stone bridge is crowded with freight cars loaded with material for repairing the structure and with people who are eager to see something horrible.

That Funeral Pyre.

The further half of the bridge which was swept away has been replaced by a trembling wooden affair, wide enough only for two persons to walk abreast. To the left of the bridge and across the river are the great brick mills of the Cambria Iron and Steel Company, crushed and torn out of a semblance to workshops. Just in front of the office is what has been called the "funeral pyre," and which threatens to become a veritable breeding spot of pestilence.

Just before me a group of red-capped firemen are

directing a stream of water upon such portions of the mass as can be reached from the shore.

Where Death Was Busiest.

Over to the right, at the edge of a muddy lagoon which marks the limit of the levelling rush of the mad torrent, there are dozens and dozens of buildings leaning against each other in the oddest sort of jumble. The spectacle would be ludicrous if it were not so awfully suggestive of the tragic fate of the inmates. Behind this border land are the regions where death was wofully busy. In some streets a mile from any railroad track locomotives and cars are scattered among the smouldering ruins. In the river the rescuers are busy, and so are the Hungarians and native born thieves.

Men take queer souvenirs away sometimes. One came up the bank a short time ago with a skull and two leg bones, all blackened and burned by the fire.

There is, of course, no business done, and those who have been spared have little to do save watch for a new phase of the greatest tragedy of the kind in modern history. On Prospect Hill is a town of tents where the homeless are housed and fed, and where also a formidable city of the dead has been just prepared. Such are some of the scenes visible from the window.

The Skeleton of Its Former Self.

The water has receded in the night almost as rapidly as it came, and behind it remains the sorriest sight imaginable. The dove that has come has no green leaf of promise, for its wings are draped with the hue of mourning and desolation. There now lies the great skeleton of dead Johnstown. The great ribs of rocky sand stretch across the chest scarred and covered with abrasions. Acres of mud, acres of wreckage, acres of unsteady, tottering buildings, acres of unknown dead, of ghastly objects which have been eagerly sought for since Friday; acres of smoky, streaming ruin, of sorrow for somebody, lie out there in the sunshine.

Like Unto Arcadia After the Fire.

The awful desolation of the scene has been described often enough already to render a repetition of the attempt here unnecessary. These descriptions have been as truthful and graphic as it is possible for man to make them; but none have been adequate—none could be. Where once stood solid unbroken blocks for squares and squares, with basements and subcellars, there is now a level plain as free from obstruction or excavation as the fair fields of Arcadia after they had been swept by the British flames. The major and prettier portion of the beautiful city has literally been blotted from the face of the earth.

Disease Succeeds to Calamity.

Up the ragged surface of Prospect Hill, whither hundreds of terrified people fled for safety Friday night, I scrambled this afternoon. I came upon a pneumonia scourge which bids fair to do for a number of the escaped victims what the flood could not. Death has pursued them to their highest places, and terror will not die. Every little house on the hill—and there are a hundred or two of them—had thrown its doors open to receive the bruised, half-clad fugitives on the dark day of the deluge, and every one was now a crude hospital. Half the women who had scaled the height were so overcome with fright that they have been bedridden ever since. There had been pneumonia on the hill, but only a few cases To-day, however, several fresh cases developed among the the flood fugitives, and a local physician said the prospects for a scourge are all too promising. The enfeebled condition of the patients, the unhealthy atmosphere pervading the valley and the necessarily close quarters in which the people are crowded render the spread of the disease almost certain.

The Military Called Out.

At the request of the Sheriff, Adjutant General Hastings called out the Fourteenth regiment of Pittsburgh, who are to be stationed at Johnstown proper, to guard the buildings and against emergencies. Other reasons are known to exist for this precaution. Bodies were recovered to-day that have been robbed by the ghouls. It is known that one lady had several hundred dollars in her possession just before the disaster, but when the body was recovered there was not a cent in her pocket.

The Hungarians attacked a supply wagon between Morrellville and Cambria City to-day. The drivers of the wagon repulsed them, but they again returned. A second fight ensued, but after lively scrambling the

Hungarians were again driven away. After that drivers and guards of supply wagons were permitted to go armed.

General Hastings was seen later in the day, and when asked what caused him to order the militia said: "There is no need of troops to quell another disturbance, but now there are at least two thousand men at work in Johnstown clearing up the débris, and I think that it will not hurt to have the Fourteenth regiment here, as they can guard the banks and all valuables. The Sheriff consulted me in the matter. He stated that his men were about worn out, and he thought that we had better have some soldiers. So I ordered them."

The people, aroused by repeated outrages, are bitterly hounding the Hungarians, and a military force is essential to see that both sides preserve order.

Indignant Battery B.

A number of the members of Battery B and the Washington infantry, who were ordered back from Johnstown, are very indignant at Adjutant General Hastings, who gave the order. They claim that General Hastings not only acted without a particle of judgment, but when they offered to act as picket, do police duty or anything else that might be required of them, they state that they were treated like dogs.

They also insist that their services are badly needed for the reason that the hills surrounding Johnstown, are swarming with tramps, who are availing themselves of every opportunity to secure plunder from the numerous wrecks or dead bodies.

They told the General that they came more as private citizens than as soldiers, and were willing to do what they could. The General abruptly ordered them back to Pittsburgh. Lieutenant Gammel, who had charge of the men, said: "We would like to have stayed but we had to obey orders and we took the first train for home. Even the short time we were there the fifty-five men had pulled out thirty-five bodies."

Members of the battery said: "This is a fine Governor we have, and as for Hastings, the least said about his actions the better."

The Adjutant General's order calling out the Fourteenth regiment and ordering them to this place is not looked upon as being altogether a wise move by many citizens.

Narrow Escape from Lynching.

About eleven o'clock this morning, Captain W. R. Jones, of Braddock, and his men discovered a man struggling in the hands of an angry crowd on Main street. The crowd were belaboring the man with sticks and fists, and Captain Jones entered the house where the disturbance occurred, and the man shouted: "I have a right here, and am getting what belongs to my folks!"

The crowd then demanded that he show what he had in his possession. He reluctantly produced a handful of jewelry from his pocket, among which was a gold watch, which was no sooner shown than a gentleman who was standing nearby claimed it as his own, saying that the house where they were standing was the residence of his family. He then proceeded to identify clearly the property. The crowd, convinced of the thief's guilt, wanted to lynch him, but after an exciting scene Captain Jones pacified them. The man was escorted out of town by officers, released and ordered not to return.

Johnstown Succored.

There will be no more charity except for the helpless. The lengthening of the death roll has fearfully shortened the list to be provided for. There is now an abundance of food and clothing to satisfy the present necessities of all who are in need. Beginning to-morrow morning, June 5th, aid will not be extended to any who are able to work except in payment for work. All the destitute who are able and willing will be put to work clearing up the wreck in the river and the wastes where the streets stood. They will be paid $2.50 and $3.00 per day for ordinary laboring work, and thus obtain money with which to buy provisions, which will be sold to them at reduced prices.

Those who will not work will be driven off. The money collected will be paid out in wages, in defraying funeral expenses and in relieving those whose bread providers have been taken away.

Dainties Not Wanted.

The supplies of food and clothing are far in excess of the demand to-day. The mistake of sending large quantities of dainties has been made by some of the relief committees. Bishop Phelan has been on the ground all day in company with a number of Catholic priests from Pittsburgh.

He has ordered provisions for all the sufferers who have taken shelter in the buildings over which he has placed the Little Sisters of the Poor. There are several hundred people now being cared for by the relief corps, and as the work of rescue goes on the number increases.

Bent on Charity.

Mrs. Campbell, president of the Allegheny Woman's Christian Temperance Union, arrived this morning, and with Miss Kate Foster, of Johnstown, organized a temporary home for destitute children on Bedford street. On the same train came a delegation from the Smithfield Methodist Episcopal Church. They began relieving the wants of the suffering Methodists.

Committees from the Masonic and Odd Fellows from Pittsburgh are looking after their brethren.

Mr. Moxham, the iron manufacturer, is Mayor pro. tem. of Johnstown to-day. He is probably the busiest man in the United States; although for days without sleep, he still sticks nobly to his task. Hundreds of others are like him. Men fall to the earth from sheer fatigue. There are many who have not closed an eye in sleep since they awoke on Friday morning; they are hollow-eyed and pitiful looking creatures. Many have lost near relatives and all friends.

Shylocks.

Men and horses are what are most needed to-day. Some of the unfortunates who could not go to the relief trains endeavored to obtain flour from the wrecked stores in Johnstown. One dealer was charging $5 a sack for flour, and was getting it in one or two cases. Suddenly the crowd heard of the occurrence.

Several desperate men went to the store and doled the flour gratuitously to the homeless and stricken. Another dealer was selling flour at $1.50 a sack. He refused to give any away, but would sell it to any one who had the money. Otherwise he would not allow any one to go near it, guarding his store with a shot-gun.

Masons on the Field.

The special train of the Masonic Relief Association which left Pittsburgh at one o'clock yesterday afternoon on the Baltimore and Ohio Railroad did not reach here until just before midnight, at which time it was impossible to do anything. Under the circumstances, the party concluded to pass the night in the cars, making themselves as comfortable as possible with packing boxes for beds and candle boxes for pillows.

They spent the morning distributing the food and clothing among the Masonic sufferers. In addition to a large quantity of cooked food, sandwiches, etc., as well as flour and provisions of every description, the Relief Committee brought up 100 outfits of clothing for women and a similar number for girls, and a miscellaneous lot for men and boys. The women's outfits are complete, and include underwear, stockings, shoes, dresses, wraps and hats. They are most acceptable in the present crisis, and much suffering has already been relieved by them.

The Knights of Pythias have received a large donation of money from Pittsburgh lodges.

Appeal to President Harrison.

Adjutant General Hastings yesterday afternoon telegraphed to President Harrison requesting that government pontoons be furnished to enable a safe passageway to be made across the field of charred ruins above Johnstown Bridge for the purpose of prosecuting search for the dead. Late last night an answer was received from the President stating that the pontoons would be at once forwarded by the Secretary of War.

A despatch of sympathy has been received by Adjutant General Hastings from the Mayor of Kansas City, who states that the little giant of the West will do her duty in this time of need.

Fraternities Uniting.

The various fraternities, whose work has been referred to in various despatches, have established headquarters and called meetings of surviving local members. These meetings are held in Alma Hall, belonging to the Odd Fellows, which, owing to its solid construction, withstood the pressure of the flood. From the headquarters at Alma Hall most of the committees representing the various secret societies are distributing relief.

The first hopeful view of the situation taken by the Odd Fellows' Committee has been clouded by the dismal result of further investigations. At last night's meeting at the old schoolhouse on Prospect Hill definite tidings were received from but thirty members out of a total of 501.

Cambria Lodge, with a membership of eighty-five, mostly Germans, seems to have been entirely wiped out, not a single survivor having yet reported.

Call for Workers.

Last night Robert Bridgard, a letter carrier of Johnstown, marched at the head of three hundred men to the corner of Morrell avenue and Columbia street, where he mounted a wagon and made a speech on the needs of the hour. Chiefest of these, he considered, was good workmen to clear away the débris and extract the bodies from the wreckage.

He closed with a bitter attack on the lazy Huns and Poles, who refused to aid in the work of relief and yet are begging and even stealing the provisions that are sent here to feed the sufferers. The crowd numbered nearly one thousand, and greeted Bridgard's words with cheers.

Another resident of the city then mounted a barrel and made a ringing speech condemning the slothful foreigners, who have proven themselves a menace to the valley and its inhabitants. The feelings of the crowd were aroused to such an alarming extent that it was feared it would culminate in an attack on the worthless Poles and Hungarians.

The following resolution was adopted with a wild shout of approval, and the meeting adjourned:—

"*Resolved*, That we, the citizens of Johnstown, in public meeting assembled, do most earnestly beg the

Relief Corps of the Johnstown sufferers to furnish no further provisions to the Hungarians and Poles of this city and vicinity except in payment of services rendered by them for the relief of their unfortunate neighbors.

"*Resolved*, Further, that in case of their refusal to render such service they be driven from the doors of the relief trains and warned to vacate the premises."

Hospitals and Morgues.

Those who doubt that many thousands lost their lives in this disaster have not visited the morgues. There are three of these dreadful places crowded so full of the unidentified dead that there is scarcely room to move between the bodies. To the largest morgue, which I visited this morning, one hundred and sixty bodies have been brought for identification. When it is remembered that most of the bodies were swept below the limits of Johnstown, that many more found here have been identified at once by their friends and that it is certain that many bodies were consumed entirely in the fire at the gorge, the fact gives some idea of the extent of the calamity.

The largest morgue is at the Fourth ward schoolhouse, a two-story brick building which stands just at the edge of the high mark of the flood. The bodies were laid across the school children's desks until they got to be so numerous that there was not room for them, excepting on the floor. Soldiers with crossed bayonets keep out the crowd of curious people who have morbid appetites to gratify. None of these people are of Johnstown. People of Johnstown do not have time to come to look for friends, and they give the morgue a wide berth. Those who do come have that dazed, miserable look that has fallen to all the residents of the unhappy town. They walk through slowly and look at the bodies and go away looking no sadder nor any less perplexed than when they came in. One of the doctors in charge at the morgue told me that many of these people had come in and looked at the bodies of their own fathers and brothers and gone away without recognizing them, though not at all disfigured.

"That's Jim."

In some instances it had been necessary for other persons, who knew the people, to point out the dead to the living and assure them positively of the identification before they could be aroused. I saw a railroad laborer who had come in to look for a friend. He walked up and down the aisles like a man in a trance. He looked at the bodies, and took no apparent interest in any of them. At last he stopped before one of them which he had passed twice before, muttered, "That's Jim," and went out just as he had come in. Two other identifications I saw during the hour I was there were just like this. There was no shedding of tears nor other showing of emotion. They gazed upon the features of their dead as if they were totally unable to comprehend it all, and reported their identification to the attendants and watched the body as it was put into a coffin and went away.

Many came to look for their loved ones, but I did not see one show more grief or realization of the dreadful character of their errand than this. Arrangements with the morgues are complete and efficient. The bodies are properly prepared and embalmed and a description of the clothing is placed upon each.

Hospital Arrangements.

The same praise cannot be given the hospital arrangements. The only hospital is a small wooden church, in which apartments have been roughly improvised, with blankets for partitions. Only twenty patients can be cared for here, and the list of wounded is more than two hundred. The rest have been taken to the private houses that were not over-crowded with the homeless survivors, to farmers in the country and to outlying towns. Two have died. It did not occur to any one until lately to get any nurses from other places to take care of the patients, and even now most of the nurses are Johnstown people who have lost relatives and have their own cares. These persons sought out the hospital and volunteered for the work.

A Procession of Coffins.

A sight most painful to behold was presented to view about noon to-day, when a procession of fifty unidentified coffined bodies started up the hill above the railroad to be buried in the improvised cemetery there. Not a relation, not a mourner was present. In fact, it is doubtful if these dead have any surviving relatives.

The different graveyards are now so crowded that it will take several days to bury all the bodies that have been deposited in them. This was the day appointed by the Citizens' Committee for burying all the unidentified dead that have been laying in the different morgues since Sunday morning, and about three hundred bodies were taken to the cemeteries to-day.

It was not an unsual sight to see two or three coffins going along, one after another. It is impossible to secure wagons or conveyances of any kind, consequently all funeral processions are on foot.

Several yellow flags were noticed sticking up from the black wreckage above the stone bridge. This was a new plan adopted by the sanitary corps to indicate at what points bodies had been located. As it grows dark the flags are still up, and another day will dawn upon the imprisoned remains. People who had lost friends, and supposed they had drifted into this fatal place, peered down into the charred mass in a vain endeavor to recognize beloved features.

Unrecognizable Victims of Fire.

There are now nearly two thousand men employed in different parts of the valley clearing up the ruins and prosecuting diligent search for the undiscovered dead, and bodies are discovered with undiminished frequency. It becomes hourly more and more apparent that not a single vestige will ever be recognized of hundreds that were roasted in the flames above the bridge.

A party of searchers have just unearthed a charred

and unsightly mass from the smouldering débris. The leader of the gang pronounced the remains to be a blackened leg, and it required the authoritative verdict of a physician to demonstrate that the ghastly discovery was the charred remains of a human being. Only the trunk remained, and that was roasted beyond all semblance to flesh. Five minutes' search revealed fragments of a skull that at once disintegrated of its own weight when exposed to air, no single piece being larger than a half dollar, and the whole resembling the remnants of shattered charcoal.

Within the last hour a half dozen discoveries in no way less horrifying than this ghastly find have been made by searchers as they rake with sticks and hooks in the smouldering ruins. So difficult is it at times to determine whether the remains are those of human beings that it is apparent that hundreds must be burned to ashes. The number that have found a last resting place beneath these ruins can at the best never be more than approximated.

A Vast Charnel House.

Every moment now the body of some poor victim is taken from the débris, and the town, or rather the remnants of it, is one vast charnel house. The scenes at the extemporized morgue are beyond powers of description in their ghastliness, while the moans and groans of the suffering survivors, tossing in agony, with bruised and mangled bodies, or screaming in a delirium of fever as they issue from the numerous temporary hospitals, make even the stoutest hearted quail with terror. Nearly two thousand bodies have already been recovered, and as the work of examining the wreckage progresses the conviction grows that the magnitude of the calamity has not yet been approximated.

The Pile of Debris Still Burning.

The débris wedged against the big Pennsylvania Railroad stone bridge is still burning, and the efforts of the firemen to quench or stay the progress of the flames are as futile as were those of Gulliver's Lilliputian firemen. The mass, which unquestionably forms a funeral pyre for thousands of victims who lie buried beneath it, is likely to burn for weeks to come. The flames are not active, but burn away in a sullen, determined fashion.

There are twenty-six firemen here now—all level-headed fellows—who keep their unwieldy and almost exhausted forces under masterful control.

Although they were scattered all over the waste places to-day, the heavy work was done in the Point district, where a couple hundred mansions lie in solid heaps of brick, stone and timbers.

One Corpse Every Five Minutes.

Here the labors of the searchers were rewarded by the discovery of a corpse about every five minutes. As a general thing the bodies were mangled and unrecognizable unless by marks or letters on their persons. In every case decomposition has set in and the work of the searchers is becoming one that will test their stomachs as well as their hearts. Wherever one turns

Pitttburghers of prominence are encountered. They are busy, determined men, rendering valuable service.

Chief Evans, of the Pitsburgh Fire Department, was hustling around with a force of twenty-four more firemen, just brought up to relieve those who have been working so heroically since Saturday. Morris M. Mead, superintendent of the Bureau of Electricity, headed a force of sixteen sanitary inspectors from Pittsburgh, who are doing great work among the dead.

How Bodies are Treated.

There are six improvised morgues now in Johnstown. They are in churches and schoolhouses, the largest one being in the Fourth Ward schoolhouse, where planks have been laid over the tops of desks, on which the remains are placed. A corpse is dug from the bank. It is covered with mud. It is taken to the anteroom of the school, where it is placed under a hydrant and the muck and slime washed off. With the slash of a knife the clothes are ripped open and an attendant searches the pockets for valuables or papers that would lead to identification. Four men lift the corpse on a rude table, and there it is thoroughly washed and an embalming fluid injected in the arm. With other grim bodies the corpse lies in a larger room until it is identified or becomes offensive. In the latter case it is hurried to the large grave, a grave that will hereafter have a monument over it bearing the inscription " Unknown Dead."

The number of the latter is growing hourly, because pestilence stalks in Johnstown, and the bloated, disfigured masses of flesh cannot be held much longer.

Levelled by Death.

Bodies of stalwart workmen lie beside the remains of refined ladies, many of whom are still decked with costly earrings and have jewels glittering on the fingers. Rich and poor throng these quarters and gaze with awe-struck faces at the masses of mutilations in the hope of recognizing a missing one, so as to accord the body a decent burial.

From Death's Gaping Jaws.

We give here the awful narrative of George Irwin's experience. Irwin is a resident of Hillside, Westmoreland county, and was discovered in a dying condition in a clump of bushes just above the tracks of the Pennsylvania Railroad, about a mile below Johnstown. When stretched upon two railroad ties near the track his tongue protruded from his mouth and he gasped as if death was at hand. With the assistance of brandy and other stimulants he was in a degree revived. He then told the following story:

"I was visiting friends in Johnstown on Friday when the flood came up. We were submerged without a moment's warning. I was taken from the window of the house in which I was then a prisoner by Mr. Hay, the druggist at Johnstown, but lost my footing and was not rescued. I clung to a saw log until I struck the works of the Cambria Iron Company, when I caught on the roof of the building. I remained there for nearly an hour, when I was knocked again from my position by a piece of a raft. I floated on top of this until I got down here and I stuck in an apple tree.

Preferred Death to Such Sights.

"I saw and heard a number of other unfortunate victims when swept by me appealing for some one to save them. One woman and two children were floating along in apparent safety; then they struck the corner of a building and all went down together.

"I would rather have died than have been compelled to witness that sight.

"I have not had a bit to eat since Friday night, but I don't feel hungry. I am afraid my stomach is gone and I am about done for."

He was taken to a hospital by several soldiers and railroad men who rescued him.

A Young Lady's Experiences.

Miss Sue Caddick, of Indiana, who was stopping at the Brunswick Hotel, on Washington street, and was rescued late Friday evening, returned home to-day. She said she had a premonition of danger all day and had tried to get Mrs. Murphy to take her children and leave the house, but the lady had laughed at her fears and partially dissipated them.

Miss Caddick was standing at the head of the second flight of stairs when the flood burst upon the house. She screamed to the Murphys—father, mother and seven children—to save themselves. She ran up stairs and got into a higher room, in which the little children, the oldest of whom was fourteen years, also ran. The mother and father were caught and whirled into the flood and drowned in an instant.

The waters came up and the children clung to the young lady, who saw that she must save herself, and she was compelled to push the little ones aside and cling to pieces of the building, which by this time had collapsed and was disintegrating. All of the children were drowned save the oldest boy, who caught a tree and was taken out almost unhurt near Blairsville. Miss Caddick clung to her fraction of the building, which was pushed into the water out of the swirl, and in an hour she was taken out safe. She said her agony in having to cut away from the children was greater than her fear after she got into the water.

An Old Lady's Great Peril.

Mrs. Ramsey, mother of William Ramsey and aunt of Lawyer Cassidy, of Pittsburgh, was alone in her house when the flood came. She ran to the third story, and although the house was twisted off its foundation, it remained intact, and the old lady was rescued after being tossed about for twenty-four hours.

James Hines, Jr., of Indiana, one of the survivors, to day said that he and twelve of the other guests took refuge on the top of the Merchants' Hotel. They were swept off and were carried a mile down the stream, then thrown on the shore. One of the party, James Ziegler, he said, was drowned while trying to get to the top of the building.

One hundred and seventy-five of the corpses

brought to Nineveh by the flood were buried this afternoon and to-night on the crest of a hill behind the town. Three trenches were dug two hundred feet long, seven feet wide and four feet deep. The coffins were packed in very much as grocers' boxes are stored in a warehouse. Of the two hundred bodies picked up in the fields after the waters subsided 117 were unidentified and were buried marked "Unknown." Twenty-five were shipped to relatives at outside points. In many cases friends of those who were recognized were unable to do anything to prevent their consignment to the trenches. Altogether twenty-seven were identified to-day. The bodies as fast as they were found were taken to the storehouse of Theodore F. Nimawaker, the station agent here, and laid out on boards. It was impossible on account of their condition to keep them any longer. The County Commissioners bought an acre of ground for $100, out of which they made a cemetery.

By Locomotive Headlights.

It was sad to see the coffins going up the steep hill on farm wagons, two or three on each wagon. No tender mourners followed the mud-covered hearses. Enough laborers sat on each load to handle it when it reached its destination. The Commissioners of Cumberland county have certainly behaved very handsomely. The coffins ordered were of the best. Some economical citizens suggested that they buy an acre of marsh land by the river, which could be had for a few dollars, but they declared that the remains should be placed in dry ground. The lifeless clay reposes now far out of the reach of the deadly waters which go suddenly down the Conemaugh Valley. It is a pretty spot, this cemetery, and one that a poet would choose for a resting place. Mountains well wooded are on every hand; no black factory smoke defaces the sky line.

Two locomotive headlights shed their rays over the cemetery to-night and gave enough light for the men to work by. They rapidly shoveled in the dirt. No priests were there to consecrate the ground or say a prayer over the cold limbs of the unknown. Upon the coffins I noticed such inscriptions as these: "No. 61, unknown girl, aged eight years, supposed to be Sarah Windser." "No. 72, unknown man, black hair, aged about thirty-five years, smooth face." Some of the bodies were more specifically described as "fat," "lean," and to one I saw the term "lusty" applied.

CHAPTER XII.

Pathetic Scenes.

Some of the really pathetic scenes of the flood are just coming to the public ear. John Henderson, his wife, his three children, and the mother of Mrs. Henderson remained in their house until they were carried out by the flood, when they succeeded in getting upon some drift. Mr. Henderson took the babe from his wife, but the little thing soon succumbed to the cold and the child died in its father's arms. He clung to it until it grew cold and stiff and then, kissing it, let it drop into the water. His mother-in-law, an aged lady, was almost as fragile as the babe, and in a few minutes Mr. Henderson, who had managed to get near to the board upon which she was floating saw that she, too, was dying. He did what little he could to help her, but the cold and the shock combined were too much. Assuring himself that the old lady was dead, Mr. Henderson turned his attention to his own safety and allowed the body to float down the stream.

In the meantime Mrs. Henderson, who had become separated from her husband, had continued to keep her other two children for some time, but finally a great wave dashed them from her arms and out of her sight. They were clinging to some driftwood, however, and providentially were driven into the very arms of their father, who was some distance down the stream quite unconscious of the proximity of his loved ones. Another whirl of the flood and all were driven over into some eddying water in Stony Creek and carried by backing water to Kernville, where all were rescued. Mrs. Henderson had nearly the same experience.

Dr. Holland's Awful Plunge.

Dr. Holland, a physician who lived on Vine street, saw both of his children drown before his eyes, but they were not washed out of the building. He took both of them in his arms and bore them to the roof, caring nothing for the moment for the rising water. Finally composing himself, he kissed them both and watched them float away. His father arrived here to-day to assist his son and take home with him the bodies of the children, which have been recovered. Dr. Holland, after the death of his children, was carried out into the flood and finally to a building, in the window of which a man was standing. The doctor held up his hands; the man seized them and dextrously slipping a valuable ring from the finger of one hand, brutally threw him out into the current again. The physician was saved, however, and has been looking for the thief and would-be murderer ever since.

Crushed in His Own House.

David Dixon, an engineer in the employ of the Cambria Iron Works, was with his family in his house on Cinder Street, when the flood struck the city. The shock overturned his house against that of his neighbor, Evans, and he, with his infant daughter, Edith, was pinned between the houses as a result of the upturning Both houses were carried down against the viaduct of the Pennsylvania Railroad and there, in sight of his wife and children, excepting a 15-year-old lad, he was drowned, the water rising and smothering him because of his inability to get from between the buildings. His wife was badly crushed and it is thought will be an invalid the remainder of her days. The children, including the babe in its father's arms, were all saved, and the other boy, Joe, one of the brightest, bravest, handsomest little fellows in the world, was in his news-stand near the Pennsylvania passenger station, and was rescued with difficulty by Edward Decker, another boy, just as the driftwood struck the little store and lifted it high off its foundation.

Babies who Died Together.

This morning two little children apparently not over three and four years old, were taken from the water clasped in each other's arms so tightly that they could not be separated, and they were coffined and buried together.

A bright girl, in a gingham sun-bonnet and a faded calico dress came out of the ruins of a fine old brick house next the Catholic church on Jackson street this afternoon. She had a big platter under her arm and announced to a bevy of other girls that the china was all right in the cupboard, but there was so much water in there that she didn't dare go in. She chatted away quite volubly about the fire in the Catholic church, which also destroyed the house of her own mother, Mrs. Foster. "I know the church took fire after the flood," she said, "for mother looked out of the window and said: 'My God! Not only flood, but fire!'" It was a burning house from Conemaugh that struck the house the other side of the church and set it on fire.

Aunt Tabby's Trunk.

"I didn't think last Tuesday I'd be begging to-day, Emma," interrupted a young man from across the stream of water which ran down the centre of Main Street. "I'm sitting on your aunt Tabby's trunk." The girl gave a cry, half of pained remembrance, half of pleasure. "Oh, my dear Aunt Tabby!" she cried, and, rushing across the rivulet, she threw herself across the battered leather trunk—sole surviving relic of Aunt Tabby; but Aunt Tabby and the finding thereof was a light among other shadows of the day.

Nothing but a Baby.

Gruesome incidents came oftener than pathetic ones or serio-comic. General Axline, the Adjutant General of Ohio, was walking down the station platform this afternoon, when a boy came sauntering up from the viaduct with a bundle in a handkerchief. The handkerchief dripped water. "What have you there, my boy?" asked the General. The boy cowered a minute, though the General's tone was kindly, for the boy, like every one else in Johnstown, was prepared for a gruff accostal every five minutes from some official, from Adjutant General to constable.

Finally he answered: "Nothing but a baby, sir," and began to open his bundle in proof of the truth of his statement. But the big soldier did not put him to the proof He turned away sick at heart. He did not even ask the boy if he knew whose baby it was.

How the Coffins Were Carried.

A strangely utilitarian device was that of a Pittsburgh sergeant of Battery B. With one train from the West came several hundred of the morbidly curious, bent upon all the horrors which they could stomach. A crowd of them crossed the viaduct and stopped to gaze round-eyed upon a pile of empty coffins meant for the bodies of the identified dead found up and across the river in the ruins of Johnstown proper. As they gazed the Sergeant, seeking transportation for the coffins, came along. A somewhat malicious inspiration of military genius lighted his eye. With the best imitation possible of a regular army man, he shouted to the idlers, " Each of you men take a coffin." The idlers eyed him.

"What for?" one asked.

"You want to go into town, don't you?" replied the Sergeant. "Well, not one of you goes unless he takes a coffin with him."

In ten minutes time way was made at the ticklish rope bridge for a file of sixteen coffins, each borne by two of the Sergeant's unwilling conscripts, while the Sergeant closed up the rear.

Some of the scenes witnessed here were neartrending in the extreme. In one case a beautiful girl came down on the roof of a building which was swung in near the tower. She screamed to the operator to save her and one big, brave fellow walked as far into the river as he could and shouted to her to try to guide herself into the shore with a bit of plank. She was a plucky girl, full of nerve and energy, and stood upon her frail support in evident obedience to the command of the operator. She made two or three bold strokes and actually stopped the course of the raft for an instant.

Then it swerved and went out from under her. She tried to swim ashore, but in a few seconds she was lost. Something hit her, for she lay quietly on her back, with face pallid and expressionless. Men and women in dozens, in pairs and singly; children, boys, big and little, and wee babies were there in among the awful confusion of water, drowning, gasping, struggling and fighting desperately for life.

Two men on a tiny raft shot into the swiftest part of the current. They crouched stolidly, looking at the shores, while between them, dressed in white and kneeling with her face turned heavenward was a girl seven years old. She seemed stricken with paralysis until she came opposite the tower and then she turned her face to the operator. She was so close they could see big tears on her cheeks and her pallor was as death. The helpless men on shore shouted to her to keep up courage, and she resumed her devout attitude and disappeared under the trees of a projection a short distance below. "We could not see her come out again," said the operator, "and that was all of it."

"Do you see that fringe of trees?" said the operator, pointing to the place where the little girl had gone out of sight.

"Well, we saw scores of children swept in there. I believe that when the time comes they will find almost a hundred bodies of children in there among those bushes."

Floated to their Death.

A bit of heroism is related by one of the telegraph operators at Bolivar. He says: "I was standing on the river bank about 7.30 last evening when a raft swept into view. It must have been the floor of a dismantled house. Upon it were grouped two women and a man. They were evidently his mother and sister, for both clung to him as though stupefied with fear as they were whirled under the bridge here. The man could save himself if he had wished by simply reaching up his hand and catching the timber of the structure. He apparently saw this himself, and the temptation must have been strong for him to do so, but in one second more he was seen to resolutely shake his head and clasp the women tighter around the waist.

On they sped. Ropes were thrown out from the tree tops, but they were unable to catch them, though they grasped for the lines eagerly enough. Then a tree caught in their raft and dragged after them. In this way they swept out of view."

Still finding bodies by scores in the burning debris; still burying the dead and caring for the wounded; still feeding the famishing and housing the homeless, and this on the fourth day following the one on which Johnstown was swept away. The situation of horror has not changed; there are hundreds, and it is feared thousands, still buried beneath the scattered ruins that disfigure the V-shaped valley in which Johnstown stood. A perfect stream of wagons bearing the dead as fast as they are discovered is constantly filing to the improvised morgues, where the bodies are taken for identification. Hundreds of people are constantly crowding to these temporary houses, one of which is located in each of the suburban boroughs that surround Johnstown. Men armed with muskets, uniformed sentinels, constituting the force that guard the city while it is practically under martial law, stand at the doors and admit the crowd by tens.

In the Central Dead House.

In the Central dead house in Johnstown proper, as early as 9 o'clock to-day there lay two rows of ghastly dead. To the right were twenty bodies that had been identified. They were mostly women and children and they were entirely covered with white sheets, and a piece of paper bearing the name was pinned at the feet. To the left were eighteen bodies of the unknown dead. As the people passed they were hurried along by an attendant and gazed at the uncovered faces seeking to identify them. All applicants for admission if it is thought they are prompted by idle curiosity, are not allowed to enter. The central morgue was formerly a school-house, and the desks are used as biers for the dead bodies. Three of the former pupils yesterday lay on the desks dead, with white pieces of paper pinned on to the white sheets that covered them, giving their names.

Looking for Their Loved Ones.

But what touching scenes are enacted every hour about this mournful building. Outside the sharp voices of the sentinels are constantly shouting: "Move on." Inside, weeping women and sad-faced, hollow-eyed men are bending over loved and familiar faces. Back on the steep grassy hill which rises abruptly on the other side of the street are crowds of curious people who come in from the country round about to look at the wreckage strewn around where Johnstown was. "Oh, Mr. Jones," a pale-faced woman asks, walking up, sobbing, "can't you tell me where we can get a coffin to bury Johnnie's body?"

"Do you know," asks a tottering old man, as the pale-faced woman turns away, "whether they have found Jennie and the children?"

"Jennie's body has just been found at the bridge," is the answer, "but the children can't be found." Jennie is the old man's married daughter, and she was drowned, with her two children, while her husband was at work over at the Cambria Mills.

They Ran for Their Lives.

Miss Jennie Paulson, who was on the Chicago day express, is dead. She was seen to go back with a companion into the doomed section of the day express in the Conemaugh Valley, and is swept away in the flood.

Last evening, after the evening train had just left Johnstown for Pittsburgh, it was learned that quite a number of the survivors of the wrecked train, who have been at Altoona since last Saturday, were on board. After a short search they were located, and quite an interesting talk was the result. Probably the most interesting interview, at least to Pittsburghers, was that had with Mrs. Montgomery Wilcox, of Philadelphia, who was on one of the Pullman sleepers attached to the lost express train. She tells a most exciting tale and confirms beyond the shadow of a doubt the story of Miss Jennie Paulson's tragic death.

A Fatal Pair of Rubbers.

She says: "We had been making but slow progress all the day. Our train laid at Johnstown nearly the whole day of Friday. We then proceeded as far as Conemaugh, and had stopped for some cause or other, probably on account of the flood. Miss Paulson and a Miss Bryan were seated in front of me. Miss Paulson had on a plaid dress with shirred waist of red cloth goods. Her companion was dressed in black. Both had lovely corsage bouquets of roses. I had heard that they had been attending a wedding before they left Pittsburgh. The Pittsburgh lady was reading a novel. Miss Bryan was looking out of the window. When the alarm came we all sprang toward the door, leaving everything behind us. I had just reached the door when poor Miss Paulson and her friend, who were behind me, decided to return for their rubbers, which they did.

Chased as by a Serpent.

"I sprang from the car into a ditch next the hillside in which the water was already a foot and a half deep and with the others climbed up the mountain side for our very lives. We had to do so as the water glided up after us like a huge serpent. Any one ten feet behind us would have been lost beyond a doubt. I glanced back at the train when I had reached a place of safety, but the water already covered it and the Pullman car in which the ladies were was already rolling down the valley in the grasp of the angry waters. Quite a number of us reached the house of a Mr. Swenzel, or some such name, one of the railroad men, whom we afterward learned had lost two daughters at Johnstown. We made ourselves as comfortable as possible until the next day, when we proceeded by conveyances as far as Altoona, having no doubt but what we could certainly proceed east from that point. We found the middle division of the Pennsylvania Railroad was, if anything, in a worse condition than the western, so we determined to go as far as Ebensburg by train, whence we reached Johnstown to-day by wagon."

Mrs. G. W. Child's Escape.

Mrs. George W. Childs, of Philadelphia, was also a member of the party. She was on her way West, and reached Altoona on Friday, after untold difficulties.

She is almost prostrated by the severe ordeal through which she and many others have passed, and therefore had but little to say, only averring that Mrs. Wilcox and her friends, who were on the lost train, had passed through perils beside which her own sank into insignificance.

Assistant Superintendent Crump telegraphs from

SWEPT AWAY ON THE TRAIN.

Blairsville Junction that the day express, eastbound from Chicago to New York, and the mail train from Pittsburgh bound east, were put on the back tracks in the yard at Conemaugh when the flooded condition of the main tracks made it apparently unsafe to proceed further. When the continued rise of the water made their danger apparent, the frightened passengers fled from the two trains to the hills near by. Many in their wild excitement threw themselves into the raging current and were drowned. It is supposed that about fifteen persons lost their lives in this way.

After the people had deserted the cars, the railroad officials state, the two Pullman cars attached to the day express were set on fire and entirely consumed. A car of lime was standing near the train. When the water reached the lime it set fire to the car and the flames reaching the sleepers they were entirely consumed.

Exhuming the Dead.

Three hundred bodies were exhumed to-day. In one spot at Main and Market streets the workmen came upon thirty, among whom were nine members of the Fitzparis family—the father, mother, seven children and the grandfather. Only one child, a little girl of nine years, is left out of a family of ten. She is now being cared for by the citizens' committee. The body of a beautiful young girl was found at the office of the Cambria Iron Company. When the corpse was conveyed to the morgue a man entered in search of some relatives. The first body he came to he exclaimed: "That's my wife," and a few feet further off he recognized in the young girl found at the Cambria Iron Company's office his daughter, Theresa Downs. Both bodies had been found within a hundred yards of each other.

A dozen instances have occurred where people have claimed bodies and were mistaken. This is due to the over-zeal of people to get their relatives and bury them. Nine children walked into one of the relief stations this morning, led by a girl of sixteen years. They said that their father, mother and two other children had been swallowed up by the flood, the family having originally comprised thirteen persons in all. Their story was investigated by Officer Fowler, of Pittsburgh, and it was found to be true. Near Main street the body of a woman was taken out with three children lying on her. She was about to become a mother.

Nursing Their Sorrows.

The afflicted people quietly bear their crosses. The calamity has been so general that the sufferers feel that everybody has been treated alike. Grouped together, the sorrows of each other assist in keeping up the strength and courage of all. In the excitement and hurry of the present, loss of friends is forgotten, but the time will come when it is all over and the world gradually drifts back to business, forgetful that such a town as Johnstown ever existed.

Then it is that sufferers will realize what they have lost. Hearts will then be full of grief and despair and the time for sympathy will be at hand. Michael Martin was one of those on the hillside when the water was rushing through the town. The spectacle was appalling. Women on the hills were shrieking and ringing their hands—in fact, people beyond reach of the flood made more noise than those unfortunate creatures struggling in the water. The latter in trying to save themselves hadn't time to shriek.

Michael Martin said: "I was on the hillside and watched the flood. You ask me what it looked like. I can't tell. I never saw such a scene before and never expect to again. On one of the first houses that struck the bridge there was standing a woman wearing a white shawl. When the house struck the bridge she threw up her hands and fell back into the water. A little boy and girl came floating down on a raft from South Fork. The water turned the raft toward the Kernville hill and as soon as it struck the bank he jumped on the hill, dragging his little sister with him. Both were saved.

"I saw three men and three women on the roof of a house. When they were passing the Cambria Iron Works the men jumped off and the women were lost. Mr. Overbeck left his family in McM. row and swam to the club house, then he tried to swim to Morrell's residence and was drowned. His family was saved. At the corner of the company's store a man called for help for two days, but no one could reach him. The voice finally ceased and I suppose he died.

A Brave Girl.

"Rose Clark was fastened in the débris at the bridge. Her coolness was remarkable and she was more calm than the people trying to get her out. She begged the men to cut her leg off. One man worked six hours before she was released. She had an arm and leg broken. I saw three men strike the bridge and go down. William Walter was saved. He was anchored on Main street and he saw about two hundred people in the water. He believes two-thirds of them were drowned. A frightened woman clung to a bush near him and her long hair stood straight out. About twenty people were holding to those in the neighborhood, but most of them were lost.

"John Reese, a policeman, got out on the roof of his house. In a second afterward the building fell in on his wife and drowned her. She waved a kiss to her husband and then died. Two servant girls were burned in the Catholic priest's house. The church was also consumed.

Along the Valley of Death.

Fifteen miles by raft and on foot along the banks of the raging Conemaugh and in the refugee trains between Johnstown and Pittsburgh. Such was the trip, fraught with great danger, but prolific of results, which the writer has just completed. All along the line events of thrilling interest mingled with those of heartrending sadness transpired, demonstrating more than ever the magnitude of the horrible tragedy of last Friday.

Just as the day was dawning I left the desolate city of Johnstown, and, wending my way along the shore of the winding Conemaugh to Sheridan, I succeeded in persuading a number of brave and stout-hearted men, who had constructed a raft and were about to start on an extended search for the lost who are known to be strewn all along this fated stream, to take me with them.

The river is still very high, and while the current is

not remarkably swift, the still flowing débris made the expedition one of peril. Between the starting point and Nineveh several bodies were recovered. They were mostly imbedded in the sand close to the shore, which had to be hugged for safety all the way. Indeed the greater part of the trip was made on foot, the raft being towed along from the water's edge by the tireless rescuers.

Just above Sang Hollow the party stopped to assist a little knot of men who were engaged in searching amid the ruins of a hut which lay wedged between a mass of trees on the higher ground. A man's hat and coat were fished out, but there was no trace of the human being to whom they once belonged. Perhaps he is alive; perhaps his remains are among the hundreds of unidentified dead, and perhaps he sleeps beneath the waters between here and the gulf. Who can tell?

Died in Harness.

A little farther down we came across two horses and a wagon lying in the middle of the river. The dumb animals had literally died in harness. Of their driver nothing is known. At this point an old wooden rocker was fished out of the water and taken on shore.

Here three women were working in the ruins of what had once been their happy home. When one of them spied the chair it brought back to her a wealth of memory and for the first time, probably, since the flood occurred she gave way to a flood of tears, tears as welcome as sunshine from heaven, for they opened up her whole soul and allowed pent-up grief within to flow freely out and away.

One Touch of Nature.

"Where in the name of God," she sobbed, "did you get that chair? It was mine—no, I don't want it. Keep it and find for me, if you can, my album; in it are the faces of my dead husband and little girl." When the rough men who have worked days in the valley of death turned away from this scene there was not a dry eye in the crowd. One touch of nature, and the thought of little ones at home, welded them in heart and sympathy to this Niobe of the valley.

At Sang Hollow we came up with a train-load of refugees en route for Pittsburgh. As I entered the car I was struck by two things. The first was an old man, whose silvered locks betokened his four-score years, and the second was a little clump of children, three in number, playing on a seat in the upper end of the coach.

Judge Potts' Escape.

The white-haired patriarch was Judge James Potts, aged 80, one of the best known residents of Johnstown, who escaped the flood's ravages in a most remarkable manner. Beside him was his daughter, while opposite sat his son. There was one missing to complete the family party, Jennie, the youngest daughter, who went down with the tide and whose remains have not yet been found. The thrilling yet pathetic story of the escape of the old Judge is best told in his own language. Said he:

"You ask me how I was saved. I answer, God alone knows. With my little family I lived on Walnut street, next door to the residence of President McMillan, of the Cambria Iron Company. When the waters surrounded us we made our way to the third floor, and huddled together in one room, determined, if die we must, to perish together.

Encircled by Water.

"Higher and higher rose the flood, while our house was almost knocked from its foundations by the ever-increasing mountain of débris floating along. At last the bridge at Woodvale, which had given way a short time before, struck the house and split it asunder, as a knife might have split a piece of paper.

"The force of the shock carried us out upon the débris, and we floated around upon it for hours, finally landing near the bridge. When we looked about for Jennie (here the old man broke down and sobbed bitterly) she was nowhere to be seen. She had obeyed the Master's summons."

A Miraculous Escape.

The three little girls, to whom I have referred, were the children of Austin Lountz, a plasterer, living back of Water street. They were as happy as happy could be and cut up in childish fashion all the way down. Their good spirits were easily accounted for when it was learned that father, mother, children and all had a miraculous escape, when it looked as if all would be lost. The entire family floated about for hours on the roof of a house, finally landing high upon the hillside.

Elmer G. Speck, traveling salesman of Pittsburgh, was at the Merchants' Hotel when the flood occurred, having left the Hurlburt House but a few hours before. He said:

"With a number of others I got from the hotel to the hill in a wagon. The sight from our eminence was one that I shall never forget—that I can never fully describe. The whole world appeared to be topsy-turvy and at the mercy of an angry and destroying demon of the elements. People were floating about on house-tops and in wagons, and hundreds were clinging to tree-trunks, logs and furniture of every imaginable description.

"My sister, Miss Nina, together with my step-brother and his wife, whom she was visiting, drifted with the tide on the roof of a house a distance of two blocks, where they were rescued. With a number of others I built a raft and in a short time had pulled eleven persons from the very jaws of death." Continuing, Mr. Speck related how a number of folks from Woodvale had all come down upon their house-tops. Mr. Curtis Williams and his family picked their way from house to house, finally being pulled in the Catholic church window by ropes.

Three of a Family Drowned.

William Hinchman, with his wife and two children, reached the stone bridge in safety. Here one of the babies was swept away through the arches. The others were also swept with the current, and when they came out on the other side the remaining child was missing, while below Mrs. Hinchman disappeared, leaving her husband the sole survivor of a family of four.

"Did your folks all escape alive?" I asked of George W. Hamilton, late assistant superintendent of the Cambria Iron Company, whom I met on the road near New Florence.

"Oh, no," was his reply. "Out of a family of sixteen seven are lost. My brother, his wife, two children, my sister, her husband and one child, all are gone; that tells the tale. I escaped with my wife by jumping from a second story window onto the moving débris. We landed back of the Morrell Institute safe and sound."

Hairbreadth Escapes.

The stories of hairbreadth escapes and the annihilation of families continue to be told. Here is one of them. J. Paul Kirchmann, a young man, boarded with George Schrœder's family in the heart of the town, and when the flood came the house toppled over and went rushing away in the swirling current. There were seven in all in the party and Kirchmann found himself wedged in between two houses, with his head under water. He dived down, and when he again came to the surface succeeded in getting on the roof of one of them. The others had preceded him there, and the house floated to the cemetery, over a mile and a half away, where all of them were rescued. Kirchmann, however, had fainted, and for seven or eight hours was supposed to be dead. He recovered, and is now assisting to get at the bodies buried in the ruins.

Saloon-keeper Fitzharris and his family of six had the lives crushed out of them when their house collapsed, and early this morning all of them, the father, mother and five children were taken from the wreck, and are now at the morgue. Emil Young, a jeweler, lived with mother, wife, three sons and daughter over his store on Clinton street, near Main. They were all in the house when the wild rush of water surrounded their home, lifted it from its foundation and carried it away. Young and his daughter were drowned and it was then that his mother and wife showed their heroism and saved the life of the other members of the family.

The mother is 80 years of age, but her orders were so promptly given and so ably executed by the younger Mrs. Young that when the house floated near another in which was a family of nine all were taken off and eventually saved. Even after this trying ordeal the younger woman washed the bodies of her husband and nineteen others and prepared them for burial.

The Whole Family Escaped.

Another remarkable escape of a whole family was that of William H. Rosensteel, a tanner, of Woodvale, a suburb of Johnstown. His house was in the track of the storm, and, with his two daughters, Tillie and Mamie, his granddaughter and a dog, he was carried down on the kitchen roof. They floated into the Bon

Ton Clothing House, a mile and a half away, on Main street. Here they remained all night, but were taken off by Mrs. Emil Young and went to Pittsburgh.

Jacob I. Horner and his family of eight had their house in Hornerstown thrown down by the water and took refuge in a tree. After awhile they returned to their overturned house, but again got into the tree, from which they were rescued after an enforced stay of a number of hours.

Charles Barnes, a real estate dealer on Main street, was worth $10,000 last Friday and had around him a family of four. To-day all his loved ones are dead and he has only $6 in his pockets.

The family of John Higson, consisting of himself, wife, and young son, lived at 123 Walnut street. Miss Sarah Thomas, of Cumberland, was a visitor, and a hired man, a Swede, also lived in the house. The water had backed up to the rear second-story windows before the great wave came, and about 5 o'clock they heard the screaching of a number of whistles on the Conemaugh. Rushing to the windows they saw what they thought to be a big cloud approaching them. Before they could reach a place of safety the building was lifted up and carried up Stony creek for about one-quarter of a mile. As the water rushed they turned into the river and were carried about three-quarters of a mile further on. All the people were in the attic and as the house was hurled with terrific force against the wreckage piled up against the Pennsylvania Railroad bridge Higson called to them to jump. They failed to do so, but at the second command Miss Thomas leaped through the window, the others followed, and after a dangerous walk over fifty yards of broken houses safely reached the shore.

CHILD FOUND THUMPING ON A WRECKED PIANO.

CHAPTER XIII.

Digging for the Dead.

A party started in early exploring the huge mass of débris banked against the Pennsylvania Railroad bridge. This collection, consisting of trees, sides of houses, timber and innumerable articles, varies in thickness from three or four feet to twenty feet. It is about four hundred yards long, and as wide as the river. There are thousands of tons in this vast pile. How many bodies are buried there it is impossible to say, but conservative estimates place it at one thousand at least.

The corps of workmen who were searching the ruins near the Methodist Church late this evening were horrified by unearthing one hundred additional bodies. The great number at this spot shows what may be expected when all have been recovered.

When the mass which blazed several days was extinguished it was simple to recover the bodies on the surface. It is now a question, however, of delving into the almost impenetrable collection to get at those lodged within. The grinding tree trunks doubtless crushed those beneath into mere unrecognizable masses of flesh. Those on the surface were nearly all so much burned as to resemble nothing human.

Meanwhile the searchers after bodies, armed with

spikes, hooks and crowbars, pry up the débris and unearth what they can. Bodies, or rather fractions of them, are found in abundance near the surface.

Tracing Bodies by the Smell.

I was here when the gang came across one of the upper stories of a house. It was merely a pile of boards apparently, but small pieces of a bureau and a bed spring from which the clothes had been burned, showed the nature of the find. A faint odor of burned flesh prevailed exactly at this spot. "Dig here," said the physician to the men. "There is one body at least quite close to the surface." The men started in with a will. A large pile of underclothes and household linen was brought up first. It was of fine quality and evidently such as would be stored in the bedroom of a house occupied by people quite well to do. Shovels full of jumbled rubbish were thrown up, and the odor of flesh became more pronounced. Presently one of the men exposed a charred lump of flesh and lifted it up on the end of a pitchfork. It was all that remained of some poor creature who had met an awful death between water and fire.

The trunk was put on a cloth, the ends were looped up making a bag of it, and the thing was taken to the river bank. It weighed probably thirty pounds. A stake was driven in the ground to which a tag was attached giving a description of the remains. This is done in many cases to the burned bodies, and they lay covered with cloths upon the bank until men came with coffins to remove them. Then the tag was taken from the stakes and tacked on the coffin lid, which was immediately closed up, as identification was of course out of the question. There is a stack of coffins by the railroad bridge. Sometimes a coffin is carried to the spot on the charred débris where the find is made.

Prodding Corpses with Canes.

The searchers by thrusting down a stick or fork are pretty sure to find a corpse. I saw a man run a cane in the débris down to the hilt and it came up with human flesh sticking to it. Another ran a stick into the thoroughly cooked skull of a little boy two feet below the surface. There are bodies probably as far down as seventy feet in some cases, and it does not seem plain now how they are to be recovered. One plan would be to take away the top layers of wood with derricks, and of course the mass beneath will rise closer to the surface. The weather is cold to-day, and the offensive smell that was so troublesome on the warm days is not noticeable at a distance.

Saved From Disfiguration.

The workers began on the wreck on Main street just opposite the First National Bank, one of the busiest parts of the city. A large number of people were lost here, the houses being crushed on one side of the street and being almost untouched on the other, a most remarkable thing considering the terrific force of the flood. Twenty-one bodies were taken out in the early morning and removed to the morgue. They were not very much injured, considering the weight of lumber above them. In many instances they were wedged in crevices. They were all in a good state of preservation, and when they were embalmed they looked almost lifelike. In this central part of the city examination is sure to result in the unearthing of bodies in every corner. Cottages which are still standing are banked up with lumber and driftwood, and it is like mining to make any kind of a clear space. I have seen relations of people who are missing, and who are supposed to be in the ruins of their homes, waiting patiently by the hour for men to come and take away the débris.

When bodies are found, the location of which was known, there are frequently two or three friends on the spot to see them dug up. Four and five of the same family have been taken from a space of ten feet square. In one part of the river gorge this afternoon were found the bodies of a woman and a child. They were close together and they were probably mother and infant. Not far away was the corpse of a man looking like a gnarled and mis-shapen section of a root of a tree. The bodies from the fire often seem to have been twisted up, as if the victims died in great agony.

Rapidly Burying the Dead.

The order that was issued last night that all unidentified dead be buried to-day is being rapidly carried out. The Rev. Mr. Beall, who has charge of the morgue at the Fourth ward school-house, which is the chief place, says that a large force of men has been put at work digging graves, and at the close of the afternoon the remains will be laid away as rapidly as it can be done.

In the midst of this scene of death and desolation, a relenting Providence seems to be exerting a subduing influence. Six days have elapsed since the great disaster, and the temperature still remains low and chilly in the Conemaugh Valley. When it is remembered that in the ordinary June weather of this locality from two to three days are sufficient to bring an unattended body to a state of decay and putrefaction that would render it almost impossible to prevent the spread of disease throughout the valley, the inestimable benefits of this cool weather are almost beyond appreciation.

The emanations from the half mile of débris above the bridge are but little more offensive than yesterday, and should this cool weather continue a few days longer it is possible hundreds of bodies may yet be recovered from the wreck in such a state of preservation as to render identification possible. Many hundreds of victims, however, will be roasted and charred into such shapeless masses as to preclude a hope of recognition by their nearest relative.

Getting Down to Systematic Work.

The work of clearing up the wreck and recovering the bodies is now being done most systematically. Over six thousand men are at work in the various portions of the valley, and each little gang of twenty men is directed by a foreman, who is under orders from the general headquarters. As the rubbish is gone over and the bodies and scattered articles of value are recovered, the débris is piled up in one high mass and the torch applied. In this way the valley is assuming a less devastated condition. In twenty-four hours more every mass of rubbish will probably have been searched, and the investigations will be confined to the smoking wreck above Johnstown bridge.

The Westmoreland Relief Committee complained of the Indiana county authorities for not having a committee to search the shores on that side for bodies. They say that all that is being done is by parties who are hunting for anything valuable they can find.

Up to two o'clock this afternoon only eight bodies had been taken out of the drift above the bridge. None of them was recognized. The work of pulling it out goes on very slowly. It has been suggested that a stationary engine should be planted on the east side of the pile and a rope and pulley worked on it.

The Keystone Hotel, a huge frame structure, was rapidly being pulled to pieces this morning, and when this had been done the work of taking out the bodies will be begun at this point.

The immense wreck will most undoubtedly yield up many bodies. The bodies of a woman and three children were taken from the débris in front of the First National Bank at ten o'clock this morning. The woman was the mother of the three children, ranging in age from one to five years, and she had them all clasped in her arms.

Booth & Flinn, the Pittsburgh contractors, have just put to work another large force of men. They have divided the town into districts, and the work is being conducted in a systematic manner. Main street is being rapidly opened up, and scores of bodies have been taken out this morning from under the Hurlburt House.

Only Found One of Her Family.

The first body taken from the ruins was that of a boy named Davis, who was found in the débris near the bridge. He was badly bruised and burned. The remains were taken to the undertaking rooms at the Pennsylvania Railroad station, where they were identified as those of William Davis. The boy's mother has been making a tour of the different morgues for the past few days, and was just going through the undertaking rooms when she saw the remains of her boy being brought in. She ran up to the remains and demanded the child. She seemed to have lost her mind, and caused quite a scene by her actions. She stated that she had lost her husband and six children in the flood, and that this was the first one of the family that had been recovered. At the First Presbyterian Church, which is being used as a morgue, seventeen bodies taken from the débris and river have been brought in.

The relief corps from Altoona found a body near Stony Bridge this morning. On his person was found a gold watch and chain, and $250 in money, which was turned over to the proper authorities. This corps took out some thirty-two bodies or more from the ruins yesterday.

A. J. Hayes, whose wife's body was taken out of the river last night, had the body taken up into the mountains where he dug her grave and said:—"I buried all that is dear to me. As for myself I don't care how soon death overtakes me."

At quarter past one this afternoon, fifty bodies had been taken from the débris in front of the Catholic Church in Johnstown borough. About forty of the bodies were those of women. They were immediately removed to the morgue for identification.

Dr. Beall, who has the supervision of the morgues in Johnstown, said that so far 2,300 bodies had been recovered in Johnstown proper, most of which had been identified and buried.

Dynamite and Derricks Used.

At one o'clock this afternoon the use of dynamite was resumed to burst the logs so that the débris in the dam at the bridge can be loosened and floated down the river. The dynamite is placed in holes bored into the massive timbers. When the log has been broken a chain is attached to its parts and it is then hoisted by a machine on the bridge and dropped into the current of the river. Contractor Kirk has abandoned the idea of constructing a dam to overflow the mass of ruins at the bridge. The water has fallen and cannot be raised to a serviceable height. A powerful windlass has been constructed at a point about one hundred feet below the bridge, and a rope attached to it is fastened to logs at the edge of the débris. In this way the course between one of the six spans of the railroad bridge has been cleared out. Where dynamite has been used to burst the logs another span has been freed of the débris, a space of about twenty by forty feet being cleared. The men are now well supplied with tools, but the force is not large enough to make rapid headway. It is believed that many more bodies will be found when the débris is loosened and started down the river.

Dynamite Tears the Bodies.

Thirteen bodies were taken from the burning débris at the stone bridge at one time this afternoon. None of the bodies were recognizable, and they were put in coffins and buried immediately. They were so badly decomposed that it was impossible to keep them until they could be identified. During a blast at the bridge this afternoon two bodies were almost blown to pieces. The blasting has had the effect of opening the channel under the central portion of the bridge.

In Unwholesome Company.

I came up here from Nineveh last night with the most disreputable crowd I ever traveled with. They were human buzzards flocking to the scene of horrors.

There was danger of a fight every moment, and if one had been started there is little doubt that it would have been short and bloody, for the conduct of the rowdy portion of the travellers had enraged the decent persons, to whom the thought of drunkenness and ribaldry at such a time was abhorrent, and they were quite ready to undertake the work of pitching the demoralized beings off the cars.

Wedged in here and there between intoxicated ruffians, who were indulging in the foulest jests about the corpses on which they were about to feast their eyes, were pale faced women, sad and red eyed, who looked as if they had had little sleep since the horrible collapse of the dam. Some of them were bound for Johnstown to claim and bring back bodies already identified, while others were on a trip for the ruins to commence a long and perhaps fruitless search for whatever might be left of their relatives. Some of those who misbehaved were friends of the lost, who, worn out with loss of sleep, had taken to drink and become madmen, but the greater part were merely sightseers or robbers of the dead.

Avaricious Tramps.

There were many tramps whose avarice had been stimulated by hearing of diamond rings and watches found on the dead. There was one little drunken hunchback who told those in the car who listened to him that years ago he had quarrelled with his parents in Johnstown and had not seen them since. He was on the way now to see if anything was left of them. One moment he was in maudlin tears and the next he was cracking some miserable joke about the disaster. He went about the car shaking dice with other inebriated passengers, and in the course of half an hour had won $6. Over this he exhibited almost the glee of a maniac, and the fate of his people was lost sight of. Then he would presently forget his gains and go sobbing up the aisle looking for listeners to his pitiful story.

There were two sinister looking Hungarians in the smoking car and their presence excited the anger of a handful of drunken maniacs. They made loud speeches, denouncing the conduct of Hungarians who robbed the Johnstown dead, levelling their remarks at the particular two. As they grew more excited they demanded that the passengers make a move and lynch the fellows. A great deal of trouble would have ensued, doubtless, if the train had not at that moment stopped at Sang Hollow, four miles from Johnstown. The conductor shouted out that the passengers must leave the car and walk along the track the remainder of the distance.

A Strange Procession.

We started out in the fast gathering darkness and the loiterers who held back made a long string. The drunken ruffians staggered along the tracks, howling with glee and talking about corpses, showing what their object was in coming. The tired out and disheartened women crowded under the shelter of the more respectable men. There was one member of the Pennsylvania National Guard in the troop with his bayonet, and he seemed to be the rallying point for the timid.

When the mob reached the outskirts of Johnstown they came across a little camp of military with outposts. I had been told that soldiers were keeping people who had no business there out of the lost city, and to insure my passage through the lines I had procured an order from Mr. McCreery, chairman of the

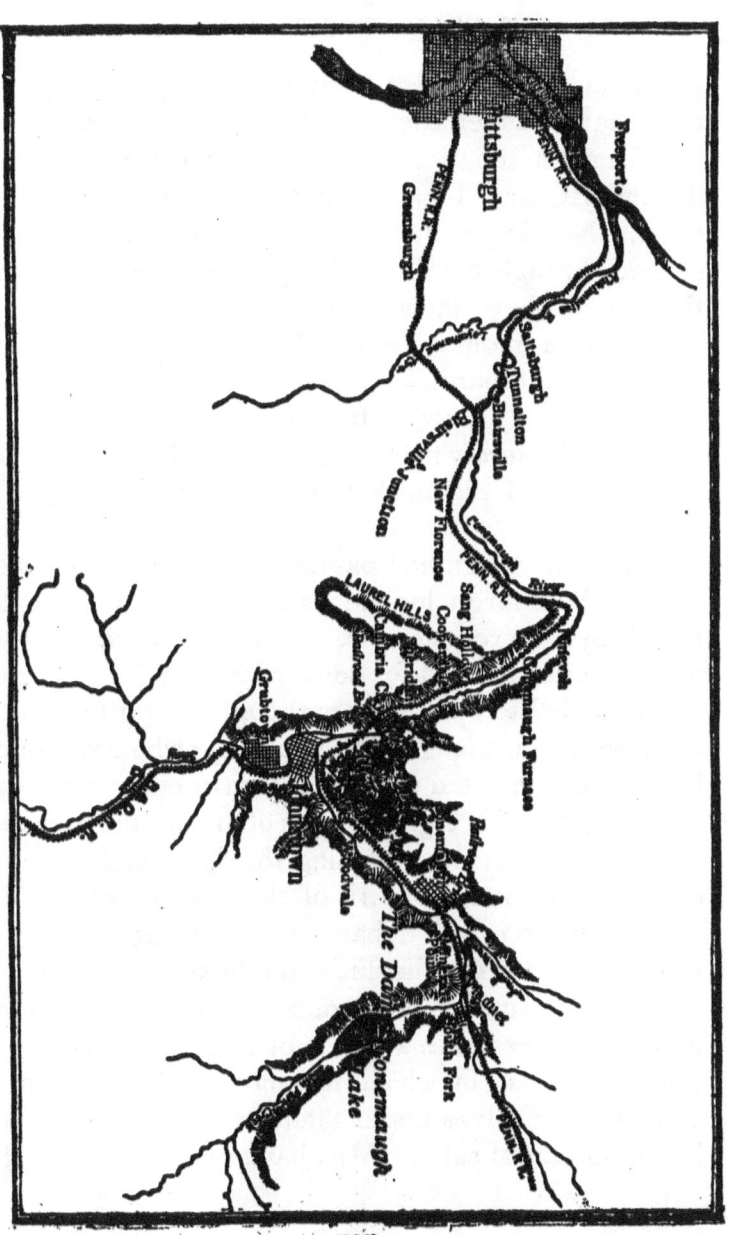

MAP OF THE DISTRICT SWEPT BY THE FLOOD.

Chamber of Commerce Committee at Pittsburgh, stating that I was entitled to go through. I knew that the drunken lunatics behind me could have no such documents, and I imagined the soldiers would stop them. Nothing of the kind happened. Whole troops surged through the line. No passes were asked from them and they showed none. They only quieted down for a moment when they saw the uniforms of the National Guard.

Reinforcing Disorder.

The mob merely helped to swell the host of thieves, cutthroats and pickpockets with which the region is infested.

The trains which had passed us going from Johnstown to Pittsburgh looked as if they might be made up of joyous excursionists. The cars were crowded to the platforms, and for some reason or other dozens of the inebriated passengers thought it appropriate to cheer and yell, though God knows the whole surroundings were calculated to make a human being shed tears of anguish. The sight of the coffins in the baggage cars, some of them containing the dead, had no dampening effect upon the spirit of these roysterers.

The reaction from debauches and excitement is terrible, and there can be little doubt that many minds will give way under the strain. One of the wonders of the disaster is the absence of suicide and the apparently calm way in which the most wofully bereaved support themselves under their terrible loss. It must be an unnatural calm. Men have quietly told me that they have lost their entire families and then have suddenly changed the subject and talked of some absurdly trivial matter with an air of great interest, but it was easy to see that there was some numbing influence over the mechanism of the mind. It is unnatural and awful. It is almost impossible to realize that the troops of workmen leisurely digging in the ruins as if engaged in everyday employment are really digging for the dead, and it is only in the actual sight of death and its emblems that one can persuade one's self that it is all true. The want of sleep conduces to an unnatural condition of the mind, under which these awful facts are bearable to the bereaved.

Picketing the Ruins.

It was like a military camp here last night. So many citizens have been knocked down and robbed that the soldiers had special instructions to see that no queer characters got through to the centre of the town. I had an excellent chance of seeing how impossible it was for an unauthorized person to move about the town easily, although he could get into the interior. I had been kindly invited to sleep on a wisp of hay in a neighboring barn, but being detained late in the valley reached the press headquarters after my host had left. It was a question of hunting shelter or sleeping on the ground.

A gentleman whom I met told me that he was living in a Baltimore and Ohio day passenger coach about a mile out, and that if we could find our way there I was welcome to a soft place on the floor. We spoke to the nearest picket. He told us that it would be madness to try to cross one part of the ground unless we had revolvers, because a gang of Huns were in hiding ready to knock down passengers and hold up any one who seemed defenceless. However, after a little cogitating, he said that he would escort us to General Hastings' headquarters, and we started, picking our way over the remains of streets and passing over great obstructions that had been left by the torrent. Ruin and wreck were on every hand. You could not tell where one street began and another left off, and in some places there was only soft mud, as devoid of evidence of the former presence of buildings as a meadow is, though they had been the sites of business blocks. It was washed clean.

A Weird Journey.

Our guide told us the details of the capture of five marauders who had been robbing the dead. They had cut off the head of a woman found in the débris to get her earrings. He said that a number of deputy sheriffs had declared that at dawn they would march to the place where the prisoners were and take them out and hang them. My military friend said that he and his comrades would not be particularly anxious to interfere. The scene as we picked our way was lighted up by camp fires, around which sat groups of deputy sheriffs in slouch hats. They were a grim looking set, armed with clubs and guns. A few had rifles and some wore revolvers in their belts in regular leather cowboy pockets. The camp fires were about two hundred yards apart and to pass them without being challenged was impossible. At the adjutant general's office we got a pass entitling us to pass the pickets, and bidding our guardsman good-night we started off escorted by a deputy sheriff. There were long lines of camp fires and every few rods we had to produce credentials. It was a pretty effect that was produced by the blazing logs. They lighted up the valley for some distance, throwing in relief the windowless ruins of what were once fine residences, bank buildings or factories. Embedded in the mud were packages of merchandise, such as sugar in barrels, etc., and over these we stumbled continually.

A Muddy Desert.

Streams were running through the principal streets of the city. In some parts all that was left of the thoroughfares were the cobble stones—by which it was possible to trace streets for a short distance—and the street railway tracks remaining in places for spaces of a hundred feet or so. There were some buildings outside of the track of the full force of the torrent, the roofs of which seemed not to have been reached. Others had been on fire and had lost parts of their walls. It was a dismal sight, this desolation, as shown up by the fitful camp fires. It was only after climbing over perilous places, crossing streams and narrowly escaping with our necks, that we came within sight of the car at two o'clock this morning. We passed by a school house used as a morgue. Several people were inside gazing by lamp light at the silent bodies in a hunt for lost ones. Piles of coffins, brown and white, were in the school playground, which resounded not many days ago with the shouts of children, some of whom lie there now. There are heaps of coffins everywhere throughout the city. Conversation with the deputy sheriffs showed a deep-rooted hatred against the Huns, and a determination to shoot them down like dogs if they were caught prowling about near the exposed property. While we were toiling over débris we heard three shots about a quarter of a mile off. We could learn nothing of their report. The service done by the deputy sheriffs was excellent.

Mistaken Identification.

At St. Columba's Catholic Church the scenes were striking in their individual peculiarities. One woman came in and identified a body as that of Katie Frank. The undertakers labeled it accordingly, but in a few moments another woman entered the church, raised the lid of the coffin, scanned the face of the corpse, and then tore the label from the casket. The undertakers were then warned by the woman to be more careful in labelling coffins in the future. She then began to weep, and left the church in despair. She was Katie's mother, and Katie is yet among the wreck in the river below.

The lot of bodies held and coffined at Morrellville presented a different feature. The mud was six inches deep, and the drizzling rain added gloom to the scene. Here and there could be seen, kneeling in the mud, broken hearted wives and mothers who sobbed and prayed. The incidents here were heartrending.

At the Fourth ward schoolhouse morgue a woman from Erie, whose name could not be learned, went to the morgue in search of some one, but fainted on seeing the long line of coffins. At the Kernville morgue, one little boy named Elrod, on finding his father and mother both dead, seized a hatchet, and for some time would let no one enter the place, claiming that the people were lying to him and wanted to rob him of his father and mother.

One sad incident was the sight of two coffins lying in the Gautier graveyard with nobody to bury them. A solitary woman was gazing at them in a dazed manner, while the rain beat on her unprotected head.

CHAPTER XIV.

Hairbreadth Escapes.

So vast is the field of destruction that to get an adequate idea from any point level with the town is simply impossible. It must be viewed from a height. From the top of Kernville Mountain just at the east of the town the whole strange panorama can be seen.

Looking down from that height many strange things about the flood that appear inexplicable from below are perfectly plain. How so many houses happened to be so queerly twisted, for instance, as if the water had a whirling instead of a straight motion, was made perfectly clear.

The town was built in an almost equilateral triangle, with one angle pointed squarely up the Conemaugh Valley to the east, from which the flood came. At the northerly angle was the junction of the Conemaugh and Stony creeks. The Southern angle pointed up the Stony Creek Valley. Now about one-half of the triangle, formerly densely covered with buildings, is swept as clean as a platter, except for three or four big brick buildings that stand near the angle which points up the Conemaugh.

Course of the Flood.

The course of the flood from the exact point where it issued from the Conemaugh Valley to were it disappeared below in a turn in the river and above by spreading itself over the flat district of five or six miles, is clearly defined. The whole body of water issued straight from the valley in a solid wave and tore across the village of Woodvale and so on to the business part of Johnstown at the lower part of the triangle. Here a cluster of solid brick blocks, aided by the conformation of the land, evidently divided the stream. The greater part turned to the north, swept up the brick block and then mixed with the ruins of the villages above down to the stone arch bridge. The other stream shot across the triangle, was turned southward by the bluffs and went up the valley of Stony Creek. The stone arch bridge in the meantime acted as a dam and turned part of the current back toward the south, where it finished the work of the triangle, turning again to the northward and back to the stone arch bridge. The stream that went up Stony Creek was turned back by the rising ground and then was reinforced by the back water from the bridge again and started south, where it reached a mile and a half and spent its force on a little settlement called Grubbtown.

Work of the Water.

The frequent turning of this stream, forced against the buildings and then the bluffs, gave it a regular whirling motion from right to left and made a tremendous eddy, whose centrifugal force twisted everything it touched. This accounts for the comparatively narrow path of the flood through the southern part of the town, where its course through the thickly clustered frame dwelling houses is as plain as a highway. The force of the stream diminished gradually as it went south, for at the place where the currents separated every building is ground to pieces and carried away, and at the end the houses were only turned a little on their foundations. In the middle of the course they are turned over on their sides or upside down. Further down they are not single, but great heaps of ground lumber that look like nothing so much as enormous pith balls.

To the north the work of the waters is of a different sort. It picked up everything except the big buildings that divided the current and piled the fragments down about the stone bridge or swept them over and soon down the river for miles. This left the great yellow, sandy and barren plain so often spoken of in the despatches where stood the best buildings in Johnstown—the opera house, the big hotel, many wholesale warehouses, shops and the finest residences. In this plain there are now only the Baltimore and Ohio Railroad train, a schoolhouse, the Morrell Company's stores and an adjoining warehouse and the few buildings at the point of the triangle. One big residence, badly shattered, is also standing.

Houses Changed Base.

These structures do not relieve the shocking picture of ruin spread out below the mountain, but by contrast making it more striking. That part of the town to the south where the flood tore the narrow path there used to be a separate village which was called Kernville. It is now known as the South Side. Some of the queerest sights of the wreck are there, though few persons have gone to see them. Many of the houses that are there, scattered helter skelter, thrown on their sides and standing on their roofs, were never in that neighborhood nor anywhere near it before. They came down on the breast of the wave from as far up as Franklin, were carried safely by the factories and the bridges, by the big buildings at the dividing line, up and down on the flood and finally settled in their new resting places little injured. A row of them, packed closely together and every one tipped over at about the same angle, is only one of the queer freaks the water played.

I got into one of these houses in my walk through the town to-day. The lower story had been filled with water, and everything in it had been torn out. The carpet had been split into strips on the floor by the sheer force of the rushing tide. Heaps of mud stood in the corners. There was not a vestige of furniture. The walls dripped with moisture. The ceiling was gone, the windows were out, and the cold rain blew in and the only thing that was left intact was one of those worked worsted mottoes that you always expect to find in the homes of working people. It still hung to the wall, and though much awry the glass and frame were unbroken. The motto looked grimly and sadly sarcastic. It was:—

"There is no place like home."

A melancholy wreck of a home that motto looked down upon.

A Tree in a House.

I saw a wagon in the middle of a side street sticking tongue, and all, straight up into the air, resting on its tail board, with the hind wheels almost completely buried in the mud. I saw a house standing exactly in the middle of Napoleon street, the side stove in by crashing against some other house and in the hole the coffin of its owner was placed. Some scholar's library had been strewn over the street in the last stage of the flood, for there was a trail of good books left half sticking in the mud and reaching for over a block. One house had been lifted over two others in some mysterious way and then had settled down between them and there it stuck, high up in the air, so its former occupants might have got into it again with ladders.

Down at the lower end of the course of the stream, where its force was greater, there was a house lying on one corner and held there by being fastened in the deep mud. Through its side the trunk of a tree had been driven like a lance, and there it stayed sticking out straight in the air. In the muck was the case and key board of a square piano, and far down the river, near the débris about the stone bridge, were its legs. An upright piano, with all its inside apparatus cleanly taken out, stood straight up a little way off. What was once a set of costly furniture was strewn all about it, and the house that contained it was nowhere.

The remarkable stories that have been told about people floating a mile up the river and then back two or three times are easily credible after seeing the evidences of the strange course the flood took in this part of the town. People who stood near the ruins of Poplar Bridge saw four women on a roof float up on the stream, turn a short distance above and come back and go past again and once more return. Then they went far down on the current to the lower part of the town and were rescued as they passed the second story window of a school house. A man who was imprisoned in the attic of his house put his wife and two children on a roof that was eddying past and stayed behind to die alone. They floated up the stream and then back and got upon the roof of the very house they had left, and the whole family was saved.

At Grubbtown there is a house that came all the way from Woodvale. On it was a man who lived near Grubbtown, but was working at Woodvale when the flood came. He was carried right past his own house and coolly told the people at the bridge to bid his wife good-bye for him. The house passed the bridge three times, the man carrying on a conversation with the people on shore and giving directions for his burial if his body should be found. The third time the house went up it grounded at Grubbtown, and in an hour or two the man was safe at home. Three girls who went by on a roof crawled into the branches of a tree and had to stay there all night before they could make any one understand where they were. At one time scores of floating houses were wedged in together near the ruins of Poplar street bridge. Four brave men went out from the shore, and, stepping from house roof to house roof, brought in twelve women and children.

Starvation Overcomes Modesty.

Some women crawled from roofs into the attics of houses. In their struggles with the flood most of their clothes had been torn from them, and rather than appear on the streets they stayed where they were until hunger forced them to shout out of the windows for help. At this stage of the flood more persons were lost by being crushed to death than by drowning. As they floated by on roofs or doors the toppling houses fell over upon them and killed them.

Nineveh was Spared.

The valley of death, twenty-three miles long, practically ends at Nineveh. It begins at Woodvale, where the dam broke, and for the entire distance to this point the mountains make a canyon—a water trap, from which escape was impossible. The first intimation this city had of the impending destruction was at noon on Friday, when Station Agent Nunamaker got this despatch:—

"We just received word from South Fork that water is coming over dam at Conemaugh Lake, and is liable to burst at any moment. Notify people to look out."

"J. C. WAUKEMSHAW,
"Despatcher at Conemaugh."

Nunamaker started on a dead run to the water front, along which most of the houses are situated, crying :—

"The dam is breaking. Run for your lives!"

Every spring, the station agent tells me, there have been a score of such alarms, and when the people heard Nunamaker they laughed and called him an old fogy for his pains. They had run too often to the mountains to escape some imaginary flood to be scared by anything less than the actual din of the torrent in their ears. Two hours and a half later a despatch came saying that the dam had indeed broken.

Again the station agent went on a trot to the residential part of the town. That same despatch had gone thundering down the whole valley. Johnstown heard the news and so did Conemaugh. No one believed it. It was what they called "a chestnut." But the cry had put the people a little on the alert. One hour after the despatch came the first warning note of the disaster. Mr. Nunamaker tells me that it took really more than that time for the head of the leaping cataract to travel the twenty-three miles. If that is so the people of Johnstown must have had half an hour's warning at least, for Johnstown is half way between here and the fatal dam.

Awful Scenes.

Nineveh is very flat on the river side where the people live, though, fortunately, the main force of the current was not directed on this side of the stream. In a second the river rose two feet at a jump. It then reared up like a thing of life, then it steadily rose inches at a time, flooding the whole town. But the people had had warning and saved themselves. Pitiful cries were heard soon from the river. People were floating down on barrels, roofs, beds, anything that was handy. There were pitiful shrieks from despairing women. The people of Nineveh could do nothing. No boat could have stemmed the cataract. During the night there were shrieks heard from the flooded meadows. Next morning at nine o'clock the flood had fallen three feet. Bodies could be seen on the trees by the Nineveh people, who stayed up all night in the hope of being able to do some act of humanity.

The Living and the Dead.

Only twenty-five were taken alive from the trees and drift on this side. Across the stream a score were secured and forty-seven corpses taken out. This, with the 200 corpses here, makes a total of 300 people who are known to have come down to this point. There are perhaps a hundred and fifty bodies within a mile. Only a few were actually taken from the river bed. They sank in deep water. It is only when they have swollen by the effect of the water that they rise to the surface. Most of those recovered were found almost on dry land or buried in drift. There are tons of wood, furniture, trees, trunks, and everything that is ever likely to float in a river, that must be "dug over." It will be work of the hardest kind to get at the remaining corpses. I went over the whole ground along the river bank between here and Johnstown to-day.

The Force of the Flood.

The trees on the banks were levelled as if by battering rams, telegraph poles were snapped off as a boy breaks a sugar stick, and parts of the Pennsylvania Railroad track were wrenched, torn and destroyed.

Jerry McNeilly, of this place, says he was at the Johnstown station when the flood came down, preceded by a sort of cloud or fog. He saw people smoking at their windows up to the last moment, and even when the water flooded their floors they laughed and seemed to think that the river had risen a few feet and that was all. Jerry, however, ran to the hills and saved himself while the water rose and did its awful work. Some houses were bowled over like ninepins. Some floated to the surface and started with the flood; others stood their ground and were submerged inch by inch, the occupants climbing from story to story, from the top story to the roof, only to be swept away from their foothold sooner or later.

The Dam's History.

I asked a gathering of men here in what light they had been accustomed to look upon the dam. They say that from the time it was built, somewhere about 1831, by the Commonwealth of Pennsylvania to collect water for the canals, it has been the "bogie" of the district. Babies were frightened when naughty by being told the dam would break. Time and time again the people of Nineveh have risen from their beds in the night and perched upon the mountains through fear. A body of water seven miles or more long, from eighty to one hundred and twenty feet deep, and about a mile wide, was indeed something to be dreaded. This lake had a circumference of about eighteen miles, which gives some idea of the volume of water that menaced the population. The dam was thick enough for two carriages to drive abreast on its top, but the people always doubted the stability of that pile of masonry and earth.

Morrellville was for a few days in a state of starvation, but Sheridan, Sang Hollow and this town are in no distress.

Nineveh has lost no life, although wild rumors said it had. Though the damage to property is very great, the Huns have been kept away, and robbers and marauders find nothing to tempt them.

What "Chal" Dick Saw.

"I'll kill the first man that dares to cross the bridge."

"Chal" Dick, lawyer, burgess and deputy sheriff and sportsman, sat upon his horse with a Winchester rifle across his saddle and a thousand or two of fiends dancing a war dance in his eyes. Down in Johnstown proper they think "Chal" Dick is either drunk or crazy. Two newspaper men bunked with him last night and found he was not afflicted in either sense. He is the only recognized head in the borough of Kernville, where every man, woman and child know him as "Chal," and greet him as he passes by.

THE JOHNSTOWN HORROR. 299

"Yes," he said to me last night, "I saw it all. My house was on Somerset street. On Thursday night it rained very hard. My wife woke me and called my attention to the way the water was coming down. I said nothing, but I got up about five o'clock and took a look around. In a little while Stony Creek had risen three feet. I then knew that we were going to have a flood, but I did not apprehend any danger. The water soon flooded the streets, and boards and logs began coming down.

Sport Before Sorrow.

"A lot of us turned in to have some sport. I gave my watch and what money I had to a neighbor and began riding logs down the stream. I had lots of company. Old men acted like boys, and shouted and shouted, and splashed about in the water like mad. Finally the water began to rise so rapidly that I became alarmed. I went home and told my wife that it was full time to get out. She was somewhat incredulous, but I made her get ready, and we took the children and we went to the house of Mr. Bergman, on Napoleon street, just on the rise of Kernville. I got wet from head to foot fooling in the water, and when I got to Bergman's I took a chill. I undressed and went to bed and fell asleep. The first thing I knew I was pulled out of bed on to the floor, by Mr. Bergman, who yelled, 'the dam has burst.' I got up, pulled on my pantaloons and rushed down stairs, I got my youngest child and told my wife to follow with the two others. This time the water was three feet in the house and rising rapidly. We waded up to our waists out through it, up the hill, far beyond the reach of danger.

A Stupendous Sight.

"From the time I left Bergman's till I stopped is a blank. I remember nothing. I turned and looked, and may my eyes never rest on another such sight. The water was above the houses from the direction of the railroad bridge. There came a wave that appeared to be about twelve feet high. It was perpendicular in its face and moved in a mist. I have heard them speak of the death mist, but I then first appreciated what the phrase meant. It came on up Stony Creek carrying on its surface house after house and moving along faster than any horse could go. In the water there bobbed up and down and twisted and twirled the heads of people making ripples after the manner of shot dropped into the water. The wave struck houses not yet submerged and cut them down. The frames rose to the surface, but the bricks, of course, were lost to sight. When the force of the water spent itself and began retracing its course, then the awfulness of the scene increased in intensity. I have a little nerve, but my heart broke at the sight. Houses, going and coming, crashed up against each other and began grinding each other to pieces. The buildings creaked and groaned as they let go their fastenings and fairly melted.

"At the windows of the dwellings there appeared the faces of people equally as ill-fated as the rest.

God forbid that I should ever again look upon such intensity of anguish. Oh, how white and horror-stricken those faces were, and such appeals for help that could not come. The woman wrung their hands in their despair and prayed aloud for deliverance. Down stream went houses and people at the rate of twenty-five miles an hour and stopped, a conglomerate mass, at the stone abutment of the railroad bridge. The first buildings that struck the bridge took fire, and those that came after were swept into a sea of flame. I thought I had already witnessed the greatest possible climax of anguish, but the scene that followed exceeded in awfulness anything I had before looked upon. The flames grew, hundreds of people were wedged in the driftwood and imprisoned in the houses. Rapidly the fire approached them, and then they began to cry for aid, and hundreds of others stood on the bank, powerless to extend a single comfort.

Judgment Day.

"As the fire licked up house after house and pile after pile, I could see men and women bid each other good-by, and fathers and mothers kiss their children. The flames swallowed them up and hid them from my view, but I could hear their shrieks as they roasted alive. The shrieks mellowed into groans, and the groans into silence, only to be followed by more shrieks, more groans and more silence, as the fire caught up and destroyed its victims. Heavens! but I was glad when the end came. My only anxiety was to have it come quickly, and I prayed that it might come, oh! so quick! It was a splendid realization of the judgment day. It was a magnificent realization of the impotency of man in a battle with such a combination of fire and flood."

Some Have Cause for Joy.

In the midst of the confusion of the disaster and the strain of excitement which followed it was but natural that every one who could not readily be found was reported dead. Amid the throng of mourners now an occasional soul is made happy by finding that some loved one has escaped death. To-day a few of the living had time to notify their friends throughout the country of their safety.

General Lew Wallace, now at West Point, telegraphed President Harrison, in response to an inquiry last night, that his wife was "coming out of the great calamity at Johnstown safe." Several reports have been sent out from Johnstown, one as late as last night, to the effect that Mrs. Wallace was believed to be among the victims of the disaster. Private Secretary Halford received a telegram this afternoon from his wife at Altoona, announcing that Mrs. Lew Wallace was with her and safe.

Did Not Lose Their Presence of Mind.

A dispatch from Carthage, Ill., says:—"Mrs. M. J. Smith, a traveling saleslady for a book concern in New York city, was at Johnstown at the time of the flood and was swept away with others. Her brothers, Lieutenant P. and James McKee, received the following telegram at Carthage yesterday from Johnstown:

THE JOHNSTOWN HORROR. 303

...ped with my life on housetop; am all right.
"M. J. SMITH.'
"The lady is well known in this county."

Rich Made Poor.

John Kelly, the prominent Odd Fellow of Conenaugh, who was supposed to be lost, escaped with his entire family, though his house and store were swept down the river.

John Rowley, who stands high among the Masons and Odd Fellows, tells me that out of $65,000 worth of property which he could call his own on Friday last he found just two bricks on the site of his residence this morning. He counts himself wealthy, however, in the possession of his wife and children who were all saved. His wife, who was very ill, was dragged through the water in her nightclothes. She is now in a critical condition, but has the best of medical attendance and may pull through.

In a frame house which stood at No. 121 Union street, Johnstown, were Mrs. O. W. Byrose, her daughters Elsie, Bessie and Emma, and sons Samuel and Ray. When the flood struck the house they ran to the attic. The house was washed from its foundation and carried with the rushing waters. Mrs. Byrose and her children then clung to each other, expecting every minute to meet death. As the house was borne along the chimney fell and crashed through the floors, and the bricks were strewn along the course of the river. The house was caught in the jam and held about two hundred feet above the bridge and one hundred and fifty feet from the shore. The terrified inmates did not lose all presence of mind, and they made their escape to the hole made by the fallen chimney. They were seen by those on shore, and after much difficulty each was rescued. A few minutes later the house caught fire from the burning buildings, and was soon consumed.

Swept from His Side.

At ten o'clock this morning an old gray bearded man stood amid the blackened logs and ashes through which the polluted water of the Conemaugh made its way, wringing his hands and moaning in a way that brought tears to the eyes of all about him. He was W. J. Gilmore, whose residence had stood at the corner of Conemaugh and Main streets. Being on low ground the house was flooded by the first rush of water and the family, consisting of Mr. Gilmore, his brother Abraham, his wife, four children and mother-in-law, ran to the second story, where they were joined by Frances, the little daughter of Samuel Fields, and Grandmother Maria Prosser. When the torrent from South Fork rushed through the town the side of the house was torn out and the water poured into the second floor. Mr. Gilmore scrambled upon some floating débris, and his brother attempted to pass the women and children out to him. Before he could do so, however, the building sank and Mr. Gilmore's family was swept from his side. His brother disappeared for a moment under the water, but came to the surface and was hauled upon the roof. The brothers then strove frantically to tear a hole in the roof of the house with their bare hands, but their efforts were, of course, unavailing, and they were soon struggling for their own lives in the wreck at the viaduct. Both finally reached the shore. The body of Mrs. Gilmore, when taken from the ruins this morning, was but little mutilated, although her body was bloated by the water. Two of the children had been almost burned to cinders, their arms and legs alone being something like their original shape.

Statue of the Virgin.

St. Mary's German Catholic Church, which is badly wrecked, was temporarily used as a morgue, but a singular circumstance connected with the wrecking having been noticed, the duty of becoming a receptacle for the dead is transferred to the Church of St. Columba. The windows of St. Mary's are all destroyed. The floor for one-third of its extent on St. Mary's side is torn up to the chancel rail in one piece by the water and raised toward the wall. One-half the chancel rail is gone, the mud is eighteen inches deep on the floor, St. Joseph's altar is displaced and the statue gone. The main altar, with its furniture for Easter, is covered with mud, and some fine potted flowers are destroyed. Nearly all the other ornaments are in place, even to the candlesticks. Strange to relate, the statue of the Virgin in her attire is unsoiled; the white vestments with silken embroidery are untarnished. This discovery led to the change of morgue. The matter being bruited abroad the desolated women of Cambria and Johnstown, as well as those who had not been sufferers from the flood, visited the church, and with most affecting devoutness adored the shrine. Some men also were among the devout, and not one of those who offered their prayers but did it in tears. For several hours this continued to be the wonder of the parishioners of the Catholic churches.

The entire family of Mr. Howe, the wealthiest man in Cambria, with some visitors from Pittsburgh and Ohio, were hurried to death by the collapse of their residence on that fatal Friday night.

In the rubbish heaped high on the shore near the stone arch bridge is a flat freight car banged and shattered and with a hole stove in its side. One of the workmen who were examining the debris to-day got into the car and found a framed and glazed picture of the Saviour. It was resting against the side of the car, right side up. Neither frame nor glass were injured. When this incident got noised about among the workmen they dropped their pickaxes and ran to look at the wonderful sight with their hats off.

Saved His Mother and Sister.

A man who came up from Lockport to-day told this:—"On the roof of a house were a young man, his mother and a young girl apparently his sister. As they passed the Lockport bridge, where the youth hung in an eddy for a moment, the men on the bridge threw them a rope. The young man on the house caught and tried to make it fast around his mother and then around his sister. They were afraid to use it or they were unwilling to leave him, for they would not take the rope. They tried to make him take it, but he threw it away and stayed on the roof with them. The house was swept onward and in another moment was lodged against a tree. The youth seized his mother and sister and placed them in safety among the branches. The next instant the house started again. The young man's foot slipped. He fell into the water and was not seen again.

Where Death Lay in Wait.

A great deal has been written and published about the terrible disaster, but in all the accounts nothing has been said about South Fork, where in proportion to its size as much damage has been done as at any other point.

For the purpose of ascertaining how the place looked which in the annals of history will always be referred to as the starting point of this great calamity, I came here from Johnstown. I left on Monday morning at half-past six, and being unable to secure a conveyance of any character was compelled to walk the entire distance. Thinking the people of Johnstown knew whereof they spoke, I started over the Edensburg turnpike and tramped, as a result, six more miles than was absolutely necessary. After I left Johnstown it began raining and continued until I reached South Fork.

Two miles out from Johnstown I passed the Altoona Relief Committee in carriages, with their supply train following, and from that until I reached Fair

View, where I turned off toward the Conemaugh river, it was a continuous line of vehicles of all kinds, some containing supplies, others passengers, many of whom were ladies. I followed a cow-path along the mountain until I reached Mineral Point. Here is where the flood did its first bad work after leaving South Fork. There had been thirty-three dwelling houses, a store and a large sawmill in the village, and in less than one minute after the flood struck the head of the place there were twenty-nine of these buildings wiped out; and so sudden had been the coming of the water that but a few of the residents succeeded in getting away.

As a Boy would Marbles.

Jacob Kohler, one of the residents of the place, said he had received a telegram stating that the flood was coming, but paid no attention to it as they did not understand its significance. "I saw it coming," he said, "with the water reaching a height of at least twenty-five feet, tearing trees up by the roots and dashing big rocks about as a boy would marbles. I hardly had time to grab a child and run for the hills when it was upon us, and in less time than it takes for me to tell it our village was entirely wiped out and the inhabitants were struggling in the water and were soon out of sight. I never want to see such a sight again."

From Mineral Point another cow-path was taken over the mountains. I came just below the viaduct within about one mile of South Fork, and here the work of destruction had been as complete as it was possible for it to be. The entire road-bed of the Pennsylvania Railroad had been washed away.

At this point a freight train had been caught and all the men on it perished, but the names could not be learned. The engine was turned completely upside down and the box cars were lifted off the track and carried two hundred feet to the side of the hill. Fifteen of them are there with the trucks, about one hundred feet from the old road-bed, and turned completely upside down.

Another freight train just ahead of it was also swept away in the same manner, all excepting two cars and the engine. One of the cars was loaded with two heavy boilers from the works of James Witherow, Newcastle.

Rails Twisted Double.

Coming in to South Fork the work of destruction on the railroad was found to be even greater, the rails being almost bent double. The large iron bridge over the river at this point is gone, as is also one of the piers. The lower portion of this place is completely wiped out, and two men were lost. This is all the loss of life here, excepting two Italians who were working at the lake proper. The loss in individual property to the people of this place will reach $75,000, and at Mineral Point $50,000.

For the purpose of seeing how the lake looked after all the water was out of it, a trip was taken to it, fully three miles distant. The driveway around it is fully thirty-five feet wide, and that was the width at the point of the dam where the break occured.

Like a Thunderbolt.

Imagine, if you can, a solid piece of ground, thirty-five feet wide and over one hundred feet high, and then, again, that a space of two hundred feet is cut out of it, through which is rushing over seven hundred acres of water, and you can have only a faint conception of the terrible force of the blow that came upon the people of this vicinity like a clap of thunder out of a clear sky. It was irresistible in its power and carried everything before it. After seeing the lake and the opening through the dam it can be readily understood how that outbreak came to be so destructive in its character.

The lake had been leaking, and a couple of Italians were at work just over the point where the break occurred, and in an instant, without warning, it gave way, and they were down in the whirling mass of water and were swept into eternity. The people of this place had been told by some of those who had been to the lake that it was leaking, but paid no attention any more than to send telegrams to Johnstown and Mineral Point.

Here's Another Paul Revere.

The first intimation the people had of the approach of the water was from the seventeen-year-old son of John Baker. He was on the road on horseback and noticed the water coming out of a cavity about five feet in diameter, and not waiting to see any more he

RESCUES AT THE SIGNAL TOWER.

put spurs to his horse and dashed for the town at breakneck speed. Some of the people of this place saw him coming at great speed, waving his hat, and knowing something was wrong at once gave the alarm, and grabbing their children started for the high parts. When he arrived almost at Railroad street, his own home, the water was already in the roadway, and in less than one minute its whole bulk was coming, twisting trees and rolling rocks before it.

In just eight minutes from the time he first saw it the water had carried away the bridge and was on its career of death and destruction. A train of Pullman cars for the East, due at South Fork at 2.55, was standing on the track on the west side of the bridge waiting to pull into the station. At first the engineer paid no attention to the wild gesticulations of the station agent, but finally started out, pulling slowly into the station, and not one moment too soon, for had he remained where he was a minute longer all would have been swept away.

Thrilling Escapes.

A local freight train with a passenger coach attached, standing on the east side of the track, was compelled to run into the rear end of the passenger train so as to get out of the way of the flood. A young man who was on the rear end of the train grabbed a young lady who was floating by and thus saved her life. The house of an old man, eighty-two years of age, was caught in the whirlpool, and he and his aged wife climbed on the roof for safety. They were floating down the railroad track to certain death, when their son-in-law, from the roof of the Pennsylvania Railroad station-house, pulled them off and saved their lives as the house was dashed to pieces.

Mr. Brown, a resident of this place, said: "I was just about opposite the mouth of the lake when it broke. When I first saw it the water was dashing over the top of the road just where it broke about a foot high, and not eight or ten feet, as has been stated, and I told Mr. Fisher, who lived there, that he had better get his family out at once, which he did, going to the hillside, and it was lucky for him that he did, because in a half minute after it broke his home was wiped away."

No Safety Outlet.

Mr. Burnett, who was born and raised a mile from the lake, and is now a resident of Hazelwood, and who was at South Fork, said: "When the State owned this lake they had a tower over the portion that gave way and a number of pipes by which they were enabled to drive off the surplus water, and had the present owners had an arrangement of that kind this accident would not have occurred. The only outlet there was for the water was a small waterway around to the right of the lake, which is totally inadequate. The people of this valley have always been afraid of this thing, and now that it is here it shows that they had every reason for their fears."

In company with Mr. Burnett I walked all over the place, and am free to confess that it looks strong, but experience shows the contrary.

Mr. Moore, who has done nearly all the hauling for the people who lived at the lake in summer, said:—
"About eight years ago this dam broke, but there was not as much water in it as now, and when it broke they were working at it and hauled cart load after cart load of dirt, stone and logs, and finally about ten tons of hay, and by that means any further damage was prevented. That was the time when they should have put forth strenuous efforts to have that part strengthened where the break occurred. This lake is about three miles long and about a mile wide and fully ninety feet deep, and of course when an opening of any kind was forced it was impossible to stop it.

Thirsting for Vengeance.

"The indignation here against the people who owned that place is intense. I was afraid that if the people here were to hear that you were from Pittsburgh they would jump to the conclusion that you were connected with the association, and I was afraid they would pull you from the carriage and kill you. That is the feeling that predominates here, and we all believe justly."

Mr. Ferguson, of the firm of J. P. Stevenson & Co., said: "It is a terrible affair, and shows the absolute necessity of people not fooling with matters of that kind. We sent telegrams to Mineral Point, Johnstown and Conemaugh, notifying them that the lake was leaking and the water rising and we were liable to have trouble, and two minutes before the flood reached here a telegram was sent to Mineral Point that the dam had broken. But you see for the past five years so many alarms of that kind have been sent that the people have not believed them."

Broke Forty-one Years Ago.

Mrs. McDonald, who lives between Johnstown and South Fork, said: "I am an old woman and lived in Johnstown forty-two year ago, when there but two or three houses here. I have always contended, ever since this club of dudes took charge of this place, that it would end in a terrible loss of life. It broke about forty-one years ago, and I was in my house washing and it actually took my tub away and I only saved myself after a desperate struggle. At that time there were no lives lost. On Friday night, when it was raining so hard, I told my son not to go near Johnstown, as it was sure, from the telegrams I heard of, which had come in the afternoon, that there would be a terrible disaster.

I was told that when the viaduct went a loud report was heard just as a couple of freight cars were dashing against it, and the people say that they were loaded with dynamite.

The Pennsylvania Railroad officials are rushing in all the men at this point possible to repair the road and are working day and night, having electric lights all along the road; but with all of that it looks as though it will be utterly impossible to have even a single track ready for business before ten days or two weeks, as there is not the slightest vestige of a railroad track to be seen. The railroad people around here are of the opinion that it will take as long as that.

The railroad men say that it is the most complete destruction of the kind that they have ever witnessed.

Wealth Borne Away.

I had an interview to-night with Colonel James A. McMillan, the consulting director and principal owner of the Cambria Iron Works. He said:—

"What will be the total loss sustained by the Cambria Company is rather hard to state with perfect accuracy just yet, but from the examinations already made of our works I would place our loss at from $3,000,000 to $4,000,000. That includes, of course, the loss of our Gautier Steel Department, above Johnstown, which is completely swept away.

"Day before yesterday I took the liberty of determining the action which the company will pursue in the matter of reconstruction and repairs. I accordingly telegraphed for Mr. Lockhart, the secretary of the company. He arrived here to-day and said to me: 'McMillan, I'm glad to see you intend to stand by the company and push the work of repairs at once.'

"I think his words voice the sentiment of all the stockholders of the company.

Reconstruction Begun.

"All day we have had at least eight hundred men cleaning away the débris about our works, and we have made so much progress that you can say we will have our entire clerical force at work to-morrow evening. Our large pieces of machinery are uninjured, and we will have to send away for only the smaller pieces of our machines and smaller pipes, which compose an enormous system of pipe connections through the works. In from ten to twelve days we will have our works in operation, and I feel confident that we will be making rails at our works inside of fifty days. As we employ about five thousand men, I think our renewal of operations will give the people more encouragement than can be imagined. Besides, we have half the amount of cash needed on deposit in our local bank here, which was brought over by the Adams Express Company on Monday to pay our men. This will be paid them as soon as we can get access to the bank.

"Our immediate work of reconstruction and repair will, of course, be confined to the company's Cambria iron works proper, and not extended to the Gautier steel works above."

Twelve Millions More.

The Colonel was then asked his estimate of the total loss sustained by the towns of Mineral Point, Franklin borough, Woodvale, Conemaugh, Johnstown, Cambria City, Coopersdale and Morrellville. He said:

"I should place it at nothing lower than $12,000,000, besides the loss sustained by our company. That is only an estimate, but when you take the different towns as they were before the flood, and knowing them as I do, you could not fail to see that this is a very reasonable estimate of the loss."

As to the South Fork dam, he said: "For the present I don't care to be interviewed on that question as representing any one but myself. Personally, I have always considered it a dangerous trap, which was likely at any time to wipe us out. For the last ten years I have not hesitated to express this opinion in regard to the dam, and I guess it is pretty well understood that all of our leading citizens held similar views. There is not a man in Johnstown who will deny that he has lived for years in constant dread of its bursting down on us."

Fifteen Years to Recover.

"What do you think will be the time required for the Conemaugh Valley to recover from the shock of the flood?"

"At least fifteen years, and vigilant efforts will be required at that. I speak now from a financial standpoint. Of course we will never recover fully from the terrible loss of life which is now being revealed in its dreadful entirety.

Survivors in Camp.

There are two camps on the hillside to the north of Johnstown, and they are almost side by side. One is a camp for the living, for the most woebegone and unfortunate of the refugees from the Conemaugh Valley of the shadow of death, and the other is for the dead. The camp of the living is Camp Hastings and the ministering spirits are members of the Americus Republican Club of Pittsburgh. The camp for the dead is the new potters' field that was laid out on Monday for the bodies of unknown victims. The former is populous and stirring, but the latter has more mounds already than the other has living souls. The refugees are widely scattered; some are in the hospital, some are packed as closely as the logs and dead bodies, at the stone bridge in the houses yet tenable, and the rest are at Camp Hastings.

In the despairing panic and confusion of Saturday the first thought that presented itself to those who were hurried in to give relief was to prepare shelter for the survivors. The camp has been in operation ever since, and will be for days and may be weeks to come.

Gloomy Pictures of Despair.

It looked desolate enough to-day after the soaking downpour of last night, and groups of shivering mothres, with their little ones, stood around a smoky fire at either end of the streets. The members of the Americus Committee, for the time being cooks, waiters, grocery dealers and dry goods men, were in striking contrast to their usual appearance at home. Major W. Coffey, one of the refugees, who was washed seven miles down the Conemaugh, was acting as officer of the guard, and limped up and down on his wooden leg, which had been badly damaged by the flood.

Palefaced women looked out through the flaps of tents on the scene, and the only object that seemed to be taking things easy was a lean, black dog, asleep in front of one of the fires.

In one of the tents a baby was born last night. The mother, whose husband was lost in the flood, was herself rescued by being drawn up on the roof of the Union Schoolhouse. One of the doctors of the Altoona Relief Corps at the Cambria Hospital attended her, and mother and babe are doing better than thousands of the flood sufferers who are elsewhere. There are other babies in Camp Hastings, but none of them receive half of the attention from the people in the camp that is bestowed upon this little tot, whose life began just as so many lives were ended. The baby will probably be named Johnstown Camp O'Connor.

The refugees who are living along the road get their supplies from the camp. They pour into the wretched city of tents in a steady stream, bearing baskets and buckets of food.

He Wanted Tobacco or Nothing.

An old Irishman walked up to the tent early in the day. "Well, what can we do for you?" was asked.

"Have yez any tobaccy?"

"No, tobacco don't go here."

"I want tobaccy or nothin'. This is no relief to a non at all, at all."

The aged refugee walked away in high dudgeon.

Just down the row from the clothing tent are located two little girls, named Johnson, who lost both father and mother. They had a terrible experience in the flood, and were two of the forty-three people pulled in on the roof of the house of the late General Campbell and his two sons, James and Curt.

"How do you fare?" one of the little girls was asked.

"Oh, very well, sir; only we are afraid of catching the measles," she answered; and with a grimace she tossed her head toward a tent on the other side and further up. A baby in the tent indicated has a slight attack of the measles, but is getting better, and is next door to a tent in which is a young woman shaking with the ague.

A Multitude to be Fed.

In the houses along the road above the camp are several hundreds of refugees. In one of them are thirty or forty people rendered homeless by the flood. These are all supplied with food from the camp. Some idea of the number of people who have to be fed can be gathered from the fact that 350 pounds of coffee have been given out since yesterday. In the hills back of Cambria there are many hundreds of survivors. Dr. Findley, of the Altoona Relief Corps, went there to-day and found that they were without a physician. One from Baltimore had been there, but had gone away. He found many people needing medical care, and they will be looked after from day to day.

"Wherever we go," said one of the doctors yesterday, "we find that there is an alarming spread of pneumonia." Of the refugees at the Cambria Hospital but two have died.

Bayonets in Control.

The ruined city lies to-night within a girdle of steel —the bayonets of the 14th Regiment. The militia has captured Johnstown and to-night over the desolate plain where the city proper stood, through the towering wrecks and by the river passes, marches the patrol, crying "Halt" and challenging vagabonds, vandals and ghouls, who cross their path. General Hastings, being the highest officer in rank, is in command, and when the survivors of the flood awake to-morrow morning, when the weary pickets are relieved at sunrise a brigade headquarters will be fully established on

ENCAMPMENT OF RELIEF PARTIES.

the slope of Prospect Hill overlooking the hundreds of white tents of the regiments that will lie down below by the German Catholic Church.

First this afternoon arrived Governor Beaver's staff, mostly by way of Harper's Ferry on the Baltimore and Ohio. All the officers in brilliant uniform and trappings reported to General Hastings. They found their commander in a slouch hat, a rough-looking cutaway and rubber boots.

The 14th Regiment, reinforced this morning until it is now 600 strong, is still camped in freight cars beyond the depot, opposite the late city proper. Space is being rapidly cleared for its tents, however, over by the German Catholic Church, and near the ruins of the Irish Catholic Church, which was on fire when the deluge came.

Early this morning the 14th Regiment went into service, but it was a volunteer service of two young officers and three privates when at noon they dragged gently from the rushing Conemaugh the body of a beautiful young girl. She was tenderly borne through the lines by regimental headquarters to the church house morgue, while the sentinels stood aside with their bayonets and the corporal ordered "Halt!" Guards were placed at the Johnstown stations and all the morgues.

Marched out of Camp.

During the day many people of questionable character, indeed all who were challenged and could not satisfactorily explain their business here, had a military escort to the city limits, where they were ordered not to return. Every now and then two of the National Guard could be seen marching along with a rough fellow between them to the post where such beings are made exiles from the scene of desolation. To-night the picket lines stretch from brigade headquarters down Prospect Hill past General Hastings' quarters even to the river. The patrol across the river is keeping sharp vigilance in town. At the eastern end of the Pennsylvania Railroad's stone bridge you must stop and give the countersign. If you don't no man can answer for your safety.

A Lieutenant's Disgrace.

Down the Cambria Road, past which the dead of the River Conemaugh swept into Nineveh in awful numbers, was another scene to-day—that of a young officer of the National Guard in full uniform and a poor deputy sheriff, who had lost home, wife, children and all, clinched like madmen and struggling for the former's revolver. If the officer of the Guard had won, there might have been a tragedy, for he was drunk. The homeless deputy sheriff with his wife and babies swept to death past the place where they struggled was sober and in the right.

The officer of the National Guard came with his regiment into this valley of distress to protect survivors from ruffianism and maintain the peace and dignity of the State. The man with whom he fought for the weapon was Peter Fitzpatrick, almost crazy in his own woe, but singularly cool and self-possessed regarding the safety of those left living.

A Man who had Suffered.

It was one o'clock this afternoon when I noticed on the Cambria road the young officer with his long military coat cut open leaning heavily for support upon two privates of Company G, Hawthorn and Stewart (boys). He was crying in a maudlin way, "You just take me to a place and I'll drink soft stuff." They entreated him to return at once to the regimental quarters, even begged him, but he cast them aside and went staggering down the road to the line, where he met the grave-faced deputy face to face. The latter looked in the white of his eyes and said: "You can't pass here, sir."

"Can't pass here?" he cried, waving his arms. "You challenge an officer? Stand aside!"

"You can't pass here," this time quietly, but firmly; "not while you're drunk."

"Stand aside," yelled the Lieutenant. "Do you you know who I am? You talk to an officer of the National Guard."

"Yes; and listen," said the man in front of him so impatiently that it hushed his antagonist's tirade; "I talk to an 'officer' of the National Guard—I, who have lost my wife, my children and all in this flood no man has yet described; we, who have seen our dead with their bodies mutilated and their fingers cut from their hands by dirty foreigners for a little gold, are not afraid to talk for what is right, even to an officer of the National Guard."

A Big Man's Honest Rage.

While he spoke another great, dark, stout man, who looked as if he had suffered, came up, and upon taking in the situation every vein in his forehead swelled purple with rage.

"You dirty cur," he cried to the officer; "you dirty, drunken cur, if it was not for the sake of peace I'd lay you out where you stand."

"Come on," yelled the Lieutenant, with an oath.

The big man sent out a terrible blow that would have left the Lieutenant senseless had not one of the privates dashed in between, receiving part of it and warding it off. The Lieutenant got out of his military coat. The privates seized the big man and with another, who ran to the scene, held him back. The Lieutenant put his hand to his pistol pocket, the deputy Fitzpatrick seized him and the struggle for the weapon began. For a moment it was fierce and desperate, then another private came to the deputy's assistance. The revolver was wrested from the drunken officer and he himself was pushed back panting to the ground.

The Victor was Magnanimous.

Deputy Fitzpatrick seized the military coat he had thrown on the ground, and with it and the weapon started to the regimental headquarters. Then the privates got around him and begged him, one of them with tears in his eyes, not to report their officer, saying that he was a good man when he was sober. He studied a long while, standing in the road, while the officer slunk away over the hill. Then he threw the disgraced uniform to them, and said: "Here, give them to him ; and, mind you, if he does not go at once to his quarters, I'll take him there, dead or alive."

Sanitarians at Work.

Dr. Benjamin Lee, secretary of the State Board of Health, has taken hold with a grip upon the handle. When he surveyed the ground to-day he found that there were no disinfectants in town, and no utensils in which to distribute them had there been any disinfectants, so he sent a squad across the river to the supply train, below the viaduct, and had all the copperas and chloride of lime to be had carried across the bridges in buckets. He sent another squad hunting the ruins for utensils, and in the wreck of a general store on Main street they discovered pails, sprinkling pots and kettles. The copperas and chloride were promptly set heating in the kettles over the streets and in a short time a squad was out sprinkling the débris which chokes Main street almost to the housetops for three squares.

The reason of this was that a brief inspection had satisfied Dr. Lee that under the wreckage were piled the bodies of scores of dead horses. Meantime other men were at work collecting the bodies of other dead horses, which were hauled to the fire and with the aid of rosin burned to the number of sixty. A large number of dead horses were buried yesterday, but this course did not meet the State Board's approval and Dr. Lee has ordered their exhumation for burning.

Dr. R. Lowrie Sibbett, of Carlisle, was made medical inspector and sent up through the boroughs up the river. To-morrow a house-to-house inspection will be made of the remaining and inhabited portion of the cities and boroughs. The overcrowding makes this necessary.

"It will take weeks of unremitting labor and thousands of men," said Dr. Lee, "to remove the sources of danger to the public health which now exist. The principal danger to people living here is, of course, from the contamination of putrifying flesh. They have an excellent water-supply from the hills, but there is a very grave danger to the health of all the people who use the Allegheny river as a water-supply. It is in the débris above the viaduct, which is full of decomposing animal matter. Every ripple of water that passes through or under it carries the germs of possible disease with it."

At the Schoolhouse Morgue.

Away from the devastation in the valley and the gloomy scenes along the river, on Prospect Hill, stands the schoolhouse, the morgue of the unidentified dead. People do not go there unless they are hunting for a friend or relative. They treat it as a pest house. They have seen enough white faces in the valley and the living feel like fleeing from the dead.

This afternoon at sunset every desk in every class-room supported a coffin. Each coffin was numbered and each lid turned to show the face within. On the blackboard in one of the rooms, between the pretty drawing and neat writing of the school children, was scrawled the bulletin "Hold No. '59' as long as possible; supposed to be Mrs. Paulson, of Pittsburgh." "But '59' wasn't Mrs. Paulson," said a little white-faced woman. "It is Miss Frances Wagner, of Market street, Johnstown." Her brother found her here. "Fifty-nine" has gone—one of the few identified to-day, and others had come to take its place.

Strongly appealing to the sympathies of even those looking for friends and relatives was the difference in the size of the coffins. There were some no larger than a violin case hidden below large boxes, telling of the unknown babies perished, and there were coffins of children of all years. On the blackboards were written such sentences as "Home sweet home;" "Peace on earth, good will toward men." For all the people who looked at their young faces knew, they might have stood by the coffin of the child who helped to write them.

The bodies found each day are kept as long as possible and then are sent away for burial with their numbers, where their names should be, on rough boards, their only tombstones.

Just as a black storm-cloud was driving hard from the West over the slope of the hills yesterday the body of young Henry G. Rose, the district attorney of Cambria County, was lowered into a temporary grave beside unknown victims. Three people attended his burial—his father-in-law, James A. Lane, who saw him lost while he himself was struggling for life in their floating house; the Rev. Dr. H. L. Chapman, of the Methodist Episcopal Church, and the Rev. L. Maguire. Dr. Chapman read the funeral services, and while he prayed the thunder rumbled and the cloud darkened the scene. The coffins are taken there in wagonloads, lowered quickly and hidden from sight.

Miss Nina Speck, daughter of Rev. David Speck,

pastor of the First United Brethren Church of Chambersburg, was in Johnstown visiting her brother last week and narrowly escaped death in the flood.

She arrived to-day clad in nondescript clothing, which had been furnished by an old colored washerwoman and told the following story of the flood ;

"Our house was in Kernville, a part of Johnstown, through which Stony Creek ran. Although we were a square from the creek, the backwater from the stream had flooded the streets in the morning and was up to our front porch. At 4 o'clock on Friday afternoon we were sitting on the front porch watching the flood, when we heard a roar as of a tornado or mighty conflagration.

"We rushed upstairs and got out upon the bay-window. There an awful sight met our eyes. Down the Conemaugh Valley was advancing a mighty wall of flame and mist with a terrible roar. Before it were rolling houses and buildings of all kinds, tossing over and over. We thought it was a cyclone, the roar sounding like a tempest among forest trees. At first we could see no water at all, but back of the mist and flames came a mighty wall of water. We started downstairs and through the rear of the house to escape to the hill-side nearby. But before we could get there the water was up to our necks and we could make no progress. We turned back and were literally dashed by the current into the house, which began to move off as soon as we were in it again. From the second-story window I saw a young man drifting toward us.

I broke the glass from the frames with my hands and helped him in, and in a few moments more I pulled in an old man, a neighbor, who had been sick.

Miraculous Escape.

"Our house moved rapidly down the stream and fortunately lodged against a strong building. The water forced us out of the second story up into the attic. Then we heard a lot of people on our roof begging us for God's sake to let them in. I broke through the roof with a bed slat and pulled them in. Soon we had thirteen in all crouched in the attic.

"Our house was rocking, and every now and then a building would crash against us. Every moment we thought we would go down. The roofs of all the houses drifting by us were covered with people, nearly all praying and some singing hymns, and now and then a house would break apart and all would go down. On Saturday at noon we were rescued, making our way from one building to the next by crawling on narrow planks. I counted hundreds of bodies lying in the débris, most of them covered over with earth and showing only the outlines of the form.

A Sad Hospital Story.

On a cot in the hospital on Prospect Hill there lies at present a man injured almost to death, but whose mental sufferings are far keener than his bodily pains. His name is Vering. He has lost in the flood his whole family—wife and five children. In an interview he said:

"I was at home with my wife and children when the

alarm came. We hurried from the house, leaving everything behind us. As we reached the door a gentleman friend was running by. He grasped the two smaller children, one under each arm, and hurried on ahead of us. I had my arm around my wife, supporting her. Behind us we could hear the flood rushing upon us. In one hurried glance, as I passed a corner, I could see the fearful crunching and hear the crackling of the houses in its fearful grasp. I then could see that there was no possibility of our escape, as we were too far away from the hill-side. In a few moments it was upon us. In a flash I saw the three dear children licked up by it and they disappeared from sight as I and my wife were thrown into the air by the vanguard of the rushing ruins. We found ourselves in a lot of drift, driving along with the speed of a race-horse. In a moment or two we were thrown with a crash against a frame building whose walls gave way before the flood as easily as if they were made of pie-crust, and the timbers began to fall about us in all directions.

Up to this time I had retained a firm hold upon my wife, but as I found myself pinned between two heavy timbers the agony caused my senses to leave me momentarily. I recovered instantly in time to see my wife's head just disappearing under the water. Like lightning I grasped her by the hair and as best I could, pinioned as I was above the water by the timber, I raised her above it. The weight proved too much and she sank again. Again I pulled her to the surface and again she sank. This I did again and again with no avail. She drowned in my very grasp, and at last she dropped from my nerveless hands to leave my sight forever. As if I had not suffered enough, a few moments after I saw some objects whirling around in an eddy which circled around, until, reaching the current again, they floated past me. My God, man, would you believe me? it was three of my children, dead. Their dear little faces are before me now, distorted in a look of agony that, no matter what I do, haunts me. O, if I could only have released myself at that time I would have willingly died with them. I was rescued some time after, and have been here ever since. I have since learned that my friend who so bravely endeavored to save two of the children was lost with them."

CHAPTER XV.

Terrible Pictures of Woe.

The proportion of the living registered since the flood as against the previous number of inhabitants is even less than was reported yesterday. It was ascertained to-day that many of the names on the list were entered more than once and that the total number of persons registered is not more than 13,000 out of a former population of between 40,000 and 50,000.

A new and more exact method of determining the number of the lost was inaugurated this morning. Men are sent out by the Relief Committee, who will go to every abode and obtain the names of the survivors, and if possible those of the dead.

The lack of identification of hundreds of bodies strengthens the inference that the proportion of the dead to the living is appalling. It is argued that the friends who might identify these unclaimed bodies are themselves all gone.

Another significant fact is that so large a number of those whom one meets in the streets or where the streets used to be are non-residents, strangers who have come here out of humane or less creditable motives. The question that is heard very often is, "Where are the inhabitants?" The town does not appear to have at present a population of more than 10,000.

It is believed that many of the bodies of the dead have been borne down into the Ohio, and perhaps into the Mississippi as well, and hence may finally be deposited by the waters hundreds of miles apart, perhaps never to be recovered or seen by man again.

The General Situation.

Under the blue haze of smoke that for a week has hung over this valley of the shadow of death the work which is to resurrect this stricken city has gone steadily forward. Here and there over the waste where Johnstown stood in its pride black smoke arises from the bonfires on which shattered house-walls, rafters, doors, broken furniture and all the flotsam and jetsam of the great flood is cast.

Adjutant General Hastings, who believes in heroic measures, has been quietly trying to persuade the "Dictator"—that is, the would-be "Dictator"—to allow him to burn up the wrecked houses wholesale without the tedious bother of pulling them down and handling the débris. The timorous committees would not countenance such an idea. Nothing but piecemeal tearing down of the wrecked houses tossed together by the mighty force of the water and destruction by never-dying bonfires would satisfy them. Yet all of them must come down. Most of the buildings reached by the flood have been examined, found unsafe and condemned. Can the job be done safely and successfully wholesale or not? That is the real question for the powers that be to answer, and no sentiment should enter into it.

Four thousand workmen are busy to-day with ropes and axe, pick and shovel. But the task is vast, it is herculean, like unto the cleaning of the Augean stables.

"To clean up this town properly," said General Hastings to-day, "we shall need twenty thousand workmen for three months."

The force of the swollen river upturned the town in a half hour. These same timorous managers weakened to-day, after having the facts before their eyes brought home to their understanding by constant iteration. They have found out that they have, vulgarly speaking, bitten off more than they can chew. Poisons of the foulest kind pollute the water which flows down the turgid Conemaugh into the Allegheny River, whence is Pittsburgh's water-supply, and thence into the Ohio, the water-supply of many cities and towns. Fears of a pestilence are not to be pooh-poohed into the background. It is very serious, so long as the river flows through the clogged and matted mass of the bridge so long it will threaten the people along its course with pestilence. The committee confess their inability to do this needed work, and to-day voted to ask the Governors of the several States to co-operate in the establishment of a national relief committee to grapple with the situation. Action cannot and must not be delayed.

Hope Out of Despair.

The fears of an outbreak of fever or other zymotic diseases appear to be based on the alleged presence

GENERAL HASTINGS DIRECTING THE POLICE.

of decomposed animal matter, human and of lower type, concealed amid the débris. The alleged odor of burnt flesh coming from the enormous mass of conglomerated timber and iron lodged in the cul-de-sac formed by the Pennsylvania Railroad bridge is extremely mythical. There is an unmistakable scent of burnt wood. It would not be strange if the carcasses of domestic animals, which must be hidden in the enormous mass, were finally to be realized by the olfactory organs of the bystanders.

Blasting Continues.

All day long the blast of dynamite resounded among the hills. Cartridges were let off in the débris, and a cloud of dust and flying spray marked the result of the mining operation. The interlaced timbers in the cul-de-sac yielded very slowly even to the mighty force of dynamite. There were no finds of especial import. At the present rate of clearing, the cul-de-sac will not be free from the wreckage in two months.

There was a sad spectacle presented this morning when the laborers were engaged in pulling over a vast pile of timber and miscellaneous matter on Main street. A young woman and a little puny baby girl were found beneath the mass, which was as high as the second story windows of the houses near by.

Together in Death.

The girl must have been handsome when in the flush of youth and health. She had seized the helpless infant and endeavored to find safety by flight. Her closely cut brown hair was filled with sand, and a piece of brass wire was wound around the head and neck. A loose cashmere house-gown was partially torn from her form, and one slipper, a little bead embroidered affair, covered a silk-stockinged foot. Each arm was tightly clasped around the baby. The rigidity of death should have passed away, but the arms were fixed in their position as if composed of an unbendable material instead of muscle and bone. The fingers were imbedded in the sides of the little baby as if its protector had made a final effort not to be separated and to save if possible the fragile life. The faces of both were scarred and disfigured from contact with floating débris. The single garment of the baby—a thin white slip—was rent and frayed. The body of the young woman was identified, but the babe remained unknown. Probably its father and mother were lost in the flood, and it will never be claimed by friendly hands.

A Strange Discovery.

This is only one among the many pathetic incidents of the terrible disaster. There were only nine unidentified bodies at the Adams street morgue this afternoon, and three additions to the number were made after ten o'clock. Two hundred and eight bodies have been received by the embalmers in charge. The yard of the school house, which was converted into a temporaay abode of death, contains large piles of coffins of the cheaper sort. They come from different cities within two or three hundred miles of Johnstown, and after being stacked up they are pulled out as needed. Coffins are to be seen everywhere about the valley, ready for use when a body is found. A trio of bodies was found near the Hurlburt House under peculiar circumstances. They were hidden beneath a pile of wreckage at least twenty-five feet in height. They were a father, a mother and son. Around the waist of each a quarter inch rope was tied so that the three were bound together tightly. The hands of the boy were clasped by those of the mother, and the father's arms were extended as if to ward off danger. The father probably knotted the rope during the awful moments of suspense intervening between the coming of the flood and the final destruction of the house they occupied. The united strength of the three could not resist the mighty force of the inundation, and like so many straws they were swept on the boiling surge until life was crushed out.

Child and Doll in One Coffin.

I beheld a touching spectacle when the corpse of a little girl was extricated and placed on a stretcher for transportation to the morgue. Clasped to her breast by her two waxen hands was a rag doll. It was a cheap affair, evidently of domestic manufacture. To the child of poverty the rag baby was a favorite toy. The little mother held fast to her treasure and met her end without separating from it. The two, child and doll, were not parted when the white coffin received them, and they will moulder together.

I saw an old-fashioned cupboard dug out of a pile of rubbish. The top shelf contained a quantity of jelly of domestic manufacture. Not a glass jar was broken. Indeed there have been some remarkable instances of the escape of fragile articles from destruction. In the débris near the railroad bridge you may come upon all manner of things. The water-tanks of three locomotives which were borne from the roundhouse at Conemaugh, two miles away, are conspicuous. Amid the general wreck, beneath one of these heavy iron tanks, a looking glass, two feet by one foot in dimensions, was discovered intact, without even a scratch on the quicksilver.

Johnstown people surviving the destruction appear to bewail the death of the Fisher family. "Squire" Fisher was one of the old time public functionaries of the borough. He and his six children were swept away. One of the Fisher girls was at home under peculiar circumstances. She had been away at school, and returned home to be married to her betrothed. Then she was to return to school and take part in the graduating exercises. Her body has not yet been recovered.

Something to be Thankful For.

There is much destitution felt by people whose pride prevents them from asking for supplies from the relief committees. I saw a sad little procession wending up the hill to the camp of the Americus Club. There was a father, an honest, simple German, who had been employed at the Cambria works during the past twelve years. Behind him trooped eight children, from a girl of fourteen to a babe in the arms of the mother, who brought up the rear. The woman and children were hatless, and possessed only the calico garments worn at the moment of flight. Forlorn and weary, they ranged in front of the relieving stand and implored succor.

"We lost one only, thank God!" exclaimed the mother. "Our second daughter is gone. We had a comfortable house which we owned. It was paid for by oui savings. Now all is gone.' Then the unhappy woman sat down on the wet ground and sobbed hysterically. The children crowded around their mother and joined in her grief. You will behold many of these scenes of domestic distress about the ruins of Johnstown in these dolorous days.

Saw a Flood of Helpless Humanity.

Mr. L. D. Woodruff, the editor and proprietor of the Johnstown *Democrat*, tells his experiences during the night of horrors. He was at the office of the paper, which is in the upper portion of the Baltimore and Ohio Railway station. This brick edifice stands almost in the centre of the couse of the flood, and its preservation from ruin is one of the remarkable features of the occasion. A pile of freight cars lodged at the corner of the building and the breakwater thus formed checked the onslaught of floating battering rams. Mr. Woodruff, with his two sons, remained in the building until the following day. The water came up to the floor of the second story. All night long he witnessed people floating past on the roofs of houses or on various kinds of wreckage. A number of persons were rescued through the windows.

A man and his wife with three children were pulled in. After a while the mother for the first time remembered that her baby of fifteen months was left behind. Her grief was violent, and her cries were mingled with the groans of her husband, who lay on the floor with a broken leg. The next day the baby was found, when the waters subsided, on a pile of débris outside and it was alive and uninjured.

During the first few hours Mr. Woodruff momentarily expected that the building would go. As the night wore away it became evident the water was going down. Not a vestige of Mr. Woodruff's dwelling has been found.

The newspapers of Johnstown came out of the flood fairly well. The *Democrat* lost only a job press, which was swept out of one corner of the building.

The Flood's Awful Spoil.

In the broad field of débris at the Pennsylvania Railroad viaduct, where the huge playthings of the flood were tossed only to be burned and beaten to a solid, intricate mass, are seen the peculiar metal works of two trains of cars. The wreck of the day express east, running in two sections that fatal Friday, lie there about thirty yards above the bridge. One mass of wreckage is unmistakably that of the Pullman car section, made up of two baggage cars and six Pullman coaches, and the other shows the irons of five day coaches and one Pullman car. These trains were running in the same block at Johnstown and were struck by the flood two miles above, torn from their tracks and carried tumbling down the mighty torrents to their resting place in the big eddy.

Railroad Men Suppressing Information.

The train crew, who saw the waters coming, warned the passengers, escaped, and went home on foot. Conductor Bell duly made his report, yet for some unknown reasons one of Superintendent Pitcairn's subordinates has been doing his best to give out and prove by witnesses, to whom he takes newspaper men, that only one car of that express was lost and with it "two or three ladies who went back for overshoes and a very few others not lively enough to escape after the warnings." That story went well until the smoke rolled away from the wreckage and the bones of the two sections of the day express east were disclosed. Another very singular feature was the apparent inability of the conductor of the express to tell how many passengers they had on board and just how many were saved. It had been learned that the first section of the train carried 180 passengers and the second 157. It may be stated as undoubtedly true that of the number fifty, at least, swell the horrible tale of the dead.

From the wreck where the trains burned there have been taken out fifty-eight charred bodies, the features being unrecognizable. Of these seven found together were the Gilmore family, whose house had floated there. The others, all adults, which, with two or three exceptions, swell the list of the unidentified dead, are undoubted corpses of the ill-fated passengers of the east express.

The Church Loses a Missionary.

To-day another corpse was found in the ruins of a Pullman car badly burned. It was fully identified as that of Miss Anna Clara Chrisman, of Beauregard, Miss., a well-developed lady of about twenty-five years, who was on her way to New York to fill a mission station in Brazil. Between the leaves of her Greek testament was a telegram she had written, expecting to send it at the first stop, addressed to the Methodist Mission headquarters, No. 20 East Twelfth street, New York, saying that she would arrive on "train 8" of the Pennsylvania Railroad, the day express east. In her satchel were found photographs of friends and her Bible, and from her neck hung a $20 gold piece, carefully sewn in a bag.

Is it possible that the Pennsylvania Railroad is keeping back the knowledge in order simply to avoid a list of "passengers killed" in its annual report, solely to keep its record as little stained as possible? It can hardly be that they fear suits for damages, for the responsibility of the wreck does not rest on them.

Two hundred bodies were recovered from the ruins yesterday. Some were identified, but the great majority were not. This number includes all the morgues—the one at the Pennsylvania Railroad station, the Fourth ward school, Cambria city, Morrellville, Kernville and the Presbyterian Church.

At the latter place a remarkable state of affairs exists. The first floor has been washed out completely and the second, while submerged, was badly damaged, but not ruined. The walls, floors and pews were drenched, and the mud has collected on the matting and carpets an inch deep. Walking is attended with much difficulty, and the undertakers and attendants, with arms bared, slide about the slippery surface at a tremendous rate. The chancel is filled with coffins, strips of muslin, boards, and all undertaking accessories. Lying across the tops of the pews are a dozen pine boxes, each containing a victim of the flood. Printed cards are tacked on each. Upon them the sex and full description of the enclosed body is written with the name, if known.

The Nameless Dead.

The great number of bodies not identified seems incredulous and impossible. Some of these bodies have lain in the different morgues for four days. Thousands of people from different sections of the State have seen them, yet they remain unidentified.

At Nineveh they are burying all the unidentified dead, but in the morgues in this vicinity no bodies have been buried unless they were identified.

The First Presbyterian Church contains nine "unknown." Burials will have to be made to-morrow. This morning workmen found three members of Benjamin Hoffman's family, which occupied a large residence in the rear of Lincoln street. Benjamin Hoffman, the head of the family, was found seated on the

CARRYING CHILDREN TO BURIAL.

edge of the bedstead. He was evidently preparing to retire when the flood struck the building. He had his socks in his pocket. His twenty-year-old daughter was found close by attired in a night-dress. The youngest member of the family, a three-year-old infant, was also found beside the bed.

Where the Dead are Laid.

I made a tour of the cemeteries to-day to see how the dead were disposed in their last resting place. There are six burying grounds—two to the south of this place, one to the north, and three on Morrellsville to the west. The principal one is Grand View, on the summit of Kernville Hill.

But the most remarkable, through the damage done by the flood, is Sandy Vale Cemetery, at Hornersville, on Stony Creek, and about half a mile from the city of Johnstown. It is a private institution in which most of the people of the city buried their dead until two years ago, when the public corporation of Grand View was established. Its grounds are level, laid out in lots, and were quite picturesque, its dense foliage and numerous monuments attracting the eyes of every passenger entering the city by the Baltimore and Ohio Railroad, which passes along one side the creek forming its other boundary. The banks of the creek are twenty feet high, and there was a nice sandy beach through its entire length.

A Sorry Scene.

When the floods came the first of the wreckage and the backwater sent hundreds of houses, immense

THE JOHNSTOWN HORROR. 349

quantities of logs and cut lumber over it and into the borough of Hornersville. As the angry waters subsided the pretty cemetery was wrecked as badly as was the city, a portion of the débris of which has destroyed its symmetry. To make way for the burial of the numerous bodies sent there by the town committees it became necessary to burn some of the débris. This was commenced at the nearest or southern end, and at the time of my visit I had, like the corpses, to pass through an avenue of fire and over live ashes to make my inspection. There were no unknown dead sent here, consequently they were interred in lots, and here and there, as the cleared spots would allow, a body was deposited and the grave made to look as decently as four or five inches of mud on the surface and the clay soil would allow.

Masses of Debris.

Scarcely a monument was left standing. Tall columns were broken like pipe-stems, and fences and evergreen bowers were almost a thing of the past. Whole houses on their sides, with their roofs on the ground, covered the lots, the beach, or blocked up the pathways, while other houses in fragments strewed the surface of the ground from one end to the other of the cemetery, once the pride of Johnstown. I found that some of the trees which were standing had feather beds or articles of furniture up in their boughs. Here and there a dead cow or a horse, two or three wagons, a railroad baggage car. Add to this several thousand logs, heaps of lumber, piled just as they left the yards, and still other single planks by the hundred thousand of feet, and some idea of the surroundings of the victims of the flood placed at rest here can be obtained.

On Kernville Hill.

Grand View Cemetery, a beautiful spot, was started as a citizens' cemetery and incorporated two years ago, and is now the finest burying place in this section of Pennsylvania. It is situated on the summit of Kernville hill, between six hundred and seven hundred feet above the town. It is approached by a zigzag roadway about one mile and a half in length, and a magnificent view of the valley is obtained from the grounds, making it well worth a visit under any circumstances. Here those whose relatives did not hold lots are to be buried in trenches four feet deep, sixty bodies to a trench. At present the trenches are not complete, and their encoffined bodies are stored in the beautiful stone chapel at the entrance. Of the other bodies they are entombed in the lots, where more than one were buried together. A wide grave was dug to hold them side by side. A single grave was made for Squire Fisher's family, one grave and one mound holding eight of them.

Snatched from the Flood.

One of the most thrilling incidents of narrow escapes is that told by Miss Minnie Chambers. She had been to see a friend in the morning and was returning to her home on Main street, when the suddenly rising waters caused her to quicken her steps.

Before she could reach her home or seek shelter at any point, the water had risen so high and the current became so strong that she was swept from her feet and carried along in the flood. Fortunately her skirts served to support her on the surface for a time, but at last as they became soaked she gave up all hope of being saved.

Just as she was going under a box car that had been torn from its trucks floated past her and she managed by a desperate effort to get hold of it and crawled inside the open doorway. Here she remained, expecting every moment her shelter would be dashed to pieces by the buildings and other obstructions that it struck. Through the door she could see the mass of angry, swirling waters, filled with all manner of things that could be well imagined.

An Ark of Refuge.

Men, women and children, many of them dead and dying, were being whirled along. Several of them tried to get refuge in the car with her, but were torn away by the rushing waters before they could secure an entrance. Finally a man did make his way into the car. On went the strange boat, while all about it seemed to be a perfect pandemonium. Shrieks and cries from the thousands outside who were being driven to their death filled the air.

Miss Chambers says it was a scene that will haunt her as long as she lives. Many who floated by her could be seen kneeling on the wreckage that bore them, with clasped hands and upturned faces as though in prayer. Others wore a look of awful despair on their faces. Suddenly, as the car was turned around, the stone bridge could be seen just ahead of them. The man that was in the car called to her to jump out in the flood or she would be dashed to pieces. She refused to go.

He seized a plank and sprang into the water. In an instant the eddying current had torn the plank from him, and as it twisted around struck him on the head, causing him to throw out his arms and sink beneath the water never to reappear again. Miss Chambers covered her face to avoid seeing any more of the horrible sight, when with an awful crash the car struck one of the stone piers. The entire side of it was knocked out. As the car lodged against the pier the water rushed through it and carried Miss Chambers away. Again she gave herself up as lost, when she felt herself knocked against an obstruction, and instinctively threw out her hand and clutched it.

Here she remained until the water subsided, when she found that she was on the roof of one of the Cambria mills, and had been saved by holding on to a pipe that came through the roof.

A Night of Agony.

All through that awful night she remained there, almost freezing to death, and enveloped in a dense mass of smoke from the burning drift on the other side of the bridge. The cries of those being roasted to death were heard plainly by her. On Saturday some men succeeded in getting her from the perilous position she occupied and took her to the house of friends on Prospect Hill. Strange to say that with the exception of a few bruises she escaped without any other injuries.

Another survivor who told a pathetic story was John C. Peterson. He is a small man but he was wearing clothes large enough for a giant. He lost his own and secured those he had on from friends.

"I'm the only one left," he said in a voice trembling with emotion. "My poor old mother, my sister, Mrs. Ann Walker, and her son David, aged fourteen, of Bedford county, who were visiting us, were swept away before my eyes and I was powerless to aid them."

"The water had been rising all day, and along in the afternoon flooded the first story of our house, at the corner of Twenty-eighth and Walnut streets. I was employed by Charles Mun as a cigarmaker, and early on Friday afternoon went home to move furniture and carpets to the second story of the house.

"As near as I can tell it was about four o'clock when the whistle at the Gautier steel mill blew. About the same time the Catholic church bell rang. I knew what that meant and I turned to mother and sister and said, 'My God, we are lost!'

Here's A Hero.

"I looked out of the window and saw the flood, a wall of water thirty feet high, strike the steel works, and it melted quicker than I tell it. The man who stopped to blow the warning whistle must have been crushed to death by the falling roof and chimneys. He might have saved himself, but stopped to give the warning. He died a hero. Four minutes after the whistle blew the water was in our second story.

"We started to carry mother to the attic, but the water rose faster than we could climb the stairs. There was no window in our attic, and we were bidding each other good-by when a tall chimney on the house adjoining fell on our roof and broke a hole through it. We then climbed out on the roof, and in another moment our house floated away. It started down with the other stuff, crashing, twisting and quivering. I thought every minute it would go to pieces.

"Finally it was shoved over into water less swift and near another house.

"I found that less drift was forced against it than against ours, and decided to get on it. I climbed up on the roof, and in looking up saw a big house coming down directly toward ours, I called to sister to be quick. She was lifting mother up to me. I could barely reach the tips of her fingers when her arms were raised up while I lay on my stomach reaching down. At that moment the house struck ours and my loved ones were carried away and crushed by the big house. It was useless for me to follow, for they sank out of sight. I floated down to the bridge, then back with the current and landed at Vine street.

"I saw hundreds of people crushed and drowned. It is my opinion that fully fifteen thousand people perished.

When the whistles of the Gautier Steel Mill of the Cambria Iron Company blew for the shutting down of the works at 10 o'clock last Friday morning nearly 1400 men walked out of the establishment and went to their homes, which were a few hours later wiped off the face of the earth. When the men to-day answered the notice that all should present themselves ready for work only 487 reported. That shows more clearly than anything else that has yet been known the terrible nature of the fatality of the Conemaugh. The mortality wrought among these men in a few hours is thus shown to have been greater than that in either of the armies that contended for three days at Gettysburg.

"Report at 9 o'clock to-morrow morning ready for work," the notice posted read. It did not say where, but everybody knew it was not at the great Gautier Mill that covered half a dozen acres, for the reason that no mill is there. By a natural impulse the survivors of the working force of the steel plant began to move from all directions, before the hour named, toward the general office of the company.

What the Superintendent Saw.

This office is located in Johnstown proper and is the only building in that section of the town left standing uninjured. It is a large brick building, three stories high, with massive brick walls. L. L. Smith, the commercial agent of the company, arrived at eight o'clock to await the gathering of the men, pausing a minute in the doorway to look at two things. One was an enormous pile of débris, bricks, iron girders and timbers almost in front of the office door which swarmed with 200 men engaged in clearing it away. This is the ruins of the Johnstown Free Library, presented to the town by the Cambria Iron Company, the late I. V. Williamson and others, and beneath it Mr. Smith knew many of his most intimate friends were buried. The other thing he looked at was his handsome residence partly in ruins, a few hundred yards away. When he entered the office he found that the men who had been shoveling the mud out of the office had finished their work and the floor was dark and sticky. A fire blazed in the open grate. A table was quickly rigged up and with three clerks to assist him, Mr. Smith prepared to make up the roster of the Gautier forces.

The Survivor's Advance Corps.

Soon they began to come like the first reformed platoon of an army after fleeing from disaster. The leader of the platoon was a small boy. His hat was pulled down over his eyes and he looked as if he were sorely afraid. After him came half a dozen men with shambling gait. One was an Irishman, two were English, one was a German and one a colored man. Two of them carried pickaxes in their hands, which they had been using to clear away the wreckage across the street.

"Say, mister," stammered the abashed small boy, "is this the place?"

"Are you a Gautier man?" asked Mr. Smith kindly.

THE JOHNSTOWN HORROR.   357

"Yes, sir, me and me father, but he's gone.

"Give us your name, my boy, and report at the lower works at 4 o'clock. Now, my men, we want to get to work and pull each other out of the hole, this dreadful calamity has put us in. It's no use having vain regrets. It's all over and we must put a good face to the front. At first it was intended that we should go up to the former site of the Gautier Mill and clean up and get out all the steel we could. Mr. Stackhouse now wants us to get to work and clear the way from the lower mills right up the valley. We will rebuild the bridge back of the office here and push the railroad clear up to where it was before.

Not Anxious to Turn In.

The men listened attentively, and then one of them asked: "But, Mr. Smith, if we don't feel just like turning in to-day we don't have to, do we?"

"Nobody will have to work at all," was the answer, "but we do want all the men to lend a hand to help us out as soon as they can."

While Mr. Smith was speaking several other workmen came in. They, too, were Gautier employees, and they had pickaxes on their shoulders. They heard the agent's last remark, and one of them, stepping forward, said: "A good many of us are working cleaning up the town. Do you want us to leave that?"

"It isn't necessary for you to work cleaning up the town," was the reply. "There are plenty of people from the outside to do that who came here for that purpose. Now, boys, just give your names so we can find out how many of our men are left, and all of you that can, go down and report at the lower office."

All the time the members of the decimated Gautier army were filing into the muddy-floored office. They came in twos and threes and dozens, and some bore out the idea of an army reforming after disaster, because they bore grievous wounds. One man had a deep cut in the back of his head, another limped along on a heavy stick, one had lost a finger and had an ugly bruise on his cheek. J. N. Short, who was the foreman of the cold-rolled steel shafting department, sat in the office, and many of the men who filed past had been under him in the works.

Mutual Congratulations.

There were handshakes all the more hearty and congratulations all the more sincere because of what all had passed through. When the wall of water seventy-five feet high struck the mill and whipped it away like shot Mr. Short was safe on higher ground, but many of the men had feared he was lost.

"I tell you, Mr. Short," said J. T. Miller, "I'm glad to see you're safe."

"And how did you make out, old man?"

"All right, thank God."

Then came another man bolder than all and apparently a general favorite. He rushed forward and shook Mr. Smith's hand. "Mr. Smith," he exclaimed, "good morning, good morning."

"So you got out of it, did you, after all?" asked Mr. Smith.

"Indeed I did, but Lord bless my soul, I thought the wife and babies were gone." The man gave his name and hurried away, brushing a tear from his eye.

Mr. Shellenberger, one of the foremen, brought up the rear of the next platoon to enter. He caught sight of Mr. Smith and shouted: "Oh, Mr. Smith: good for you. I'm glad to see you safe."

"Here to you, my hearty," was the answer. "Did you all get off?"

"Every blessed one of us," with a bright smile. "We were too high on the hill."

He was Tired of Johnstown.

A little bit later another man came in. He looked as if he had been weeping. He hesitated in front of the desk. "I am a Gautier employee," he said, speaking slowly, "and I have reported according to orders."

"Well, give us your name and go to work down at the lower works," suggested Mr. Smith.

"No, sir, I think not," he muttered, after a pause. "I am not staying in this town any longer than I can help, I guess. I've lost two children and they will be buried to-day."

"All right, my man, but if you want work we have plenty of it for you."

The reporting of names and these quiet mutual congratulations of the men went on rapidly, but expected faces did not appear. This led Mr. Smith to ask, "How about George Thompson? Is he alive?"

"I do not know," answered the man addressed. "I do not think so."

"Who do you know are alive?" asked Mr. Smith, turning to another man. Mr. Smith never once asked who was dead.

"Well," answered the man speaking reflectively, "I'm pretty sure Frank Smith is alive. John Dagdale is alive. Tom Sweet is alive, and I don't know any more, for I've been away—at Nineveh." The speaker had been at Nineveh looking for the body of his son. Not another word was said to him.

"Say, boys," exclaimed Mr. Smith suddenly, a few minutes after he had looked over the list, "Pullman hasn't reported yet."

"But Pullman's all right," said a man quickly, "I was up at his sister's house last night and he was there. That's more than I can say of the other men in Pullman's shift though," added the speaker in a low tone. Mr. Short took this man aside, "That is a fact," said he, "yesterday I knew of a family in which five out of six were lost. To-day I find out there were twenty people in the house mostly our men and only three escaped."

Each Thought the Other Dead.

Just then two men met at the door and fairly fell on each other's necks. One wore a Grand Army badge and the other was a young fellow of twenty-three or thereabouts. They had been fast friends in the same department, and each thought the other dead. They knew no better till they met at the office door. "Well, I heard your body had been found at Nineveh," said the old man.

"And I was told you had been burned to death at the bridge," answered the other. Then the two men solemnly shook hands and walked away together.

A pale-faced woman with a shawl over her shoulders entered and stood at the table. "My husband cannot report," she said simply, in almost a whisper. "He worked for the Gautier Mill?" she was asked. She nodded, bent forward and murmured something. The man at the desk said: "Make a note of that; so-and-so's wife reports him as gone, and his wages due are to be paid to her."

The work of recording the men went on until nearly one o'clock. Then, after waiting for a long time, Mr. Smith said, "Out of 1400 men we now have 487. It may be there are 200 who either did not see the notice or who are too busy to come. Anyway, I hope so—my God, I hope so." All afternoon the greater part of the 487 men were swinging pickaxes and shovels, clearing the way for the railroad leading up to the Gautier Steel Works of the future.

The Morbidly Curious.

To-day the order "Halt!" rang out in earnest at the footbridge over the rushing river into Johnstown. It was the result of a cry as early as the reveille, that came from among the ruins and from the hoarse throats of the contractors—"For God's sake, keep the morbid people out of here; they're in the way!"

General Hastings ordered the picket out on the high embankment east of the freight depot, where every man, woman and child must pass to reach the bridge. Colonel Perchment detailed Captain Hamilton, of G Company, there with an ample guard, and all who came without General Hastings' pass in the morning were turned aside. This afternoon a new difficulty was encountered. When you flashed your military pass on the sentinel who cried "Halt!" he would throw his gun slantwise across your body, so that the butt grazed your right hip and the bayonet your left ear and say: "No good unless signed by the sheriff." The civil authorities had taken the bridge out of the hands of the militia, and the sheriff sat on a camp stool overlooking the desolate city all the forenoon making out passes and approving the General's.

No Conflict of Authority.

The military men say there was no conflict of authority, and it was deemed proper that the civil authorities should still control the pass there. The sheriff came near getting shot in Cambria City this morning during a clash with one of his deputies over a buggy. Yet he looked calm and serene. Some beg him for passes to hunt for their dead. One man cried: "I've just gotten here, and my wife and children are in that town; another said, "I belong in Conemaugh and was carried off by the flood," while an aged, trembling man behind him whispered, "Sheriff, I just wanted to look where the old home stood." When four peaceful faced sisters in convent garb, on their mission of mercy, came that way the sentinels stood back a pace and no voice ordered "Halt!"

At noon the crane belonging to the Pennsylvania

Railroad was taken away from the débris at the bridge, and Mr. Kirk had to depend on dynamite alone. Later it was ordered back, and after that the work went on rapidly. An opening 400 feet long, which runs back in some places fifty feet, was made during the afternoon. A relief party yesterday found a ladies' hand satchel containing $91 in cash, deeds for $26,000 in property and about $10,000 in insurance policies. Mrs. Lizzie Dignom was the owner, and both she and her husband perished in the flood.

Remembering the Orphans.

Miss H. W. Hinckley and Miss E. Hanover, agent of the Children's Aid Society and Bureau of Information of Philadelphia, arrived here this morning, and in twenty minutes had established a transfer agency. Miss Hinckley said:

"There are hundreds of children here who are apparently without parents. We want all of them given to us, and we will send them to the various homes and orphanages of the State, where they shall be maintained for several months to await the possibility of the reappearance of their parents when they will be returned to them. If after the lapse of a month they do not reclaim their little ones, we shall do more than we ordinarily do in the way of providing good homes for children in their cases. Think of it, in the house adjoining us are seven orphans, all of one family. We have been here only a half hour, but we have already found scores. We shall stay right here till every child has been provided for."

There is no denying that a great deal of ill-feeling is breeding here between the survivors of the flood over the distribution of the relief supplies. The supplies are spread along the railroad track down as far as Morrellville in great stacks; provisions, clothing, shoes, and everything else. The people come for them in swarms with baskets and other means of conveyance. Lines are drawn, which are kept in trim by the pickets, and in this way they pass along in turn to the point where the stock is distributed.

It was not unusual yesterday to hear women's tongues lashing each other and complaining that the real sufferers were being robbed and turned away, while those who had not fared badly by flood or fire were getting lots of everything from the committee. One woman made this complaint to a corporal.

"Prove it; prove it," he said, and walked away. She cried after him, "The pretty women are getting more than they can carry."

Twice the line of basket-carriers was broken by the guard to put out wranglers, and all through the streets of Cambria City could be heard murmurs of dissension. There is no doubt but that a strong guard will be kept in the town day and night, for in their deplorable condition the husbands may take up the quarrel of their wives.

Danger of Insanity.

The *Medical News*, of Philadelphia, with rare enterprise, despatched a member of its staff to Johnstown, and he telegraphed as follows for the next issue of that paper:

"The mental condition of almost every former resident of Johnstown is one of the gravest character, and the reaction which will set in when the reality of the whole affair is fully comprehended can scarcely fail to produce many cases of permanent or temporary insanity. Most of the faces that one meets, both male and female, are those of the most profound melancholia, associated with an almost absolute disregard of the future. The nervous system shows the strain it has borne by a tremulousness of the hand and of the lip, in man as well as in woman. This nervous state is further evidenced by a peculiar intonation of words, the persons speaking mechanically, while the voices of many rough-looking men are changed into such tremulous notes of so high a pitch, as to make one imagine that a child, on the verge of tears, is speaking. Crying is so rare that your correspondent saw not a tear on any face in Johnstown, but the women that are left are haggard, with pinched features and heavy, dark lines under their eyes.

The State Board of Health should warn the people of the portions of the country supplied by the Conemaugh of the danger of drinking its waters for weeks to come."

The Women and Children.

New Johnstown will be largely a city of childless widowers. One of the peculiar things a stranger notices is the comparatively small number of women seen in the streets. Of the throngs who walked about the place searching for dear friends there is not one woman to ten men. Occasionally a little group of two or three women with sad faces will pick their way about looking for the morgues. There are a few Sisters of Charity—their black robes the only instance in which the conventional badge of mourning is seen upon the streets—and in the parts of the town not totally destroyed the usual number of women are seen in the houses and yards.

But, as a rule, women are a rarety in Johnstown now. This is not a natural peculiarity of Johnstown nor a mere coincidence, but a fact with a terrible reason behind it. There are so many more men than women among the living in Johnstown now because there are so many more women than men among the dead. Of the bodies recovered there are at least two women to every one man. Besides the fact that their natural weakness made them an easier prey to the flood, the hour at which the disaster came was one when the women would most likely be in their homes and the men at work in the open air or in factory yards, from which escape was easy.

An Almost Childless City.

Children also are rarely seen about the town and for a similar reason. They are all dead. There is never a group of the dead discovered that does not contain from one to three or four children for every grown person. Generally the children are in the arms of the grown persons, and often little toys and trinkets clasped in their hands indicate that the children were caught up while at play and carried as far as possible toward safety.

Johnstown, when rebuilt, will be a city of many widowers and few children. In turning a schoolhouse into a morgue, the authorities probably did a wiser thing than they thought. It will be a long time before the schoolhouse will be needed for its original purpose.

The Flood on the Flat.

The flood, with a front of twenty feet high, bristling with all manner of débris, struck straight across the flat, as though the river's course had always been that way. It cut off the outer two-thirds of the city with a line as true and straight as could have been drawn by a survey. On the part over which it swept there remains standing but one building, the brewery. With this exception, not only the houses and stores, but the pavements, sidewalks and curbstones, and the earth beneath for several feet are washed away. The pavements were of cinders from the Iron Works; a bed six inches thick and as hard as stone and with a surface like macadam. Over west of the washed-out portion of the city not even the broken fragments of these pavements are left.

Aside from the few logs and timbers left by the afterwash of the flood, there is nothing remaining upon the outer edge of the flat, including two of the four long streets of the city, except the brewery mentioned before and a grand piano. The water-marks on the brewery walls show the flood reached twenty feet up its sides and it stood on a little higher ground than buildings around it at that.

Thieves Had Rifled His Safe.

Mr. Steires, who on last Friday was the wealthiest man in town, on Sunday was compelled to borrow the dress which clothed his wife. When the flood began to threaten he removed some of the most valuable papers from his safe and moved them to the upper story of the building to keep them from getting wet. When the dam burst and Conemaugh Lake came down these, of course, went with the building. He got his safe Monday, but found that thieves had been before him, they having chiseled it open and taken everything but $65 in a drawer which they overlooked. Mr. Steires said to day: "I am terribly crippled financially, but my family were all saved and I am ready to begin over again."

Rebuilding Going On Apace.

Oklahoma is not rising more quickly than the temporary buildings of the workmen's city, which includes 5,000 men at least, and who are mingling the sounds of hammers on the buildings they are putting up for their temporary accommodation, with the crash of the buildings they are tearing down. It seemed almost a waste of energy two days ago, but the different gangs are already eating their way towards the heart of the great masses of wreckage that block the streets in every direction.

A dummy engine has already been placed in position on what was the main street, and all the large logs and rafters that the men can not move are fastened with ropes and chains, and drawn out by the engine into a clear space, where they are surrounded by smaller pieces of wood and burned. Carloads of pickaxes, shovels and barrows are arriving from Baltimore for the workmen.

First Store Opened.

The first store was opened to-day by a grocer named W. A. Kramer, whose stock, though covered with mud and still wet from the flood, has been preserved intact. So far the greater part of his things have been bought for relics. The other storekeepers are dragging out the débris in their shops and shoveling the mud from the upper stories upon inclined boards that shoot it into the street, but with all this energy it will be weeks before the streets are brought to sight again.

As a proof of this, there was found this morning a passenger car fully half a mile from its depot, completely buried beneath the floor and roofs of other houses. All that could be seen of it by peering through intercepting rafters was one of the end windows over which was painted the impotent warning of "Any person injuring this car will be dealt with according to law."

Curious Finds of Workmen.

The workmen find many curious things among the ruins, and are, it should be said to their credit, particularly punctilious about leaving them alone. One man picked up a base-ball catcher's mask under a great pile of machinery, and the decorated front of the balcony circle of the Opera House was found with the chairs still immediately about its semi-circle, a quarter of a mile from the theatre's site.

The mahogany bar of a saloon, with its nickel-plated rail, lies under another heap in the city park, and thousands of cigars from a manufactory are piled high in Vine street, and are used as the only dry part of the roadway. Those of the people who can locate their homes have gathered what furniture and ornaments they can find together, and sit beside them looking like evicted tenants.

The Grand Army of the Republic, represented by Department Commander Thomas J. Stewart, have placed a couple of tents at the head of Main street for the distribution of food and clothing. A census of the people will be taken and the city divided into districts, each worthy applicant will be furnished with a ticket giving his or her number and the number of the district.

The Post-office Uniforms.

Across the street from the Grand Army tents is the temporary post-office, which is now in fairly good working order. One of the distributing clerks hunted up a newspaper correspondent to tell him that the post-office uniforms sent from Philadelphia by the employees of that city's office have arrived safely and that the men want to return thanks through this paper.

The Red Cross Army people from Philadelphia

have decided to remain, notwithstanding General Hastings' cool reception, and they have taken up their quarters in Kernville, where they say the destitution is as great as in what was the city proper.

The Tale the Clocks Tell.

The clocks of the city in both public and private houses tell different tales of the torrent that stopped them. Some of them ceased to tick the moment the water reached them. In Dibert's banking-house the marble time-piece on the mantel stopped at seven minutes after 4 o'clock. In the house of the Hon. John M. Rose, on the bank of Stony Creek, was a clock in every room of the mansion from the cellar to the attic. Mr. Rose is a fine machinist, and the mechanism of clocks has a fascination for him that is simply irresistible. He has bronze, marble, cuckoo, corner or "grandfather" clocks—all in his house. One of them was stopped exactly at 4 o'clock; still another at 4.10; another at 4.15, and one was not stopped till 9 P. M. The "grandfather" clock did not stop at all, and is still going.

The town clocks, that is the clocks in church towers, are all going and were not injured by the water. The mantel piece clocks in nearly every house show a "no tick" at times ranging from 3.40 to 4.15.

Dead in the Jail.

This morning a man, in wandering through the skirts of the city, came upon the city jail, and finding the outer door open, went into the gloomy structure. Hanging against the wall he found a bunch of keys and fitting them in the doors opened them one after another. In one cell he found a man lying on the floor in the mud in a condition of partial decomposition. He looked more closely at the dead body and recognized it as that of John McKee, son of Squire McKee, of this city, who had been committed for a short term on Decoration Day for drunkenness. The condition of the cell showed that the man had been overpowered and smothered by the water, but not till he had made every effort that the limits of his cell would allow to save himself. There were no other prisoners in the jail.

Heroes of the Night.

Thomas Magee, the cashier of the Cambria Iron Company's general stores, tells a thrilling story of the manner in which he and his fellow clerks escaped from the waters themselves, saved the money drawers and rescued the lives of nineteen other people during the progress of the flood. He says:

It was 4.15 o'clock when the flood struck our building with a crash. It seemed to pour in from every door and window on all sides, as well as from the floors above us. I was standing by the safe, which was open at the time, and snatched the tin box which contained over $12,000 in cash, and with other clerks at my heels flew up the stairs to the second floor. In about three minutes we were up to our waists in water, and started to climb to the third floor of the building. Here we remained with the money until Saturday morning, when we were taken out in boats.

Besides myself there were in the building Michael Maley, Frank Balsinger, Chris Mintzmeyer, Josepn Berlin and Frank Burger, all of whom escaped. All Friday night and Saturday morning we divided our time between guarding the money, providing for our own safety and rescuing the poor people floating by. We threw out ropes and gathered logs and timbers together until we had enough to make a raft, which we bound together with ropes and used in rescuing people. During the night we rescued Henry Weaver, his wife and two children ; Captain Carswell, wife and three children, and three servant girls ; Patrick Ravel, wife and one child ; A. M. Dobbins and two others whose names I have forgotten. Besides this we cut large pieces of canvas and oilcloth and wrapped it around bread and meat and other eatables and threw it or floated it out to those who went by on housetops, rafts, etc., whom we could not rescue without getting our raft in the drift and capsizing. We must have fed 100 people in this way alone.

When we were rescued ourselves we took the money over to Prospect Hill, and sent to the justice of the peace, who swore us all in to keep guard over our own money and that taken by Paymaster Barry from the Cambria Iron Company's general offices, amounting to $4000, under precisely the same circumstances that marked our escape. We remained on guard until Monday night, when the soldiers came over and escorted us back to the office of the Cambria Iron Company, where we placed the money in the company's vault.

So far as known at this hour only eighteen bodies have been this morning recovered in the Conemaugh Valley. One of these was a poor remnant of humanity that was suddenly discovered by a teamster in the centre of the road over which his wagons had been passing for the past forty-eight hours. The heavy vehicles had sunk deeply in the sand and broken nearly every bone in the putrefying body. It was quite impossible to identify the corpse, and it was taken to the morgue and orders issued for its burial after a few hours' exposure to the gaze of those who still eagerly search for missing friends.

Only the hardiest can bear to enter the Morgue this morning, so overwhelming is the dreadful stench. The undertakers even, after hurriedly performing their task of washing a dead body and preparing it for burial, retreat to the yard to await the arrival of the next ghastly find. A strict order is now in force that all bodies should be interred only when it becomes impossible to longer preserve them from absolute putrefaction. There is no iron-clad rule. In some instances it is necessary to inter some putrid body within a few hours, while others can safely be preserved for several days. Every possible opportunity is afforded for identification.

Four bodies were taken from the ruins at the Cambria Club House and the company's store this morning. The first body was that of a girl about seventeen years of age. She was found in the pantry and it is supposed that she was one of the servants in the house. She was terribly bruised and her face was crushed into a jelly. A boy about seven years of age was taken from the same place. Two men and a woman were taken from in front of a store on Main street. The remains were all bruised and in a terrible condition. They had to be embalmed and buried immediately, and it was impossible to have any one identify them.

Only Fifty Saved at Woodville.

The number of people missing from Woodville is almost incredible, and from present indications it looks as if only about fifty people in the borough were saved. Mrs. H. L. Peterson, who has been a resident at Woodville for a number of years, is one of the survivors. While looking for Miss Paulsen, of Pittsburg, of the drowned, she came to a coffin which was marked "Mrs. H. L. Peterson, Woodville Borough, Pa., age about forty, size five feet one inch, complexion dark, weight about two hundred pounds." This was quite an accurate description of Mrs. Peterson. She tore the card from the coffin and one of the officers was about to arrest her. Her explanations were satisfactory and she was released.

In speaking of the calamity afterward she said: "The people of Woodville had plenty of time to get out of the town if they were so minded. We received word shortly before two o'clock that the flood was coming, and a Pennsylvania Railroad conductor went through the town notifying the people. I stayed until half-past three o'clock, when the water commenced to rise very rapidly, and I thought it was best to get out of town. I told a number of women that they had better go to the hills, but they refused, and the cause of this refusal was that their husbands would not go with them and they refused to leave alone."

Terrific Experience of a Pullman Conductor.

Mr. John Barr, the conductor of the Pullman car on the day express train that left Pittsburgh at eight o'clock, May 31, gave an account of his experience in the Conemaugh Valley flood: "I was the last one saved on the train," he said. "When the train arrived at Johnstown last Friday, the water was up to the second story of the houses and people were going about in boats. We went on to Conemaugh and had to halt there, as the water had submerged the tracks and a part of the bridge had been washed away. Two sections of the day express were run up to the most elevated point.

"About four o'clock I was standing at the buffet when the whistle began blowing a continuous blast— the relief signal. I went out and saw what appeared to be a huge moving mountain rushing rapidly toward us. It seemed to be surmounted by a tall cloud of foam.

Sounding the Alarm.

"I ran into the car and shouted to the passengers, 'For God's sake follow me! Stop for nothing!'

"They all dashed out except two. Miss Paulsen and Miss Bryan left the car, but returned for their overshoes. They put them on, and as they again

WRECK OF THE DAY EXPRESS.

stepped from the car they were caught by the mighty wave and swept away. Had they remained in the car they would have been saved, as two passengers who stayed there escaped.

"One was Miss Virginia Maloney, a courageous, self-possessed young woman. She tied securely about her neck a plush bag, so that her identity could be established if she perished. Imprisoned in the car with her was a maid employed by Mrs. McCullough. They attempted to leave the car, but the water drove them back. They remained there until John Waugh, the porter, and I waded through the water and rescued them.

"The only passengers I lost were the two unfortunate young ladies I have named. I looked at the corpses of the luckless victims brought in during the two days I remained in Johnstown, but the bodies of the two passengers were not among them.

"At Conemaugh the people were extremely kind and hospitable. They threw open their doors and provided us with a share of what little food they had and gave us shelter.

Stripped of Her Clothing.

"While at Conemaugh, Miss Wayne, of Altoona, who had a miraculous escape, was brought in. She was nude, every article of her clothing having been torn from her by the furious flood. There was no female apparel at hand, and she had to don trousers, coat, vest and hat.

"We had a severe task in reaching Ebensburg,

eighteen miles from Conemaugh. We started on Sunday and were nine hours in reaching our destination. At Ebensburg we boarded the train which conveyed us to Altoona, where we were cared for at the expense of the Pennsylvania Railroad Company.

"I had a rough siege. I was in the water twelve hours. The force of the flood can be imagined by the fact that seven or eight locomotives were carried away and floated on the top of the angry stream as if they were tiny chips."

CHAPTER XVI.

Stories of the Flood.

War, death, cataclysm like tnis, America,
Take deep to thy proud, prosperous heart.

E'en as I chant, lo! out of death, and out of ooze and slime,
The blossoms rapidly blooming, sympathy help, love,
From west and east, from south and north and over sea,
Its hot spurr'd hearts and hands humanity to human aid moves on;
And from within a thought and lesson yet.

Thou ever-darting globe! thou Earth and Air!
Thou waters that encompass us!
Thou that in all the life and death of us, in action or in sleep.
Thou laws invisible that permeate them and all!
Thou that in all and over all, and through and under all, incessant!
Thou! thou! the vital, universal, giant force resistless, sleepless, calm,
Holding Humanity as in the open hand, as some ephemeral toy,
How ill to e'er forget thee!

Walt Whitman.

"Are the horrors of the flood to give way to the terrors of the plague?" is the question that is now agitating the valley of the Conemaugh. To-day opened warm and almost sultry, and the stench that assails one's senses as he wanders through Johnstown is almost overpowering. Sickness, in spite of the precautions and herculean labors of the sanitary authorities, is on the increase and the fears of an epidemic grow with every hour.

"It is our impression," said Dr. T. L. White, assistant to the State Board of Health, this morning, "that there is going to be great sickness here within the next week. Five cases of malignant diphtheria were located this morning on Bedford street, and as they were in different houses they mean five starting points for disease. All this talk about the dangers of epidemic is not exaggerated, as many suppose, but is founded upon all experience. There will be plenty of typhoid fever and kindred diseases here within a week or ten days in my opinion. The only thing that has saved us thus far has been the cool weather. That has now given place to summer weather, and no one knows what the next few days may bring forth.

Fresh Meat and Vegetables Wanted.

Even among the workmen there is already discernible a tendency to diarrhœa and dysentery. The men are living principally upon salt meat, and there is a lack of vegetables. I have been here since Sunday and have tasted fresh meat but once since that time. I am only one of the many. Of course the worst has passed for the physicians, as our arrangements are now perfected and each corps will be relieved from time to time. Twenty more physicians arrived from Pittsburgh this morning and many of us will be relieved to-day. But the opinion is general among the medical men that there will be more need for doctors in a week hence than there is now.

Sanitary Work.

Dr. R. L. Sibbel, of the State Board of Health, is in charge of Sanitary Headquarters. "We are using every precaution known to science," said he this morning, "to prevent the possibility of epidemic. Our labors here have not been confined to any particular channel, but have been extended in various directions. Disinfectants, of course, are first in importance, and they have been used with no sparing hand. The prompt cremation of dead animals as fast as discovered is another thing we have insisted upon. The immediate erection of water-closets throughout the ruins for the workmen was another work of the greatest sanitary importance that has been attended to. They, too, are being disinfected at frequent intervals. We have a committee, too, that superintends the burial of the victims at the cemeteries. It is of the utmost importance in this wholesale interment that the corpses should be interred a safe distance beneath the surface in order that their poisonous emanations may not find exit through the crevices of the earth.

"Another committee is making a house-to-house inspection throughout the stricken city to ascertain the number of inhabitants in each standing house, the number of the sick, and to order the latter to the hospital whenever necessary. One great danger is the overcrowding of houses and hovels, and that is being prevented as much as possible by the free use of tents upon the mountain side. So far there is but little contagious disease, and we hope by diligent and systematic efforts to prevent any dangerous outbreak."

Dodging Responsibility.

It is now rumored that the South Fork Hunting and Fishing Club is a thing of the past. No one admits his membership and it is doubtful if outside the cottage owners one could find more than half a dozen members in the city. Even some of the cottage owners will repudiate their ownership until it is known whether or not legal action will be taken against them. If it were not for the publicity which might follow one could secure a transfer of a large number of shares of the club's stock to himself, accompanied by a good sized roll of money. It is certain that the cottage owners cannot repudiate their ownership. None of them, however, will occupy the houses this summer.

The Club Found Guilty.

Coroner Hammer, of Westmoreland county, who has been sitting on the dead found down the river at Nineveh, concluded his inquests to-day. His trip to South Fork Dam on Wednesday has convinced him that the burden of this great disaster rests on the shoulders of the South Fork Hunting and Fishing Club of Pittsburgh. The verdict was written to-night, but not all the jury were ready to sign it. It finds the South Fork Hunting and Fishing Club responsible for the loss of life because of gross, if not criminal negligence, and of carelessness in making repairs from time to time. This would let the Pennsylvania Railroad Company out from all blame for allowing the dam to fall so badly out of repair when they got control of the Pennsylvania Canal and abandoned it. The verdict is what might have been expected after Wednesday's testimony.

Mr. A. M. Wellington, with P. Burt, associate editor of the *Engineering News*, of New York, has just completed an examination of the dam which caused the great disaster here. Mr. Wellington states that the dam was in every respect of very inferior construction, and of a kind wholly unwarranted by good engineering practices of thirty years ago. Both the original and reconstructed dams were of earth only, with no heart wall, but only riprapped on the slopes.

The original dam, however, was made in dammed and watered layers, which still show distinctly in the wrecked dam. The new end greatly added to its stability, but it was to all appearances simply dumped in like an ordinary railroad fill, or if rammed, the wreck shows no evidence of the good effect of such work. Much of the old part is standing intact, while the adjacent parts of the new work are wholly carried off. There was no central wall of puddle or masonry either in the new or old dam. It has been the invariable practice of engineers for thirty or forty years to use one or the other in building high dams of earth. It is doubtful if there is a single dam or reservoir in any other part of the United States of over fifty feet in height which lacks this central wall.

Ignorance or Carelessness.

The reconstructed dam also bears the mark of great ignorance or carelessness in having been made nearly two feet lower in the middle than at the ends. It should rather have crowned in the middle, which would have concentrated the overflow, if it should occur, at the ends instead of in the centre. Had the break begun at the ends the cut of the water would have been so gradual that little or no harm might have resulted. Had the dam been cut at the ends when the water began running over the centre the sudden breaking would have been at least greatly diminished, possibly prolonged, so that little harm would have resulted. The crest of the old dam had not been raised in the reconstruction of 1881. The old overflow channel through the rock still remains, but owing to the sag of the crest in the middle of the dam only five and a half feet of water in it, instead of seven feet, was necessary to run the water over the crest.

And the rock spillway, narrow at best, had been further contracted by a close grating to prevent the escape of fish, capped by a good-sized timber, and in some slight degree also as a trestle footbridge. The original discharge pipe indicates that it was made about half earth and half rock, but if so there was little evidence of it in the broken dam. The riprapping was merely a skin on each face with more or less loose spauls mixed with the earth. The dam was seventy-two feet above water, two to one inside slope, one and a half to one outside slope and twenty feet wide on top. The rock throughout was about one foot below the surface. The earth was pretty good material for such a dam, if it was to be built at all, being of a clayey nature, making good puddle. To this the fact of it standing intact since 1881 must be ascribed, as no engineer of standing would have ever tried to so construct it. The fact that the dam was a reconstructed one after twenty years' abandonment made it especially hard on the older part of the dam to withstand the pressure of the water.

Elder Thought it was Safe.

Cyrus Elder, general counsel for the Cambria Iron Company and a wealthy and prominent citizen of Johnstown, lost a wife and daughter in the recent disaster and narrowly escaped with his own life.

"When the rebuilding of the dam was begun some years ago," he said, "the president of the Cambria Iron Company was very seriously concerned about it, and wished, if possible, to prevent its construction, referring the matter to the solicitor of the company. A gentleman of high scientific reputation, who was then one of the general engineers, inspected the dam. He condemned several matters in the way of construction and reported that this had been changed and that the dam was perfectly safe. My son, George R. Elder, was at that time a student in the Troy Polytechnic University.

His professor submitted a problem to the class which he immediately recognized as being the question of the safety of the South Fork dam. He sent it to me at the time in a letter, which, of course, is lost, with everything else I possessed, in which he stated that the verdict of the class was that the dam was safe. The president of the Cambria Iron Company being still anxious, thought it might be good policy to have some one inside of the fishing and hunting corporation owning the dam. The funds of the company were therefore used to purchase two shares of its stock, which were placed in the name of D. J. Morrell. After his death these shares were transferred to and are still held by me, although they are the property of the Cambria Iron Company. They have not been sold because there was no market for them."

Untold Volumes of Water.

So far as the Signal Service is concerned, the amount of rainfall in the region drained by the Conemaugh river cannot be ascertained. The Signal Service authorities here, to whom the official there reported, received only partial reports last Friday. There had been a succession of rains nearly all of last week. The last rain commenced Thursday evening and was unusually severe.

Mrs. H. M. Ogle, who had been the Signal Service representative in Johnstown for several years and also manager of the Western Union office there, telegraphed at eight o'clock Friday morning that the river marked 14 feet, rising; a rise of 13 feet in wenty-four hours. At eleven o'clock she wired: "River 20 feet and rising, higher than ever before; water in first floor. Have moved to second. River gauges carried away. Rainfall, 2 3-10 inches." At twenty-seven minutes to one P. M., Mrs. Ogle wired: "At this hour north wind; very cloudy; water still rising."

Nothing more was heard from her by the bureau, but at the Western Union office here later in the afternoon she commenced to tell an operator that the dam had broken, that a flood was coming, and before she had finished the conversation a singular click of the instrument announced the breaking of the current. A moment afterward the current of her life was broken forever.

Sergeant Stewart, in charge of the bureau, says that the fall of water on the Conemaugh shed at Johnstown up to the time of the flood was probably 2 5-10 inches. He believes it was much heavier in the mountains. The country drained by the little Conemaugh and Stony Creek covers an area of about one hundred square miles. The bureau, figuring on this basis and 2 5-10 inches of rainfall, finds that 464,640,000 cubic feet of water was precipitated toward Johnstown in its last hours. This is independent of the great volume of water in the lake, which was not less than 250,000,-000 cubic feet.

Water Enough to Cover the Valley.

It is therefore easily seen that there was ample water to cover the Conemaugh Valley to the depth of from ten to twenty-five feet. Such a volume of water was never known to fall in that country in the same time.

Colonel T. P. Roberts, a leading engineer, estimates that the lake drained twenty-five square miles, and gives some interesting data on the probable amount of water it contained. He says:—"The dam, as I understand, was from hill to hill about one thousand feet long and about eighty-five feet high at the highest point. The pond covered above seven hundred acres, at least for the present I will assume that to be the case. We are told also that there was a waste weir at one end seventy-five feet wide and ten feet below the comb or top of the dam. Now we are told that with this wier open and discharging freely to the utmost of its capacity, nevertheless the pond or lake rose ten inches per hour until finally it overflowed the top, and, as I understand, the dam broke by being eaten away at the top.

Calculating the Amount of Water.

"Thus we have the elements for very simple calculation as to the amount of water precipitated by the flood, provided these premises are accurate. To raise 700 acres of water to a height of ten feet would require about 300,000,000 cubic feet of water, and while this was rising the waste dam would discharge an enormous volume—it would be difficult to say just how much without a full knowledge of the shape of its side walls, approaches and outlets—but if the rise required ten hours the waste river might have discharged perhaps 90,000,000 cubic feet. We would then have a total of flood-water of 390,000,000 cubic feet. This would indicate a rainfall of about eight inches over the twenty-five square miles. As that much does not appear to have fallen at the hotel and dam it is more than likely that even more than eight inches were precipitated in the places further up. These figures I hold tentatively, but I am much inclined to believe that there was a cloud burst."

Six thousand men were at work on the ruins to-day. They are paid two dollars a day, and have to earn it. The work seems to tell very little, however, for the mass of débris is simply enormous. The gangs have cleaned up the streets pretty thoroughly in the main part of the city, from which the brick blocks were swept like card houses before a breeze. The houses are pulled apart and burned in bonfires. Nowhere is anything found worth saving.

It is not probable that the mass of débris at the bridge, by which the water is tainted, can be removed in less than thirty days with the greatest force possible to work on it. That particular job is under the control of the State Board of Health. Every day adds to its seriousness. The mass is being cleared by dynamite at the bridge where the current is strongest, and the open place slowly grows larger. Not infrequently a body is found after an explosion has loosened the wreckage.

So-called relief corps are still moving to and fro in the city, but the most serious labor of many of the members is to carry a bright yellow badge to aid them in passing the guards while sight-seeing. The militia men are little better than ornamental. The guards do a good deal of changing, to the annoyance of workers who want to get into the lines, but they rarely stop any one. The soldiers do a vast deal of loafing. A photographer who had his camera ready to take a view among the ruins was arrested to-day and made to work for an hour by General Hastings' order. When his stent was done he did not linger, but went at once.

Signs of Improvement.

"What is the condition of the valley now?" I asked Colonel Scott.

"It is improving with every hour. The perfect organization which has been effected within the past day or two has gradually resolved all the chaos and confusion into a semblance of order and regulation."

"Are many bodies being discovered now?"

"Very few; that is to say, comparatively few. Of course, as the waters recede more and more between the banks, we have come upon bodies here and there, as they were exposed to sight. The probabilities are that there will be a great many bodies yet discovered under the rubbish that covers the streets, and our hope and expectation is that the majority of all the dead may be recovered and disposed of in a Christian manner."

"How about the movement to burn the rubbish, bodies and all?"

"I do not think that will be done—at least only as a last extremity. While there is great anxiety in regard to the sanitaty condition, all possible precautions are being taken, and we hope to prevent any disease until we shall have time to thoroughly overhaul the wreck.

Consideration for the Dead.

"The greatest consideration is being given to this matter of the recovery of the dead and treatment of the bodies after discovery. I think an impression has gone abroad that the dead are being handled here very much as one would handle cord wood, but this is a great mistake. As soon as possible after discovery they are borne from public gaze and taken to the Morgue, where only persons who have lost relatives or friends are admitted. Of course the general exclusion is not applied to attendants, physicians and representatives of the press, but it is righteously applied to careless sight-seers. We have no room for sight-seers in Johnstown now. It is earnest workers and laborers we want, and of these we can hardly have too many."

Speculating in Disaster.

Some long headed men are trying to make a neat little stake quietly out of the disaster. A syndicate has been formed to buy up as much real estate as possible in Johnstown, trusting to get a big block as they got one to-day, for one-third of the valuation placed on it a week ago. The members of the syndicate are keeping very much in the background and conducting their business through a local agent.

I asked Adjutant General Hastings to-day what he thought of the situation.

"It is very good so far as reported," was the reply. "Bodies are being gradually recovered all the time, but of course not in the large number of the first few days. Last night we arrested several ghouls that were wandering amid the wreck on evil intent, and they were promptly taken to the guard house. This morning they were given the choice of imprisonment or going to work at two dollars a day, and they promptly chose the latter. We are getting along very well in our work, and very little tendency to lawlessness, I am happy to say, is observed."

Succor for the Living.

The Red Cross flag now flies over the society's own camp beside the Baltimore and Ohio tracks, near the bridge to Kernville. The tents were pitched this morning and the camp includes a large supply tent, mess tent and offices. Miss Clara Barton, of Washington, is, of course, in charge, and the work is being rapidly gotten into shape. I found Miss Barton at the camp this morning.

"The Red Cross Society will remain here," she said, "so long as there is any work to do. There is hardly any limit to what we will do. Much of the present assistance that has been extended is, of course, impulsive and ephemeral. When that is over there will still be work to do, and the Red Cross Society will be here to do it. We are always the last to leave the field.

"We need and can use to the greatest advantage all kinds of supplies, and shall be glad to receive them. Money is practically useless here as there is no place to buy what we need."

Dr. J. Wilkes O'Neill, of Philadelphia, surgeon of the First Regiment, is here in charge of the Philadelphia division of the Red Cross Society. He is assisted by a corps of physicians, nurses and attendants. Within two hours after establishing the camp this morning about forty cases, both surgical and medical, were treated. Diphtheria broke out in Kernville to-day. Eleven cases were reported, eight of which were reported to be malignant. The epidemic is sure to extend. There are also cases of ulcerated tonsilitis. The patients are mostly those left homeless by the flood and are fairly well situated in frame houses. The doctors do not fear an epidemic of pneumonia. The Red Cross Society has established a hospital camp in Grubbtown for the treatment of contagious diseases. An epidemic of typhoid fever is feared, two cases having appeared. The camp is well located in a pleasant spot near fine water. It is supplied with cots, ambulances and some stores. They have an ample supply of surgical stores, but need medical stores badly.

Serving Out the Rations.

At the commissary station at the Pennsylvania Railroad depot there was considerable activity. A crowd of about one thousand people had gathered about the place after the day's rations. The crowd became so great that the soldiers had to be called up to guard the place until the Relief Committee was ready to give out the provisions. . Several carloads of clothing arrived this morning and was to be disposed of as soon as possible. The people were badly in need of clothing, as the weather had been very chilly since Saturday.

B. F. Minnimun, a wealthy contractor of Springfield, Ohio, arrived this forenoon with a despatch from Governor Foraker offering 2,000 trained laborers for

Johnstown, to be sent at once if needed. The despatch further stated that if anything else was needed Ohio stood ready to respond promptly to the call.

What Clara Barton Said.

"It is like a blow on the head; there are no tears, they are stunned; but, ah, sir, I tell you they will awake after awhile and then the tears will flow down the hills of this valley from thousands of bleeding hearts, and there will be weeping and wailing such as never before."

That is what Clara Barton, president of the National Red Cross, said this afternoon as she stood in a plain black gown on the bank of Stony Creek directing the construction of the Red Cross tents, and she looked motherly and matronly, while her voice was trembling with sympathy.

"You see nothing but that dazed, sickly smile that calamity leaves," she went on, "like the crazy man wears when you ask him, 'How came you here?' Something happened, he says, that he alone knows; all the rest is blank to him. Here they give you that smile, that look and say 'I lost my father, my mother, my sisters,' but they do not realize it yet. The Red Cross intends to be here in the Conemaugh Valley when the pestilence comes to them, and we are making ready with all our heart, with all our soul, with all our strength. The militia, the railroad, the Relief Committees and everybody is working for us. The railroad has completely barricaded us so that none of our cars can be taken away by mistake."

When the great wave of death swept through Johnstown the people who had any chance of escape ran hither and thither in every direction. They did not have any definite idea where they were going, only that a crest of foaming waters as high as the housetops was roaring down upon them through the Conemaugh and that they must get out of the way of that. Some

A WOMAN'S BODY LODGED IN A TREE.

in their terror dived into the cellars of their houses and clambered over the adjoining roofs to places of safety. But the majority made for the hills, which girt the town like giants. Of the people who went to the hills, the water caught some in its whirl.

The others clung to trees and roots and pieces of débris which had temporarily lodged near the banks, and managed to save themselves. These people either stayed out on the hills wet, and in many instances walked all night, or they managed to find farmhouses which sheltered them. There was a fear of going back to the vicinity of the town. Even the people whose houses the water did not reach abandoned their homes and began to think of all of Johnstown as a city buried beneath the water. But in the houses which were thus able to afford shelter there was not food enough for all. Many survivors of the flood went hungry until the first relief supplies arrived from Pittsburgh.

Struggling to Live Again.

From all this fright, destitution and exposure is coming a nervous shock, culminating in insanity, pneumonia, fever and all the other forms of disease. When these people came back to Johnstown on the day after the wreck of the town they had to live in sheds, barns and in houses which had been but partially ruined. They had to sleep without any covering, in their wet clothes, and it took the liveliest kind of skirmishing to get anything to eat. Pretty soon a citizen's committee was established, and nearly all the male survivors of the flood were immediately sworn in as deputy sheriffs. They adorned themselves with tin stars, which they cut out of pieces of the sheets of metal in the ruins, and pieces of tin with stars cut out of them are now turning up continually, to the surprise of the Pittsburgh workmen who are endeavoring to get the town in shape.

The women and children were housed, so far as possible, in the few houses still standing, and some idea of the extent of the wreck of the town may be gathered from the fact that of 300 prominent buildings only 16 are uninjured. For the first day or so people were dazed by what had happened, and for that matter they are dazed still. They went about helpless, making vague inquiries for their friends, and hardly feeling the desire to eat anything. Finally the need of creature comforts overpowered them and they woke up to the fact that they were faint and sick.

Refugees in Their Own City.

Now this is to some extent changed by the arrival of tents and by the systematic military care for the suffering. But the daily life of a Johnstown man who is a refugee in his own city is still aimless and wandering. His property, his home, in nine cases out of ten, his wife and children, are gone. The chances are that he has hard work to find the spot where he and his family once lived and were happy. He meditates suicide, and even looks on the strangers who have flocked in to help him and to put him and his town on their feet again with a kind of sullen anger. He has frequent conflicts with the soldiers and with the sight-seers, and he is crazy enough to do almost anything.

The first thing that Johnstown people do in the morning is to go to the relief stations and get something to eat. They go carrying big baskets, and their endeavor is to get all they can. There has been a new system every day about the manner of dispensing the food and clothing to the sufferers. At first the supplies were placed where people could help themselves. Then they were placed in yards and handed to people over the fences. Then people had to get orders for what they wanted from the citizens' committee and their orders were filled at the different relief stations. Now the matter has been arranged this way, and probably finally. The whole matter cf receiving and dispensing the relief supplies has been placed in the hands of the Grand Army of the Republic men.

Women Too Proud to Beg.

The Grand Army men have made the Adams Street Relief Station a central relief station and all the others at Kernville, the Pennsylvania depot, Cambria City and Jackson and Somerset Streets, sub-stations. The idea is to distribute supplies to the sub-stations from the central station and thus avoid the jam of crying and excited people at the committee's headquarters. The Grand Army men have appointed a committee of women to assist in their work. The women go from house to house ascertaining the number of people lost from there in the flood and the exact needs of the people. It was found necessary to have some such committee as this, for there were women actually starving who were too proud to take their places in lines with the other women with bags and baskets. Some of these people were rich before the flood.

Now they are not worth a dollar. One man who was reported to be worth $100,000 before the flood now is penniless and has to take his place in the line along with others seeking the necessaries of life.

Though the Adams street station is now the central relief station, the most imposing display of supplies is made at the Pennsylvania Railroad freight and passenger depots. Here on the platform and in the yards are piled up barrels of flour in long rows three and four barrels high. Biscuits in cans and boxes by the carload, crackers under the railroad sheds in bins, hams by the hundred strung on poles, boxes of soap and candles, barrels of kerosene oil, stacks of canned goods and things to eat of all sorts and kinds are here to be seen.

No Fear of a Food Famine.

The same sight is visible at the Baltimore and Ohio road and there is now no fear of a food famine in Johnstown, though of course everybody will have to rough it for weeks. What is needed most in this line are cooking utensils. Johnstown people want stoves, kettles, pans, knives and forks. All the things that have been sent so far have been sent with the evident idea of supplying an instant need, and that is right and proper. But it would be well now if instead of some of the provisions that are sent, cooking utensils should arrive. Fifty stoves arrived from Pittsburgh this morning, and it is said more are coming. At both the depots where the supplies are received and stored a big rope line encloses them in an impromptu yard so as to give room to those having the supplies in charge to walk around and see what they have got.

On the inside of this line, too, stalk back and forth the soldiers with their rifles on their shoulders, and by the side of the lines pressing against the ropes there stands every day from daylight until dawn a crowd of women with big baskets who make piteous appeals to the soldiers to give them food for their children at once before the order of the relief committee.

Where Death Rules.

The following letters from a young woman to her mother, written immediately after the disaster at Johnstown from her home in New Florence, a few miles west of that place, though not intended for publication, picture in graphic manner the agony of suspense sustained by those who escaped the flood, and give side pictures of the scenes following the disaster. They were received in Philadelphia:

Hours of Suspense.

NEW FLORENCE, PA.—My Darling Mother: I am nearly crazed, and thought I would try and be quiet and write to you, as it always comforts me to feel you are near your child, though many miles are now between us. I have said my prayers over and over again all day long, and to-night I am going to spend in the watch-tower, and am trying to be quiet and brave, although my heart is just wrung with anguish. Andrew sent me word from Johnstown this afternoon about half-past three he was safe and would be home shortly. Well, he has never come, and I have had many reports of the work train, but no one seems to know anything definite about him. I have telegraphed and telegraphed, but no news yet, and all I can find out is he was seen on the bridge just before it went down. I am trying to be brave.

Good News at Last.

SUNDAY MORNING.

You see, dearest mother, I could not write, and now I am happy, though tired, for Andrew is home and safe, and I thank God for the great mercy he has shown his child. I won't dwell on my anxiety, it can better be imagined than described. From the letter I had from him at Johnstown, written at 9 A. M. Friday, until 6.30 last evening, I never knew whether he was living or dead. Thomas, our man, brought the news. God bless him, and it nearly cost him his life to do it, poor man. Andrew got separated from the party, and was close to the bridge when it was carried away, but escaped by going up the mountain. He tried to signal to his men he was safe, but could not make them see him, nor could those men that were with him; all communication was impossible. Thomas left him at nine o'clock Friday night on the mountain and tried to get home. He got a man to ferry him across the river above Johnstown, and the boat was upset, but all managed to get ashore, and Thomas walked all night and all yesterday, and came straight to me and told me my husband was safe, and an hour later I had a telegram from Andrew. He had walked from the Conemaugh side to Bolivar. The bridge at Nineveh was the only bridge left standing. He took the first train home from Bolivar and got home about 9.30.

I telegraphed you in the morning, or rather Uncle Clem, that I was safe and Andrew reported safe, though now they tell me every one here thought he was lost and Thomas with him. Thomas's wife was met at the station and informed of his death by some of the men, and six hours afterwards Thomas came home, yet more dead than alive, poor man. It is very hard to write, as all the country people and men have been here to tell me how glad they are "I got my husband safely back, and that I am a powerful sight lucky young woman." Well, mother darling, make your mind easy about your children now. Andrew is safe and well, though pretty well exhausted, and his feet are so sore and swollen he can hardly stand, and can't wear anything but rubbers, as his mountain shoes he cut to pieces. He left early this morning, but will be back to-night. I cannot begin to tell you of the horrors, as the papers do not half picture the distress. New Florence was not flooded, though some of the people left the place on Friday night and went up on Squirrel Hill.

Scenes at the River.

I went down to the river once, and that was enough, as I knew Andrew would not like me to see the sorrow, for which there was no help. I went just after the bridge fell, saw Centreville flooded and the people make a dash for the mountain. Yesterday two hundred and three bodies were taken from the river near here, and yet every train takes away more. The freight cars have taken nothing but human freight.

and wagon load after wagon load of dead bodies have been right in front of the house. There was a child about Nellie's age, with light hair, dead in the wagon, with her hands clasped, saying her prayers, and her blue eyes staring wide open. By her side lay a man with a pipe in his mouth, naked children, and a woman with a baby at her breast. Oh, the terror on their faces. Two women and three men were rescued here, and a German family of mother, four children and father. I had them all on my hands to look after; no one could make them understand, and how I ever managed it I don't know, but I did. They lost two children and their home, but had a little money and were going to his brother's, at Hazleton. They got here in the night and left at noon, and it would have done your heart good to see them eat. One was a baby five weeks old.

Help Needed.

Now, mother, I want you to go around among the family and get me everything in the way of clothes you possibly can, and get Uncle Clem to express them to me. I should also like money, and as much as you can get can be used. I am pretty well cleaned out of everything, as all the cattle and stock have been lost and nothing can be bought here, and all I have in the way of provisions is some preserves, chocolate, coffee, olives and crackers. We can't starve, as we have the chickens. I got the last meat from the butcher's yesterday, and he said he didn't expect to have any more for a week, so I told Uncle Clem I would not mind having two hams from Pittsburgh, and was very grateful for his telegram. I telegraphed him in the morning; also, Uncle White at Germantown, so that they might know I was all right, but from Auntie's telegram I judge Uncle Clem's telegrams were the only ones that got through. If I find I need provisions I will let you know, but do not think I will need anything for myself, and the poor are being fed by the relief supplies, and what is needed now is money and clothes.

Helpers.

There's not a house in the place that is not in trouble from the loss of some dear one, nor one that does not hold or shelter some one or more of the sufferers. Tell everybody anything you can get can be used, and by the time you get this letter I will know of more cases to provide for, so take everything you can get, and don't worry about me, for I am all right now that Andrew is safe. This letter has been written by instalments, as I have been interrupted so many times, so pardon the abruptness of it, and please send it to Germantown, as I have too much to do now. My hands and heart are both full. Milk is as scarce as wine, as the pasturage was all on the other side, and cows were lost, and bread is as scarce as can be, and, instead of a dozen eggs, we only get one a day. I am proud of New Florence, as all it has done to help the sufferers no one knows, and as for Mr. Bennett, he is one in a thousand. Mr. Hay's son has worked like a Trojan. Tell Cousin Hannah that the new tracks will be sure to be straight, as Andrew will superintend the whole business. With heart full of love to one and all and a kiss to the children. Lovingly,

BETT.

The Awful After Scenes.

NEW FLORENCE, Sunday Night.

My Darling Mother: This is my second letter to you to-day. It is after 11 o'clock, and one of the men has just brought me word that Andrew will be home, he thought, by 1 o'clock; so I am waiting up for him, so as to give him his dinner, and I have been through so much I cannot go to bed until I know he is safe home again. I put him up a good lunch, and know he cannot starve.

Oh the horrors of to-day! I have only had one pleasant Sunday here, and that was the one after we were married. I have had a very busy day, as I have been through our clothes, and routing out everything possible for the sufferers and the dead, and the cry to-day for linen sheets, etc., was something awful. I have given away all my underclothes, excepting my very best things—and all my old ones I made into face-cloths for the dead. To-day they took five little children out of the water; they were playing "Ring around a rosy," and their hands were clasped in a clasp which even death did not loosen, and their faces were still smiling.

One man identified his wife among those who came ashore here, and Rose said that he was nearly crazy, and that her face was the most beautiful thing she ever saw, and that she had very handsome pearls in her ears and was so young looking. The dead are all taken from here to Johnstown and Nineveh and other places, where they will be most likely to be identified; about thirty have been identified here and taken away. I feel hardened to a great deal, and feel God has been so merciful to me I must do all I can for the unfortunate ones. I hope soon to have some help from you all, for I have given willingly of my little and my means are exhausted. I expect we will have to live on ham and eggs next week, but we are thankful to have that, as I would rather live low and give all I can, than not to give. All I care about is that Andrew gets enough to eat, as he needs a great deal to keep his strength up, working as hard as he does. Now I will close as it is nearly time for him to be home. Lovingly,

BETT.

Feeding the Hungry.

There are over 30,000 people at Johnstown who must be fed from the outside world. Of these 18,000 are natives of the town that a week ago had 29,500 inhabitants; all the others are dead or have gone away. Over 12,000 people are here clearing the streets, burying the dead, attending the sick, and feeding and sheltering the homeless; all these people have to be fed at least three times a day, for days are very long in Johnstown just now. They begin at five o'clock in the morning, two hours before the whistles in the half-mired Cambria Iron Company's building blow, and end just about the time the sun is going down. If the people who are on the outside and who are engaged in the labor of love of sending the food that is keeping strength in Johnstown's tired arms and the clothing that is covering her nakedness could understand the situation as it is they would redouble their efforts. Johnstown cannot draw on the country immediately around about her, for that was drained days ago. To be safe, there should be a week's supply of food ahead. At no time has there been a day's supply or anything like it.

A Crisis in the Commissary.

Twice within the last forty-eight hours the commissary department at the Pennsylvania Railroad Depot, where nearly 10,000 people are furnished with food, have been in a state of mind bordering on panic. They had run out of food; people who had trudged down the hill with expectant faces and empty baskets had to trudge back again with hearts heavy and baskets still empty. That was the case on Wednesday night. Then the Citizens' Committee had to send to the refugee camp, the smallest food station in the city, and take away 1500 loaves of bread. The bread supply in the central portion of the town had suddenly given out and there was a clamoring crowd demanding to be fed.

The same thing happened again last night. It was not so bad as on the night before, but there were anxious faces enough among the men under the direction of Major Spangler, who realized the awful responsibility of providing the mouths of the thousands with food. The supply had given out, but fortunately not until almost everybody had been supplied. Telegrams announced that eight carloads of provisions had been shipped from the West and were somewhere in the line between Pittsburgh and Johnstown. At midnight nothing could be heard of them. The delay was maddening. If the food did not arrive it meant fully 10,000 breakfastless and possibly dinnerless people in Johnstown to-day, with consequent suffering and possible disorder among the rough and rowdy element.

The Danger Tided Over.

Before daylight the expected cars came in from Ohio and Pittsburgh and the danger was over for the time being. This serves, however, to show the perilous condition the town is in, living as it is in a hand-to-mouth fashion. It should be remembered that the only direct access to Johnstown from the West is by way of the Pennsylvania, which is handicapped as she has never been before, and from the East and South, of the Baltimore and Ohio. If the Pennsylvania were opened through to the East a steady stream of 200 cars already loaded for the sufferers would pour over the Alleghenies, but the Pennsylvania does not see light ahead much more clearly than yesterday. The terrible breaks and washouts will require days yet to repair, and supplies that come from the interior of the State must come by means of wagons.

Crowding in the Supplies.

The Baltimore and Ohio is piling the supplies in to-day faster than the men can unload them. In the neighborhood of 100 carloads were received. The Pennsylvania during to-day has handled something like twenty-eight carloads all told. In the way of food the articles most needed are fresh, salt meats, sugar, rice, coffee, tea, and dried and canned fruits. The supply of sugar gave out entirely to-day. Twenty thousand pounds of Cincinnati hams arrived to-day and they melted like 20,000 pounds of ice beneath the scorching heat of this afternoon's sun. Much of the clothing that is received here is new and serviceable, but thousands of pieces are so badly worn that, to use the words of General Axline, of Ohio, who is doing noble service here with the thousands of other self-sacrificing men, "it is unfit to be worn by tramps." Many old shoes with the soles half torn off have been received. Shoes are badly needed at once or all Johnstown will be barefooted.

Eighteen Carloads of Relief.

Even in the rush of distribution the officials who have it in charge can find time to say a hearty word of praise for those towns which have contributed to the sufferers. Philadelphia's first installment was the first to arrive from the East, and more goods have been coming in steadily ever since. W. H. Tumblestone, the president of the Retail Grocers' Association of Pennsylvania, who was appointed first lieutenant of the Philadelphia relief by the Mayor, arrived here first. He set at work handling coffins, but as soon as the first freight car of goods arrived he was put in charge of their distribution and has been working like three men ever since. The eight freight cars from Philadel-

DISTRIBUTING CLOTHING AND OTHER SUPPLIES.

phia which arrived with the relief party on Monday, at 4 o'clock, were distributed from a great storehouse at the terminus of the Baltimo e and Ohio Railroad. The goods are carried in bulk from the cars to the warehouse by a gang of twenty-eight men, who are identified by red flannel hat-bands. When they fail to enthuse over their work Mr. Tumblestone gets off his coat and shoves boxes himself.

Distributing Supplies.

Inside the warehouse a score of volunteers and Pittsburgh policemen break open the boxes and pile the goods in separate heaps; the women's clothing, the men's, the children's and the different sizes being placed in regular order. Then the barriers are opened and the crowd surges in like depositors making a run on a savings bank. The police keep good order and the ubiquitous Tumblestone and his assistants dole out the goods to all who have orders. Special orders call for stoves, mattrasses and blankets.

If the Philadelphians could see the faces of the people they are helping before and after they have passed the distribution windows they would feel well repaid for their visible sympathy. Chairman Scott says the class of goods from Philadelphia have been of the highest quality. "We have been delighted with the thought and excellence of the selections and amiable nature of the contributions. The two miles of track lying between here and Morrellville are still blocked with cars stretched from one end to the other, and fresh arrivals are coming in daily over the Baltimore and Ohio." Although it is impossible to say how much has been received from Philadelphia, Mr. Tumblestone says that so far as many as eighteen freight cars, each filled from the sides to the roof, have arrived from the Quaker City, and their contents have been distributed.

How Rival Hotels were Crushed Together.

The principal hotels of the town were bunched in a group about the corner of Main and Clinton streets. They were the Merchants' a large old-fashioned, three-story tavern, with a stable yard behind, a relic of staging days; the Hurlburt House, the leading hotel of the place, a fine four-story brick structure with a mansard roof and all the latest wrinkles in furnishing inside and out; the Fritz House, a narrow, four-story structure, with an ornate front, and the Keystone, a smaller hotel than any of the others.

These few inns stood in the path of the flood. The Hurlburt, the largest and handsomest, was absolutely obliterated. The Keystone's ruin was next in completion. It stood across Clinton Street from Fritz's, and Landlord Charles West has not yet recovered from the surprise of seeing the rival establishment thrown bodily across the street against his second story front, tearing it completely out.

After the water subsided it fell back upon the pavement in front of its still towering rival, and in the meantime Landlord West had saved mine host of the Keystone and his family from the roof which was thrust in his windows.

Back of Fritz's there was a little alley, which made a course for a part of the torrent. Fully half a dozen houses were sent swimming in here. They crushed their way through the small hotel's outhouses straight to the rear of the Merchants', and sliced the walls off the old inn as a hungry survivor to-day cut a Philadelphia cheese. You can see the interior of the rooms. The beds were swept out into the flood, but a lonesome wardrobe fell face downward on the floor and somehow escaped. There are bodies under the rear wall. How many is not known, but Landlord West, of Fritz's, says he is certain there were people on the rear porch of the Merchants'. The story of Landlord West's rival being thrown into his front windows has its parallels.

Colonel Higgins, the manager of the Cambria Club House, was in the third story of the building with his family. Suddenly a man was hurled by the torrent rapidly through the window. He was rescued, then fainted, and upon inspection was found to have a broken leg. The leg was bandaged and the man resuscitated, and when this last act of kindness was accomplished he said faintly: "This ain't so bad. I've been in a blow-up."

A Cool Request.

This remark showed the greatest sang froid known to be exhibited during the flood, but the most irreverent was that of an old man who was saved by E. B. Entworth, of the Johnson works. On Saturday morning Mr. Entworth rowed to a house near the flowing débris at the bridge, and found a woman, with a broken arm, and a baby. After she had got into the boat she cried: "Come along, grandpap." Whereupon an old man, chilled but chipper, jumped up from the other side of the roof, slid down into the boat, and ejaculated: "Gentlemen, can any of you give me a chew of tobacco?"

Scenes Amid the Ruins.

One of the curious finds in the débris yesterday was two proofs from cabinet-size negatives of two persons —a man and a woman. The prints were found within two feet of each other in the ruins near the Merchants' Hotel. They were immediately recognized as portraits of Mamie Patton, formerly a Johnstown girl, and Charles DeKnight, once a Pullman palace car conductor. The two were found dying together in a room in a Pittsburgh hotel several months ago, the woman having shot the man and then herself. She claimed that he was her husband. The dress in which the picture showed her was the same that she wore when she killed DeKnight.

Tracks that were Laid in a Hurry.

If Pennsylvania Railroad trains ever ran over tougher-looking tracks than those used now through Johnstown it must have been before people began to ride on it. The section from the north end of the bridge to the railroad station has a grade that wabbles between 50 and 500 feet to the mile and jerks back and forth sideways as though laid by a gang of intoxicated men on a dark night. When the first engine went over it everybody held his breath and watched to see it tumble. These eccentricities are being straightened out, however, as fast as men and broken stones can do it.

The railroad bridge at Johnstown deserves attention beyond that which it is receiving on account of the way it held back the flood. It is one of the most massive pieces of masonry ever set up in this country. In a general way it is solid masonry of cut sandstone blocks of unusual size, the whole nearly 400 feet long, forty wide, and averaging about forty deep. Seven arches of about fifty feet span are pierced through it, rising to within a few feet of the top and leaving massive piers down to the rock beneath. As the bridge crosses the stream diagonally, the arches pierce the mass in a slanting direction, and this greatly adds to the heavy appearance of the bridge. There has been some disposition to find fault with the bridge for being so strong, the idea being that if it had gone out there would have been no heaping up of buildings behind it, no fire, and fewer deaths. This is probably unfair, as there were hundreds of persons saved when their houses were stopped against the bridge by climbing out or being helped out upon the structure. If the bridge had gone, too, the flood would have taken the whole instead of only half of Cambria City.

Photographers Forced to Work.

The camera fiend has about ceased his wanderings. An order was issued yesterday from headquarters to arrest and put to work the swarms of amateur photographers who are to be found everywhere about the ruins. Those who will not work are to be taken uptown under guard. This order is issued to keep down the number of useless people and thus save the fast diminishing provisions for the workers.

A man who stood on the bluff and saw the first wave of the flood come down the valley tried to describe it. "I looked up," he said, "and saw something that looked like a wall of houses and trees up the valley The next moment Johnstown seemed coming toward me. It was lifted right up and in a minute was smashing against the bridge and the houses were flying in splinters across the top and into the water beyond."

A 13-year-old girl, pretty and with golden hair, wanders about from morgue to morgue looking for ten of a family of eleven, she being the sole survivor.

There were half a dozen bulldogs in one house that was heaped up in the wreck some distance above the bridge. They were loose among the débris, and it is said by those who claim to have seen it that after fighting among themselves they turned upon the people near them and were tearing and biting them until the flames swept over the place.

Slow Time to Pittsburgh.

Irregular is a weak word for the manner in which passenger trains run between this place and Pittsburgh. The distance is seventy miles and the ordinary time is two hours. The train that left here at 4.30 yesterday afternoon reached there at midnight. This is ordinarily good time nowadays. A passage in five hours is an exceptional one.

Engine 1309, the one that faced the flood below Conemaugh and stood practically unharmed, backed down to the station as soon as the tracks were laid up to where it stood and worked all right. Only the oil cups and other small fittings, with the headlight, were broken.

The superintendent of the Woodvale Woolen Mills, one of the Cambria Iron Company's concerns, was one of the very few fortunate ones in that little place. He and all his family got into the flouring mill just below the woolen mill and upon the roof. The woolen mill was totally wrecked, though not carried away, and the flouring mill was badly damaged, but the roof held and all were saved. These two parts of the mill were the only buildings left standing in Woodvale.

A man in Kernville, on Friday last, had jet black hair, moustache and beard. That night he had a battle with the waters. On Saturday morning his hair and beard began to turn gray, and they are now well streaked with white. He attributes the change to his awful Friday night's experience.

Wounds of the Dead.

It is the impression of the medical corps and military surgeons who arrived here early in the week that hundreds, maybe thousands of men, women and children were insensible to all horror on that awful afternoon, just a week ago, before the waters of the valley closed in over them. Their opinion is based on the fact that hundreds and hundreds of the bodies already brought to light are terribly wounded somewhere, generally on the head. In many instances the wounds are sufficient in themselves to have caused death.

The crashing of houses together in the first mad rush of the flood with a force greater than the collision of railroad trains making fast time, and the hurling of timbers, poles, towers and boulders through the air is believed to have caused a legion of deaths in an instant, before the lost knew what was coming. Even the survivors bear testimony to this.

Surgeon Foster, of the 14th Regiment, who was first to have charge of the hospital, tells how he treated long lines of men, women and children for wounds too terrible to mention and they themselves know not how it happened only that they fell in a moment. In connection with his experience he speaks of the tender, yet heroic, work of four Sisters of Mercy, two from Pittsburgh and two here, who went ahead of him down the ranks of the wounded with sponges, chloroforming the suffering, before his scalpel aid reached them. Sometimes there were a dozen victims ahead of his knives.

Once these sisters stopped, for the first time showing horror, by a great pile of dead children and infants on the river bank laid one on top of the other. By one man each little body was seized and the clothing quickly cut from it. Then he passed it to another, who washed it in the river. Then a third man took it in the line of the dead. But the Sisters of Mercy saw they were too late there, and passed on among the living.

Most of the Pennsylvania Railroad passengers who left Pittsburgh for the East last Friday and were caught in the flood in the Conemaugh Valley reached Philadelphia in a long special train at 5 o'clock Friday morning, June 7th, after a week of adventure, peril and narrow escapes which none of them will ever forget. A few of their number who lost presence of mind when the flood struck the train were drowned. The survivors are unanimous in their appreciation of the kindness shown them by Pennsylvania officials, and in their praise of the hospitality and generosity of the country folk, among whom they found homes for three days. The escapes in some instances seem miraculous.

An hour before the flood the first section of the day express stopped at Conemaugh City, about ten miles below the dam at South Fork, on account of a washout farther up the valley. The second section of the express and another passenger train soon overtook the first and half an hour before the dam broke all these trains stood abreast on the four-track road. The positions now occupied seems providential. If the railroad men had foreseen the disaster they could not have shown greater prudence, for the engine of the first section of the express, on the track nearest the mountain side, stood about a car's length ahead of the second. The engine of the third train came to a stop a car's length behind the second and on the outer track, which was within a few feet of the swollen Conemaugh River, stood a heavily laden freight train.

When the flood came it struck the slanting front of the four locomotives. Most of the passengers had, in the meantime, escaped up the mountain side. Three of the locomotives were carried down by the irresistible torrent, but the fourth turned on its side and was soon buried under sand, tree trunks and other débris. This served as a breakwater for the flood and accounts for the fact that the trains of cars were not reduced to kindling wood while the railroad roundhouse and its twelve locomotives, a little farther down the valley, was taken up bodily, broken into fragments and its mighty inmates carried like chips for miles down the valley.

Weary Passengers.

From end to end of the train, upon its arrival at Philadelphia, there was an aspect of absolute exhaustion, varied in its expression according to the individual. Phlegmatic men lay upon their backs, across the seats, with their legs dangling in the aisles. One might send them spinning round or toss their feet out of the passage, and their worn faces showed no more sign than if they were lifeless. Women lay swathed in veils and wraps, sometimes alone, sometimes huddled together, and sometimes guarded by the arms of their husbands—husbands who themselves had given way and slept as heavily as if dosed with narcotics.

But here and there is the typical American girl, full

of nerve. She is worn out, too, but sleeps only fit fully, starting up at every sound and dropping uneasily off again. Now and then one encountered the man and woman of restless temperament, whose sleepless eyes looked out thinking, thinking—thinking on the trees and grass and bushes, faintly showing form now in the gray light of the very earliest dawn.

Childhood's Peaceful Sleep.

In the midst of it all a girl of six or seven, with a light shawl thrown over her figure, slept as peacefully as if she lay in the comfortable embrace of her own crib at home. She was little Bertha Reed, who had been sent out from Chicago in the care of the conductor on a trip to Brooklyn, where she was to meet her aunt. At Pittsburgh she was taken in charge by a Miss Harvey, a relative. She was a passenger on the Chicago limited, the last train to get safely across the bridge at South Fork. She was a model of patience and cheerfulness through all the discomforts and drawbacks of the voyage, and her innocent prattle made every man and woman love her.

It might have been supposed that if one were to waken any of these sleeping passengers to obtain their names and ask them of the disaster they might surlily have resented it. But they didn't. Now and then one of them would half-sleepily hand out his ticket under the mistaken notion that the reporter was the conductor. Another shake brought them round and they answered everything as kindly as if the unavoidable breaking in upon their comfort were a matter of no concern whatever. Sometimes it would seem that great sorrow must have a chastening effect upon everyone.

From All Parts of the World.

It was a strange gathering altogether, and made one think again of the remark so often repeated in "No Thoroughfare," "How small the world is." All the ends of the earth had sent their people to meet at the disaster, and the tide of human life flows on as recklessly as the current of any sea or river. Here weary, sleepy and sad, was Jacob Schmidt, of Aspen, Col. He had been a passenger on the Pittsburgh day express. He was standing on the platform when the flood came and by a lurching of the car he was thrown into the boiling torrent. He managed to seize a floating plank and was saved, but all his money and other valuables were lost. That was a particularly hard loss to him, because he was on his way to South Africa to seek his fortune. Behind him was R. B. Jones, who had come from the other side of the globe; in particular from Sydney, Australia, and met the others at Altoona. He was on the way for a visit to his parents in York County. He was on the Chicago Limited and just escaped the danger.

In a front car was Peter Sherman, of Pawtucket, R. I. He was tall and broad shouldered and his sun-browned face was shaded by a big soft hat. He was on his way from Texarkana, way down in Texas, and he too was at Conemaugh. He was a passenger on the first section of the day express. He had not slept a wink on the way down from Altoona, and he told his story spiritedly. He said: "I heard a voice in the car crying the reservoir is burst; run for your lives! I got up and made a rush for the door. A poor little cripple with two crutches sat in front of me and screamed to me to save him or he would be drowned. I grabbed him up under one arm and took his crutches with my free hand. As we stepped from the car the water was coming. I made my way up the hill toward a church. The water swooped down on us and was soon up to my knees. I told the cripple I could not carry him further; that we should both be lost. He screamed to me again to save him, but the water was gaining rapidly on us. He had a grip of my arm, but finally let go, and I laid him, hopefully, on the wooden steps of a house. I managed to reach the high land just in time. I never saw the cripple afterwards, but I learned that he was drowned."

A Great Loss.

A tall, heavily built man, with tattered garments, walked along the platform with the help of a cane. His face was covered with a beard, and his head was bowed so that his chin almost touched his breast. One foot was partially covered by a cut shoe, while on the other foot he wore a boot from which the heel was missing. This was Stephen Johns, a foreman at the Johnson Steel Rail Works at Woodvale. He was a big, strong man, but his whole frame trembled as he said: "Yes, I am from Johnstown. I lost my wife and three children there, so I thought I would leave."

It was only by the greatest effort that Mr. Johns kept the tears back. He then told his experience in this way: "I was all through the war. I was at Fair Oaks, at Chancellorsville, in the Wilderness, and many other battles, but never in my life was I in such a hot place as I was on Friday night. I don't know how I escaped, but here am I alone, wife and children gone. I was at the office of the company on Friday. We had been receiving telephonic messages all morning that the dam was unsafe. No one heeded them. I did not know anything about the dam. The bookkeeper said there was not enough water up there to flood the first floor of the office. I thought he knew, so I didn't send my family to the hills.

"I don't know what time it was in the afternoon that I saw the flood coming down the valley. I was standing at the gate. Looking up the valley I saw a great white crowd moving down upon us. I made a dash for home to try to get my wife and children to the hills. I saw them at the windows as I ran up to the house. That is the last time I ever saw their faces. No sooner had I got into the house than the flood struck the building. I was forced into the attic. It was a brick house with a slate roof. I had intended to keep very cool, but I suppose I forgot all about that.

Swept Down the Stream.

"It seemed a long time, but I suppose it was not more than a second before the house gave way and went tumbling down the stream. It turned over and over as it was washed along. I was under the water as often as I was above it. I could hear my wife and children praying, although I could not see them. I did not pray. They were taken and I was left for some purpose, I suppose. My house finally landed up against the stone railway bridge. I was then pinned down to the floor by a heavy rafter or something. Somehow or other I was lifted from the floor and thrown almost out upon the bridge. Then some people got hold of me and pulled me out and took me over to a brickyard. My eyes and nose were full of cinders. After I reached the brickyard I vomited fully a pint of cinders which I had swallowed while coming through that awful stream of water. I can't tell you what it was like. No one can understand it unless he or she passed through it."

"Did you find your wife and children?"

"No. I searched for them all of Saturday, Sunday and Monday, but could find no trace of them. I think they must have been among those who perished in the fire at the bridge. I would have staid there and worked had it not been the place was so near my old home that I could not stand it. I thought I would be better off away from there where I could not see anything to recall that horrible sight."

How the Survivors Live.

With a view of showing the character of living in and about Johnstown, how the people pass each day and what the conveniences and deprivations of domestic life experienced under the new order of things so suddenly introduced by the flood are, an investigation of a house-to-house nature was made to-day. As a result, it was noted that the degrees of comfort varied with the people as the types of human nature. As remarked by a visitor:

"The calamity has served to bring to the surface every phase of character in man, and to bring into development traits that had before been but dormant. Generally speaking all are on the same footing so far as need can be concerned. Whether houses remain to them or not, all the people have to be fed, for even should they have money, cash is of no account, provisions cannot be bought; people who still have homes nearly all of them furnish quarters for some of the visitors. Militia officers, committeemen, workmen, &c., must depend upon the supply stations for food."

At Prospect.

The best preserved borough adjoining Johnstown is Prospect, with its uniformly built gray houses, rising tier upon tier against the side of the mountain, at the north of Johnstown. There are in the neighborhood of 150 homes here, and all look as if but one architect designed them. They are large, broad gabled, two-story affairs, with comfortable porches, extending all the way across the front, each being divided by an interior partition, so as to accommodate two families. The situation overlooked the entire shoe-shaped district, heretofore described.

Nearly every householder in Prospect is feeding not only his own family, but from two to ten others, whom he has welcomed to share what he has. Said one of these "We are all obliged to go to the general department for supplies, for we could not live otherwise. Our houses have not been touched, but we have given away nearly everything in the way of clothing, except what we have on. There were two little stores up here, but we purchased all they had long ago. It does not matter whether the people are rich or poor, they are all compelled to take their chances. In Prospect are the quarters of the Americus Club, of Pittsburgh, an organization which is widely spoken of as having distinguished itself by furnishing meals to any and every hungry person who applied."

An Incident.

As two newspaper men were about to descend the hill, after visiting a number of points, a little woman approached and made an inquiry about the running of trains. She was one of the survivors and wished to reach Clearfield, where her grown-up sons were. "I'd walk it if I could," she said, "but it's too far, and I'm too old now." She was living with her friends, who have taken care of her since her home was swept away.

A Distributing Point.

At the base of the long flight of wooden steps that lead to Prospect is the path extending across to the Pennsylvania Railroad station. Here is one of the principal distributing points. Three times each day a remarkable sight is here to be witnessed. Along the track at the eastern end, from the station platform back as far as the freight house, standing upon railroad ties, resting upon piles of lumber, and trying to hold their places in the line of succession in any position possible, crowds of people wait to be served. Aged, decrepid men and women and little girls and boys hold baskets, boxes, tin cans, wooden buckets, or any receptacle handy in which they may carry off provisons for the day.

Sad Sights.

The women have, many of them, tattered or ill-fitting clothing, taken at random when the first supply of this character arrived, their heads covered with thin shawls or calico sun shades. They stand there in the chilly morning wind that blows through the valley along the mountains, patiently waiting their turn at the provision table, making no complaint of cold feet and chilled bodies. In the line are people who, ten days ago, had sufficient of this world's goods to enable them to live comfortably the remainder of their lives. They are massed in solidly.

Guards of soldiers stand at short intervals to keep them back and preserve the lines, and sentries march up and down the entire length of the station challenging the approach of any one who desires to pass along the platform. For a distance of about one hundred feet to the railroad signal tower are piled barrels of flour, boxes of provisions, and supplies of all descriptions. Under the shed of the station an incongruous collection of clothing is being arranged to allow of convenient distribution. While they waited for the signal to commence operations, a guard entered into conversation with a woman in the line. She was evidently telling a story of distress, for the guard looked about hastily to a spot where canned meats and bread were located and made a movement as if to obtain a supply for the woman, but the eyes of brother soldiers and a superior officer were upon him and he again assumed his position. It is said to be not unusual for the soldiers, under cover of dusk, to overstep their duty in order to serve some applicant who, through age or lack of physical strength, is poorly equipped to bear the strain. All sorts of provisions are asked for. One woman asks boldly for ham, canned chicken, vegetables and flour. Another approaches timidly and would be glad to have a few loaves of bread and a little coffee.

No Discrimination.

Before complete system was introduced complaint was made of discrimination by those dealing out supplies, but under the present order of things the endeavor is made to treat everybody impartially. Provisions are given out in order, so that imposition is avoided. It would seem that there could be no imposition in any case, however. The people who are here, and who are able to get within the lines at all, have a reason for their presence, and this is not curiosity. They are here for anything but entertainment, and there is no possibility of purchasing supplies. All must needs apply at the commissary department.

A big distributing point for clothing is at the Baltimore and Ohio Railroad station, in the Fourth Ward, known as Harpville, on the east bank of the Stony creek. A rudely constructed platform extends over a washed-out ditch, partially filled with débris. In the vicinity is a large barn and several smaller outhouses, thrown in a tumble-down condition. Piled against them are beams and rafters from houses smashed into kindling wood. All about the station are boxes, empty and full, scattered in confusion, and around and about these crowds are clustered as best they can. A big policeman stands upon a raised platform made of small boxes, and as he is supplied with goods from the station he throws about in the crowds socks, shoes, dresses, shirts, pantaloons, etc., guessing as rapidly as possible at proportion and speedily getting rid of his bundle. Around the corner, on a street running at right angles with the tracks, is the provision department. These two are sample stations. They are scattered about at convenient points, and number about ten in all.

CHAPTER XVII.

One Week After the Great Disaster

By slow degrees and painful labor the barren place where Johnstown stood begins again to look a little like the habitations of a civilized community. Daily a little is added to the cleared space once filled with the concrete rubbish of this town, daily the number of willing workers who are helping the town to rise again increases. To-day the great yellow plain which was filled with the best business blocks and residences before the flood is covered with tents for soldiers and laborers and gangs of men at work. The wrecks are being removed or burned up. Those houses which were left only partially destroyed are beginning to be repaired. Still, it will be months, very likely years, before the pathway of the flood ceases to be perfectly plain through the town. Its boundaries are as plainly marked now as if drawn on a map; where the flood went it left its ineffaceable track. Nearly one-half of the triangle in which Johnstown stood is plainly marked, one angle of the triangle pointing to the east and directly up the Conemaugh Valley, from which the flood descended. Its eastern side was formed by the line of the river. The second angle pointed toward the big stone arch bridge, which played such an important part in the tragedy. The western ran along the base of the mountain on the bank of Stony Creek, and the third angle was toward Stony Creek Valley.

Miles of Buildings in the Wreck.

Imagine that before the flood this triangle was thickly covered with houses. The lower or northern part was filled with solid business blocks, the upper or southern half with residences, for the most part built of wood. Picture this triangle as a mile and a half in its greatest length and three-quarters of a mile in its greatest breadth. This was the way Johnstown was ten days ago. Now imagine that in the lower half of this triangle, where the business blocks were, every object has been utterly swept away with the exception of perhaps seven scattered buildings. In their places is nothing but sand and heaps of débris. Imagine that in the upper portion of this triangle the pathway of destruction has been clearly cut. Along the pathway houses have been torn to pieces, turned upside down, laid upon their sides or twisted on their foundations. Put into the open space on the lower end of the triangle the tents and the fires of burning rubbish and you will have the picture of Johnstown to-day.

Unheeded Warnings.

The people had been warned enough about the dangers of their location. They had been told again and again that the dam was unsafe, and whenever the freshets were out there were stories and rumors of its probable breaking. The freshets had been high for many days before that fatal Friday All the creeks were over their banks and their waters were running on the streets. Cellars and pavements were flooded. Reports from the dam showed that it was holding back more water than at any other time in its history. A telegraph despatch early in the afternoon gave startling information about the cracks in the dam, but it was the old story of the wolf. They had heard it so often that they heard it this time and did not care.

The first warning that the people had of their coming doom was the roar of the advancing wave. It rushed out of the valley at four o'clock in the afternoon with incredible swiftness. Those who saw it and are still alive say that it seemed to be as high as an ordinary house. It carried in its front an immense amount of battered wreckage, and over it hung a cloud of what seemed to be fog, but was the dust from the buildings it had destroyed. Straight across the river it rushed upon the apex of the triangle. It struck the first houses and swept them away in fragments. The cries and shrieks of the frightened people began to be heard above the roar of the floods, and a few steps further the great wave struck some unusually solid structure. Its force right in the centre was already diminished. On these houses it split and the greater part of it went on diagonally across the triangle, deflecting somewhat toward the north and so on down to the stone arch bridge.

Nothing Could Withstand the Flood.

Wherever it went the houses tumbled down as if they were built of cards. It was not alone the great volume of water, but the immense revolving mass of lumber it carried, that gave it an additional and terrific force, and houses, five bridges, railroad trains, boilers and factories were whirling furiously about. What could stand against such an instrument of destruction as this? It swept the triangle as clean as a board. It tore up pavements. It dug out railroad tracks, and twisted them into strange and fantastic shapes. It carried with it thousands of human beings, crushing them against the fragments, and drove their bodies into the thick mass of mud and sand which it carried at the bottom. It went on and on straight as an arrow, and piled masses of all it had gathered against and over the solid arches of the stone bridge. The bridge sustained the shock. How it did it engineers who have seen the effects and the marvellous strength of the flood in other places wonder. An immense raft of houses and lumber and trees and rubbish of every kind, acres in extent, collected here.

Roasted in the Debris.

In these houses were imprisoned people still alive, in numbers estimated at two or three thousand, tossed about in the whirling flood which was turned into strange eddies by the obstruction it had met. In some way not explained a fire broke out.

The frame structures packed in closely together were like so much tinder wood. Those who had escaped drowning died in their prisons a more horrible death.

While this was going on that part of the divided

stream which turned to the south continued on its way. At first its violence was undiminished, but as it went on the inclination of the land and the obstacles it met somewhat broke its force. It swept across the triangle, inclining toward the south, and was turned still further in that direction by the bed of Stony Creek, at the foot of the mountain which forms the western barrier of the basin in which Johnstown lies. Its course is plainly visible now, as it was two hours afterward. Where it started everything is cleared away.

A little further along the houses are still standing, but they are only masses of lumber and laths. Still further to the north they are overturned or lying upon their sides or corners, some curiously battered and as full of great holes as if they had been shot at with cannon. They are surrounded by driftwood and timbers, ground into splinters, railroad cars, ties and beams, all in a wild, untraceable jumble.

The wave reached to the north at least a distance of a mile from the point where it was divided. Then it swept backward. It carried with it many houses that had come from every part of the river.

At the Mercy of the Waves.

Upon them and upon flooded roofs and doors and timbers were men, women and children crying, beseeching and praying for help. Those on the shore who were watching this never to be forgotten spectacle saw the sufferers in the river go sweeping by, saw them come down again and still were unable to give them the slightest assistance. The flood proceeded half a mile or more, and then was met and reinforced by a wave started backward from the eddy formed at the stone arch bridge. With redoubled force it turned once more to the south and then it went half a mile further, toppling over the houses, wrecking some and adding some to those which it had brought down from other places. For the second time it spent its force and turned back, swept to the south and to destruction those who had four times been within sight of safety. This time the whole mass of flooded wreckage was carried down to the stone arch bridge and added to the collection there and at last to the fire that was raging.

Hundreds Will Never Be Found.

The blackened timber left from this fire, wedged in tightly above the bridge, is the only gorge at which workmen have labored all this week with dynamite and monstrous cranes. In it and below it are unnumbered hundreds of bodies. How many perished in that frightful fire will never be known. Only a small proportion of the bodies can ever be found. Some were burned so that nothing but a handful of ashes remained, and that was swept away long ago with the torrent. Some were buried deep in the sand, and some have been carried down and hidden in sand banks and slews. Many will be destroyed by dynamite, and some will have disappeared long before the great flood of rubbish can be removed. Of all the **horrible features** of this dreadful story none is more heartrending than the story of that fire. It began about five o'clock that afternoon and went on all night and all the next day, and smouldered until Monday noon. Its progress was retarded somewhat by the rain and by the soaking of the material in the water, but this was only an added horror, for it prolonged the anguish for those imprisoned in the great raft who plainly saw their approaching death.

Those who saw this sight from the shore cannot speak of it now and will hardly be able to speak of it as long as they live without tears. Imagination could not picture a situation more harrowing to human feeling than to stand there and watch that horrible scene without being able to rescue the prisoners or even alleviate their sufferings.

Ruins Left to Tell the Tale.

Just below the stone bridge are the great works of the Cambria Iron Company. They occupy the eastern bank of the stream for a distance of half a mile. The flood, tearing over the bridge, descended upon these works and tore the southernmost end of them to pieces. The rest of the buildings escaped, but none of the works were swept away in the torrent. An iron bridge used jointly by the public and by the iron company to transport its coal from the mines across the river was caught by the very front of the flood and tossed away as if built of toothpicks.

Looking from the stone arch bridge, the iron company's buildings, the lower town school house, three of the buildings which divided the flood, a church, part of a brick residence and a little cluster of brick business houses, is all that can be seen above the yellow waste. Why these buildings are left it is impossible to say. The school house, except for most of the windows being battered in and the scars and dents driven into it from the passing wreckage, is almost uninjured, although it stands directly in the centre of the flood.

Locomotives Swimming in the Torrent.

It is plain from the appearance of the buildings that the direction of the flood in many places was rotary, and the houses which still stand may have escaped between the eddies. No other explanation seems possible, for the force of the torrent was tremendous. It carried five lomotives, with their tenders, several miles, and piled them up against the stone bridge as easily as it carried a box of clothespins. At the head of the iron company's works was a great pile of iron in pieces eight feet long and a foot and a half thick either way. The flood toppled these over. In the half charred raft above the bridge are found great boilers, masses of iron, twisted beams and girders from bridges, heavy safes, pieces of railroad track, a hundred car wheels, mixed with every conceivable object of household use—pianos, sofas, dressing cases, crockery, trunks and their contents.

Yet in all that mass it is impossible to find any trace of that pile of bricks built into the business houses of the town; nor yet upon the banks, nor in the heaps of sand which, when the flood went down, were left here and there, is there any trace of the material of the building except the lumber. In the opinion of experts, all this stuff must have been ground into powder and swept down the river. Johnstown will never resume its former importance. A curse will hang over this beautiful valley as long as this generation lasts. The sanitary experts who have examined the place say that in all probability it will be plague ridden for years and years.

Decomposing Bodies in the Wreck.

The massive stone bridge of the Pennsylvania Railroad, opposite the Cambria Iron Works, marks the point of demarcation between the borough of Johnstown and that of Cambria City. The changes in the situation which have occurred since the eventful Friday have not been numerous. The wreckage impacted beneath the arches has been removed from three of them, leaving four, which are closed by masses of timber and drift material. I climbed over the débris in the famous cul-de-sac and reached the second from the Johnstown side after half an hour's labor. The appearance was singular. Beneath the conglomeration of timber which filled the cavity of the arch to a distance of twenty-five feet from the top the waters of the Conemaugh flowed swiftly.

There was a network of telegraph wires, iron rods and metal work of Pullman cars stretched across from stone work to stone work on either side. The gridiron, as it were, penetrated far down into the water, and it had proved sufficiently strong to resist the onward rush of the lighter flotsam which swept before the onrolling wave. Lodged in this strange pile was the body of a horse. Deep among the meshes a terrible spectacle presented itself. There were the bodies of three people—a woman, a child and a laborer with hobnailed shoes. They were beyond the reach of the workers who are clearing the wreck near to the bridge and the latter will be unable to reach the corpses until a considerable amount of blasting with dynamite has been done. There was a faint odor of decomposition and another day will cause the vicinity of the viaduct to suggest a charnel house to the olfactory senses. There are many other bodies, no doubt, beneath the débris and prevented from floating down the stream by the ruins.

Cambria City Paralyzed.

Conemaugh City was connected with the Cambria Iron Works, on the opposite side of the Conemaugh, by a temporary suspension bridge of steel wire. The bridge was originally for two railways—a narrow and a broad gauge—and a footway. It was swept away before the reservoir burst, according to all accounts. Cambria City, or rather a fringe of houses along the higher ground of the bank, the remaining portion of a once prosperous town, is absolutely paralyzed by the stunning blow which has befallen it. There are but few people at work among the débris. The clean sweep of the flood left little wreckage behind. A few sad-faced women wandered about and poked in the sand and among the broken stone which now covers the location of their former homes. The men who were saved have returned to their work at the Cambria mills, and the survivors among their families are stowed in the houses which remain intact. There must have been at least one thousand lives lost from Cambria City.

There has been no attempt to replace the bridge at "Ten Acre," as the point below Cambria City is called. The banks of the Conemaugh remain covered with débris. In many places the masses are piled twenty-five feet high. The people are clearing their land by burning the unwonted accumulations. Only an occasional body is found. Most of the 200 corpses which have been buried at Nineveh were found in the bushes which fringe the river. All the way to Freeport the accumulation of débris may be seen.

Kindly Care for the Helpless.

There is to-day no lack of supplies, save at Cambria City, which has been overlooked and neglected, but where the destitution is great. The people there are in great want of food. Bread has given out, and ham is about the only food to be obtained. In only one of the wrecked houses left untouched by the flood I found from twenty to twenty-five refugees. The commissary at the Pennsylvania Railroad depot is heaped so high with stores that distribution goes on with difficulty. The Grubbtown commissary is in the same condition. The Red Cross people got fairly to work in their supply tent to-day, and during the morning alone distributed five hundred packages of clothing.

Their hospital on the hill, back of Kernville, is in excellent order, and the patients quartered in the village houses are comfortably situated. There have been no deaths at the Cambria hospital. The doctors there have cared for 500 cases indoors and out. Even Grandma Teeter is doing well. She was taken out of the wreck at the bridge on Saturday with her right arm crushed. It had to be amputated, and the old woman—she is eighty-three years of age—stood the operation finely.

Miss Hinckley, of Philadelphia, is busy in Kernville making known the plans of the Children's Aid Society. She does an immense amount of running about and visiting houses. Many children made orphans by the flood are now being cared for. There are a hundred or more of them ; just how many no one knows.

"I have great difficulty," said Miss Hinckley to me to-day, "to persuade the people who have taken children to care for that our society can be trusted to take charge of what will surely be a burden to them. All my work now is to inspire confidence. We have received hundreds of letters from people anxious to adopt children. They are ready now in the first flush of sympathy, but I am afraid that they will not be willing to take the children when we are ready to place them."

Many Dead Still in the Ruins.

The ruins still shelter a ghastly load of dead. Every hour at least one new body is uncovered and borne on a rough stretcher to some one of the many morgues. The sight loses none of its sadness and pathos by its commonness; only the horror is gone, giving place to apathy and stupor. Stalwart men, in mud-stained, working clothes, bring up the body, the face covered with a cloth. The crowds part and gaze at the burned corpse as it passes. At the morgue it is examined for identification, washed and prepared for burial. Not more than half of these recovered now are identified.

The vast majority fill nameless but numbered graves, and the descriptions are much too indefinite to hope for identification after burial. What can you expect from a description like this, picked out at random: "Woman, five feet four inches tall, long hair?" The body of Eugene Hannon, twenty-two, found yesterday near the First Presbyterian Church, was identified to-day by his father. He was a member of the League of American Wheelmen, and his bicycle was found within a few yards of his body. The father will lay the wrecked bicycle on the coffin of his son.

Just now a woman, still young and poorly dressed, went by the shed where I am writing, sobbing most pitifully. She lost her husband and children in the flood and is on the verge of insanity.

Finding Solace in Work.

The day opened with heavy rain and an early morning thunder storm. The hill-side streams were filled to the banks and everything was dripping. The air was chilly and damp, and daylight was slow in coming to this valley of desolation and death. At an early hour the valley, where so many have gone to rest, presented a most dismal scene. It looked, indeed, like the valley of the dead. Nothing was moving, and all remained within the meagre shelter offered them till the day had fairly begun. As the day advanced, the tented hills began to show signs of life, smoke arose from many a camp fire, and on every eminence surrounding this valley of desolation could be seen the guards moving among the tented villages.

The weather was most unpleasant for any one to be outdoors, but it apparently had no effect on the people here, for as soon as the early breakfast was over the thousands of workmen could be seen going to their work, and soon the whole valley that in the early morning hours was asleep was a teeming throng of life and activity. While the rain was far from pleasant to the workers and many helpers, it was certainly providential that the cool weather is continuing in order to prevent the much-dreaded decomposition of the hundreds of human bodies yet unrecovered and the thousands of animals that perished in the flood. The air this morning, while tainted to some extent with the fumes arising from the decaying bodies, was not near so bad as it would have been had the morning been hot and sultry.

Working on the Stone Bridge Debris.

By seven o'clock the whole valley was full of people and the scene was a most animated one. The various sections of the flooded territory were full of men busy in searching for the dead, removing and burning the débris. At eight o'clock this morning five bodies had been taken from the mass at the stone bridge. A large force of men have been working all day on this part of the wreck, but so great is the quantity of wreckage to be gone over and removed that while much work is done very slow progress is being made. The continued falling of the river renders the removal of the débris every day more arduous, and where a few days ago the timbers when loosened would float away, now they have to be moved by hand, making the work very slow.

A most welcome arrival this morning was Dr. B. Bullen of disinfectant fame. He brought with him fifty barrels more of his disinfectant. The doctor will take charge of the disinfecting of the dangerous sections of the flooded district and notably at the stone bridge. Twenty-five barrels have already been used with most favorable results. Dr. Bullen was a former resident of Johnstown and lost thirty relatives in the flood, among them three brothers-in-law, three uncles and two aunts.

Clearing the Cambria Iron Works.

The Cambria Iron Company's Works presented a busy scene to-day. At least nine hundred men are at work, and most rapid progress is being made in clearing away the wreck. It is said that the works will start up in about three weeks.

There is little change in the situation. Every one is working with the one end in view, to clear away the wreckage and give the people of Johnstown a chance to rebuild. The laborers working at the Cambria Iron Works and on the Pennsylvania Railroad seem to be making rapid progress. This is no doubt for the reason that these men are more used to this kind of work. About ten o'clock the rain was over, and the sun came out with its fierce June heat.

A number of charges of dynamite were fired during the day, and each time with good effect. The channels through to the bridge are almost clear of débris, and each charge of dynamite has loosened large quantities of the wreckage.

This is the eighth day since the demon of destruction swept down the valley of the Conemaugh, but the desolation that marks its angry flight is still visible in all its intensity and horror. The days that have been spent by weary toilers whose efforts were steeled by grief have done little to repair the devastation wrought in one short hour by the potent fury of the elements. To the watchers on the mountain side all seems yet chaos and confusion. The thousand fires that spot the valley show that the torch is being used to complete the work of annihilation where repair is impossible and the smoke curls upward. It reminds one of the peace offerings of ancient Babylon.

Uncle Sam's Men on Hand.

The corps of government engineers that arrived last night has already demonstrated the valuable assistance which it is capable of rendering in these times of emergency. With but a few hours rest, those men were up ere sunrise this morning, and by eight o'clock a pontoon bridge had been stretched across the river at Kernville. Acting in conjunction with the Pennsylvania military authorities they are pursuing their labors at various other points, and by sundown it is confidently expected that pontoon bridges will be erected at all places where the necessities of traffic demand. It is the fact, probably not generally known, that the great government of the United States owns only 500 feet of pontoon bridges, and that these are the same that were used by the federal forces in the civil war, twenty-five years ago. The bridges that are to be used at Johnstown were brought from West Point and Willet's Point, where they have been for years used in the ordinary course of instruction in the military and engineer corps.

Secret Society Relief.

The following official announcements have been made:

A Masonic relief committee has been organized and solicits aid for distressed Freemasons and their families.

WILLIAM A. DONALDSON, Chairman.

OFFICE OF SUPREME COMMANDER, KNIGHTS OF THE MYSTIC CHAIN, WILMINGTON, DEL., June 8, 1889.—In view of the great calamity that has befallen our brothers at Johnstown, Pa., and vicinity, I, H. G. Rettes, Supreme Commander, request that wherever the Order of the Knights of the Mystic Chain exists there be liberal donations made for our afflicted brothers.

Affairs at the tremendous stone bridge wreckage pile seem to have resolved themselves into a state of almost hopelessness. It is amazing the routine into which everything has fallen in this particular place. Every morning at seven o'clock a score of Lilliputs come mechanically from huts and tents or the bare hill-side, and wearily and weakly go to work clearing away this mass, and at the rate they are now proceeding it will actually be months before the débris is cleared away and the last body found. Fortunately the wind is blowing away from us or we would have olfactory evidence that what is not found is far worse than what has been exposed.

Then it may be good business and good policy to have these few workers fool around the edge of the wreckage for five or ten minutes adjusting a dynamite blast, then hastily scramble away and consume as much more time before a tremendous roar announces the ugly work is done, but the onlookers doubt it. Sometimes, when an extra large shot is used, the water, bits of wood and iron, and other shapes more fearfully suggestive, fly directly upward in a solid column at least three hundred feet high, only to fall back again in almost the same spot, to be tugged and pulled at or coaxed to float down an unwilling current that is falling so rapidly now that even this poor mode of egress will soon be shut entirely off.

The fact of the matter is simply this: They are not attempting to recover bodies at the bridge, but as one blast tears yards of stuff into flinders it is shoved indifferently into the water, be it human or brute, stone, wood or iron, to float down toward Pittsburgh or to sink to the bottom, may be a few yards from where it was pushed off from the main pile.

Up in the centre of the town the débris is piled even higher than at the stone bridge, but the work is going on fairly well. The men seem to be working more together and enter into the spirit of the thing. Besides this, horses and wagons can get at the wrecks, and it really looks as if this part of the ruins has been exaggerated, and some of the foremen there say that at the present rate of work going on through the town all the bodies that ever will be recovered will be found within the next ten days. As to the condition these bodies are in, that has become almost a matter of indifference, except as to the effect upon the health of the living.

Compared with other Calamities.

An eye-witness writes as follows:

The scene is one that cannot be described in outline—it must be told in detail to become intelligible. Never before in this country, at least, was there a disaster so stupendous, so overwhelming, so terrible in its fierce and unheralded onset and so sorrowful in its death-dealing work. I traversed the Mill River Valley the day after the bursting of the Mill River dam. I went over Wallingford, in Connecticut, a few hours after that terrible cyclone had swept through the beautiful New England village. I stood on the broken walls of the Brooklyn Theatre and looked down upon hecatombs of dead sacrificed in that holocaust to Momus. Each of these was in itself a terrible calamity, but here is not only what was most terrible in all these, but every horrifying feature of the Mill River flood, the Wallingford cyclone and the Brooklyn Theatre fire is here magnified tenfold, nay, a hundred fold. And what is even more terrible than the scenes of devastation, the piles of dead that have been unearthed from the ruins and the mangled human bodies that still remain buried in the débris, is the simple but startling fact that this disaster ought not to have happened.

The flood was not due to the rains. This calamity is not the work of the unprovoked fury of the angry elements. This fair town and the populous valley above it, all the varied industries of this thriving city, all these precious lives are a sacrifice to the selfishness of a few men whose purses were bigger than their hearts. There would have been no flood if these rich men had not built an artificial pond in which to catch fish.

The now famous dam was only a mud bank. For years it was a constant menace to Johnstown and the Conemaugh Valley. It has long been only a question of time when the calamity that has befallen these people should befall them. It came at last because the arrogance of the purse and the pleasure-seeking selfishness of wealth were blind to the safety of a populous community.

The cause of the Johnstown disaster was wholly due

to the South Fork Fishing and Hunting Club. This club was specially chartered by the Legislature, and notwithstanding there was some opposition at the time, it was accorded the privilege of making an artificial lake and fish pond by means of an embankment. The site chosen was the old dam on South Fork Creek, about two miles above the village of South Fork, on the Conemaugh river. This dam was built by the Pennsylvania Canal in 1830 as a feeder to the canal below Johnstown. When the canal was finally abandoned, after passing into the hands of the Pennsylvania Railroad Company, the dam was sold to a private buyer for the very reasonable sum of $700. By him it was afterwards conveyed to the Fishing and Hunting Club for $1,400. This was about twenty years ago. The club spent $22,000 in rebuilding the dam and erected a beautiful club house on the west bank of the artificial lake. Beside the club house there are from twelve to fifteen cottages, the summer residences of members of the club, all built since the acquisition of the property twenty years ago. Ten of these cottages are visible from the embankment where the break occurred. It was a beautiful spot before the disaster, but this artificial lake in its placid beauty was a menace to the lives and property of the people in the Conemaugh Valley from its completion to its destruction.

The South Fork Fishing and Hunting Club was a very aristocratic and exclusive organization. Not even Tuxedo puts on more airs. It was composed of about seventy members, a baker's dozen of them Pittsburgh millionaires.

These wealthy gentlemen and their associates never so much as recognized the existence of the common clay of South Fork, except to warn all intruders to keep off the land and water of the South Fork Fishing and Hunting Club. Their placards still stare sight-seers in the face. One of these reads:

PRIVATE PROPERTY.

ALL TRESPASSERS FOUND HUNTING OR FISHING ON THESE GROUNDS WILL BE PROSECUTED TO THE FULL EXTENT OF THE LAW.

Another is as follows:

PRIVATE PROPERTY.

NO FISHING OR HUNTING ON THESE PREMISES, UNDER PENALTY OF THE LAW, $100.

SOUTH FORK HUNTING AND FISHING CLUB.

Only an Earthwork.

Strenuously as the club insisted upon exacting the fnll penalties and extent of the law for encroachments upon its privileges, it was quite heedless of the rights of others. There probably never was in the world a case of such blind fatuity as that of the South Fork Fishing and Hunting Club in building and maintaining its dam. From the first it must have been known to every member of the club, as it certainly was to every resident of the South Fork and Conemaugh Valleys, that if the water ever began to run over the breast of the dam the dam itself would give way. The dam was only a clay embankment. There was no masonry whatever—at least there is none visible in the break. The bottom was of brushwood and earth—some people in the South Fork valley say hay and sand. In consequence, the people below the dam who knew how it was built have always regarded it as a menace to their safety. Indeed, one man employed in its construction was discharged by the club or its contractor for protesting against the dam as insecure. His crime consisted in declaring that an embankment made in that way could not resist the force of an overflow. He was telling the simple truth, which was clear to every one except men disposed to take chances.

CHAPTER XVIII.

A Walk Through the Valley of Death.

In the following graphic narrative one of the eye-witnesses of the fearful ruin and slaughter represents himself as a guide, and if the reader will consider himself as the party whom the guide is conducting, a vivid impression of the scene of the great destruction may be obtained.

"Hello, where on earth did you come from? And what are you doing here, anyhow? Oh! you just dropped in to see the sights, eh? Well, there are plenty of them and you won't see the like of them again if you live a century. What's that? You have been wandering around and got tangled up in the ruins and don't know where you are? Well, that's not strange. I have been lost myself a dozen times. It's a wonder you haven't got roasted by some of those huge bonfires. But here, you come with me. Let me be your guide for the afternoon and I'll put you in the way of seeing what is left of Johnstown.

"First, let's climb up this bluff just before us and we shall have a first-rate view of things. Skip across this little temporary bridge over this babbling brook and now—climb! Whew! that takes your breath, doesn't it? But it is worth the trouble. Now you see we are standing on an embankment perhaps thirty feet high.

We are in the midst, too, of a lot of tents. It is here that the soldier boys are encamped. Off to one side you see the freight depot of the Pennsylvania Railroad and the tracks, you notice, run along on the top of this embankment. It is in that freight depot that Adjutant General Hastings has his headquarters. We will walk over there presently, but first let's take a look at our surroundings.

Prospect Hill.

"You notice, I suppose, that this flat spreading out before us at the bottom of the embankment is inclosed on all sides by mountains. They are shaped something like a triangle and we are standing at the base. Here, let me make a rough sketch of it on the back of this envelope. It will help us out a little. There! That figure 1 is the freight depot, near which we are standing. Towering up above us are houses and up there a canvas city for refugees. There is a temporary hospital there, too, and a graveyard, where many a poor victim of the flood lies. The background is a high hill. The people here call it Prospect Hill. The flood! Gracious! what a view the people up the hill must have had of it as it whirled, and eddied, and roared and rushed through the town, for this great flat before us was where the main portion of Johnstown stood.

"You notice that there are gaps in the mountain chains which form the sides of the triangle. Through the gap at our left comes the Conemaugh River, flowing from the mountain on its way westward. River, did I say? I don't wonder you smile. It doesn't look much like a river—that little bubbling stream. Can you imagine it swelling into a mighty sea, that puny thing, that is smiling in its glee over the awful havoc it has created? Now you are beginning to under-

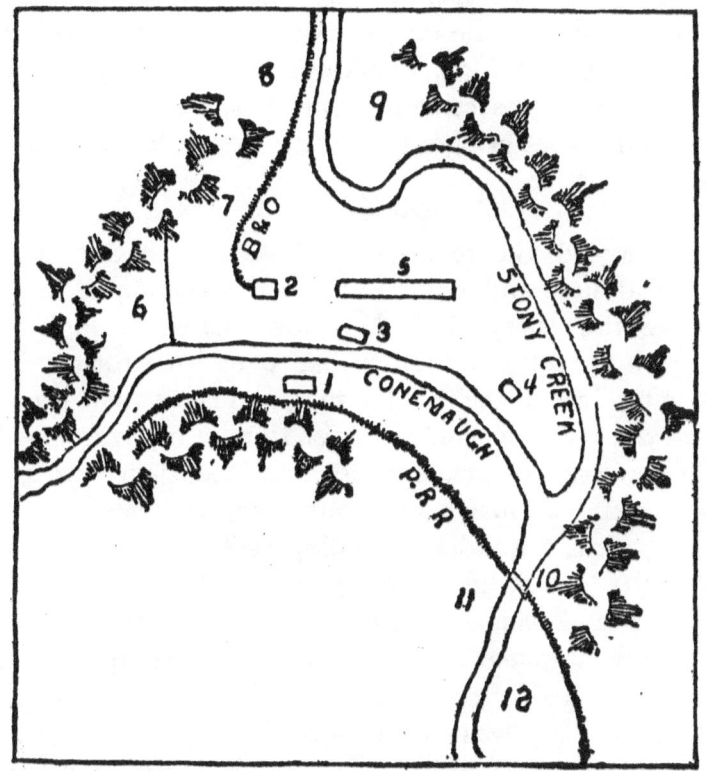

stand how it is that Johnstown proper lies within the forks of two streams. The Conemaugh runs by us at our feet to the right. See, there is a wrecked and overturned car down there. If thrown across the stream it would almost bridge it. That is Stony Creek on the other side of the flat, running down through that gap which forms the apex of the triangle. It skirts the mountains on the right and the two streams meet. You can't see the meeting point from here, for our embankment curves, but they do meet around that curve, and then the united rivers flow under the now famous stone bridge, which was built to carry this railroad across the stream. Oh! yes, we will go down there, for that bridge formed the gorge which proved so destructive.

Savage Fury.

"I would like to take you away up to the dam if we had time and point out the destruction all along down the valley until the flood rushed through that gap to the left and then spread over Johnstown. But it is too late in the day for that, and the walk is a most tiresome one, so you will have to take my word for it. Of course, you have read that the dam was constructed in a most outrageous manner. Well, that is true. It is a wonder the valley wasn't swept long ago. No, the loss of life wasn't great in the upper part of the valley because the people took the warning which the Johnstonians refused and mostly escaped. The little town of South Fork was badly shattered and Mineral Point was swept away.

"But the real fury of the flood is seen in its marks on the soil. Gracious! how it leveled forests, swept away bowlders, cut out new channels and destroyed everything in its path. I cannot begin to give you even an idea of the wonderful power of that flood.

At East Conemaugh not a vestige of the place was left. Where once stood a row of houses the river now runs, and the former river-bed is now filled with dirt and stones. It was in this vicinity, you know, where so many engines and cars were wrecked—smashed, twisted, broken and scattered along the valley for half a mile. It was here, too, where the passengers in the two trains met such a thrilling experience, and where so many of them were killed. The body of one of the passengers, Miss Bryan, of Germantown, was found away down here in Johnstown.

"It took but a few minutes for the flood to rush down upon Woodvale and sweep it out of existence, and then it made a mad break through that gap over there on the extreme left. The houses which you see on the hillside over there—figure 6—belong to Conemaugh borough, a different place from East Conemaugh, you understand. The borough also extended down over the flat. By the way, there is something very funny about all these separate boroughs. Most all of them are naturally parts of Johnstown—such as Conemaugh, Kernville, Cambria City, Prospect and the like, but there have been so many petty jealousies that they have refused to unite. But that is neither here nor there now, for in the common calamity they are one.

Laughing at Danger.

"Now you would have thought that the people on the Johnstown flat would have got out of the way when warned of danger, wouldn't you? But they simply laughed. You must remember that a good portion of the place was flooded long before the dam broke. The rise of the two rivers did that. The water ran from two to five or six feet high in some of the houses. But, bless you, that was nothing. The place had been flooded so many times and escaped that everybody actually howled down all suggestions of danger. Telegrams had been coming into town all the afternoon and they were received by Miss Ogle, the brave lady operator, who stuck to her post to the last, but they might as well never have been sent for all the good they did.

"Well, now with Johnstown spread out before you you can readily understand what happened when the flood burst through the gap. There was no time to run then. No time to pray, even. You notice the river makes a sharp curve, and naturally enough the impetus of the water spread it over a wide territory. The Conemaugh houses on the flat went down like so many pasteboard houses. A portion of the flood followed the stream and the other portion went tearing along the line of the hills which form the left side of the triangle.

Wiped Out of Existence.

"Now look away over to the left and then away over to the hills on the right, and what do you see? That distance is how great? Two miles, do you say? Yes, fully that and probably more. Well, now for two or three squares inland from this stream at our feet there is nothing but a barren waste of sand—looks like a desert, doesn't it? Can you imagine that all that immense strip was covered with stores, business houses and dwellings? Where are they now? Why, just look at that circular hole just beneath us on the other side of the stream. That was the gas works once. The great iron receiver, or whatever you call it, went rolling, dashing, crashing away before the flood, and not a vestige of it has been found yet. Can you ask, then, what became of the houses? Simply wiped out of existence.

"There! I put down the figure 2 on the map. It is a brick building, as you see, but there is a big hole knocked in it. That is the B. and O. depot. Figure 3—Two more brick buildings with one end completely gone. These are the Cambria Iron Company's offices and the company's stores. What else can you see? Just around the curve where I mark down figure 4 is another brick building—the Millvale school-house. It is out of range from this point, but you shall see it by and by. These buildings are actually the only ones left standing in all that desert of sand, a covering four or five feet deep left by the flood and hiding whatever is underneath as effectually as the ashes of Mt. Vesuvius blotted out Pompeii. There may be a thousand bodies under that sand for all that anybody knows. Just ahead of us in the great area roughly shown by this figure 5 lie the tents of the workmen engaged in putting Johnstown in order. Now, if you draw a line from the Conemaugh hills right down back of the B.

and O. depot through the camp of the workmen, and thence to Stony Creek, the only buildings you will find standing between us and that imaginary line are these I have already marked with figures as 2, 3 and 4 on the map. Did you ever see anything so destructive in your life?

A Famous Morgue.

"You say you see a good many buildings in what appears to be the centre of the town. So you do, but just wait until you stroll among them. There are many there, it is true, but after all, how many are good for anything? Oh! the water has been doing a tremendous amount of damage. Why, over there, up to the very foot of the hills—I will mark the spot No. 7—behind the buildings which you see, it has simply torn things up by the roots. That is the Fourth ward, and the ruins are full of the dead, and the Fourth Ward Morgue has had more bodies in it than any of the others.

"You remember that I told you that one current swept over that way. It caught up houses and they began to drift all over the place, crashing into each other and grinding people between the timbers. All this time the houses down here by the Conemaugh had been floating toward the bridge. Logs, boards, lumber and houses from the banks of Stony Creek had been coming down, too, and thus formed that tremendous jam above the stone bridge, which actually turned the current of the creek back upon itself. Some of the houses from the centre of the city and from the Fourth ward got into Stony Creek and actually went up the stream. Others floated all over town in circles and finally, having reached the Conemaugh, got caught in the jam at last and were destroyed by the fire which broke out there. After a

SELLING DAMAGED GOODS.

time, too, the pressure at the bridge became so tremendous that the river burst a new channel for itself and then many houses came down again.

"But I am anticipating. Let us walk down to the bridge—it is not far—for the bridge is the key to the situation. We must pass the freight depot, for we follow the track. You see it is a busy place. You know we have had a change of administration here, and Adjutant General Hastings is in command. We are all heartily glad of it, too, for the worst kind of red tapeism prevailed under the Pittsburgh regime.

"And then the deputies—a lot of brutes appointed by the Sheriff. What an ignorant set they were. Most of them couldn't even read. They were the only toughs in town. They had captured all the tomato cans left over from the great flood which the Bible tells about and had cut out tin stars to decorate themselves with. Anybody who could find a piece of tin could be a deputy. And how they did bulldoze.

"But all this is changed now. The deputies—we called them the tin policemen—have been bounced and the place is now guarded by the soldiers. Business has taken the place of red tape, and General Hastings has turned the freight depot into offices for his various departments, for a system has been established which will reach all the victims, bury all the dead, discover all the living and clean up the town. There is now a central bureau, into which reports are turned, and the old haphazard way of doing things has been swept as clean as the sand before us. There is General Hastings' horse standing at the steps, for the general is in the saddle most of the time, here, there, everywhere, directing and ordering.

"Dinner! hello, dinner is ready. Now you will see

how the officers at headquarters live. You see, the table has been spread on the platform facing the railroad tracks. Ah! there is Hastings himself—white slouch hat, white shirt, blue flannel trousers, and boots. He looks every inch a soldier, doesn't he? There! he is beckoning to us. What do you suppose he wants. Oh! he wants us to dine with him. Shall we? It will be plain fare, but as good as can be found. A dudish society reporter from Philadelphia dropped into town the other morning. He met a brother reporter from the same paper.

"'Oh!' he groaned. 'Where can I find a restaurant?'

"'Restaurant!' shrieked the other. 'Where do you think we are? Restaurant! You come with me and I'll try to steal you a ham sandwich, and you'll be mighty lucky to get that.'

"'Oh! but I am so hungry. Can you direct me to the nearest hack stand?'

"The brother reporter turned and fled in dismay, and the society man hasn't been seen around here since. But it illustrates the time the boys have been having getting anything to eat. So we had better accept the general's invitation. What have we here? Oh! this is fine. You don't mind tin plates and spoons and coffee cups, of course, especially as we have ham and potatoes, bread and coffee for dinner. That's a right good meal; but I tell you I have eaten enough ham to last me for a year, and when I get out of Johnstown and get back to Philadelphia I am going to make a break for the Bellevue and eat. And there wont be any ham in that dinner, you can bet.

A Renowned Building.

"Now, have you had enough? Then we will continue our walk along the tracks to the bridge. First we pass the Pennsylvania Railroad passenger station. What a busy place it is! The tracks are filled with freight cars packed with supplies, and the platform is filled with men and women ready to take them. In this station a temporary morgue was established. It has been moved now to the school-house, No. 4, you know, on the map. Now, as we round the curve you see it. That is the famous building that saved so many lives—the only one left in the great barren waste of sand. You know the water formed an eddy about it, and thus, as house after house floated and circled about it men and women would clutch the roof and climb upon it. The water reached half way to the ceiling on the second floor on a dead level.

"Now you can see where the two rivers come together. What a jam that was. It extended from the fork down to the bridge—No. 10. When the flames began to demolish it the pile towered far above the bridge. Now it is level with the water, but so thickly is it packed that the river runs beneath it. Let us stand here on the railroad embankment at the approach to the bridge, and watch the workmen. You notice how high the approaches are on either side, and you can readily understand how these high banks caught the drift. The stone arches of the bridge are low, you perceive. When the flood was at its height houses were actually swept over the bridge. From the débris left in the river and on the sides you can imagine what an immense dam it was that was formed, and just how it happened that the rivers turned back on themselves. I met a woman up Stony Creek early this morning. She was laughing over the adventure she and her children had. They floated down the creek to the bridge and then floated back again, and were finally rescued in boats. I asked her how she could joke about it.

"'Oh!' she said, 'I am never bothered about anything. I was as cool then as I am now, and rather enjoyed it.'

"But she wasn't very cool. She was bordering on the hysterical. She and her children are now living with friends, for their house was completely wrecked.

A Telegraph Office.

"A good many people had experiences similar to hers before the river broke through the railroad embankment just above the bridge here and swept tracks and everything else down upon the Cambria Iron Works. There they are, just behind us. I will mark them on the map—No. 11. Then the flow rushed through Cambria City, just below. That place is in a horrible condition—houses wrecked and streets full of débris. But there is no necessity of going there. You can see all the horrors you want right here.

"Look across the bridge, up the hill a little way. Do you see that old, tumble-down coal shed? It is where the Western Union established its office, and in that neighborhood most of the reporters have been living —sleeping in brick-kilns, hay lofts, tents, anywhere in fact. What a nice time they have had of it. They have suffered as much as the flood victims.

"Phew! What a stench. It comes from the débris in the river. It is full of the dead bodies of horses, dogs; yes, and of human beings. We hear stories occasionally of women being taken from that mass alive. They are false, of course, but there was one instance that is authentic. A woman was found one week after the flood still breathing. She had been caught in some miraculous way. She was taken to Pittsburgh, where she died. I was kicking about over the débris a day or two ago, and heard a cat mewing under the débris somewhere. I know half a dozen people who have rescued kittens and are caring for them tenderly. A flood cat will command a premium before long, I have no doubt.

"Ha! What's that? Yes, it is a body. The sight is so common now that people pay no attention to it. We have been living in the midst of so much death, of so many scenes of a similar character, that I suppose the sensibilities have become hardened to them. There, they are placing the body on a window shutter and are carrying it up to the school house. It will be laid on a board placed over the tops of the children's desks. You will notice coffins piled up all about the school house. Of course, the body is awfully disfigured and cannot be identified. The clothing will be described and the body hurried away to its nameless grave.

Fragment of a Bible.

"Have you enough? Then let us walk back toward headquarters and go down upon the flat into the centre of the town. What is that you have there? A piece of a Bible? Yes, you will find lots of leaves lying around. There is a story—I don't know how true it is—that many people have thrown their Bibles away since the flood, declaring that their belief, after the horrors they have witnessed, is at an end. I can hardly credit this. But there is one curious thing that is certain, and everybody has noticed it. Books and Bibles have been found in the rubbish all over the town, and in a great many instances they are open at some passage calling attention to flood and disaster. I have found these myself a dozen times. It is a remarkable coincidence, to say the least.

"Some people may find a warning in all this. I don't pretend to say, but as we walk along here let me tell you of a conversation I had with a man who was worth nearly $20,000 before the flood. He has lost every cent, and is glad enough to get his daily meals from the supplies sent here.

"'I don't know what to think of Johnstown,' he said. 'We have been called a wicked place. Perhaps all this is a judgment. Just when we have been most prosperous some calamity has come upon us. We were never more prosperous than when this flood overwhelmed us.'

"Well here we are back at General Hastings' headquarters. Now we will go down the embankment, cross the river and plunge ahead into town.

"Over this loose sand we will trudge and strike in by the Baltimore and Ohio depot. Now we are in the camp of the workingmen. Here are the stalls for the horses, too. The men, you see, live in tents. There are not as many of them as there will be; probably not over fifteen hundred to-day, but there will be twice that to-morrow, and five thousand men will be employed here steadily for a long time to come. Now let us jump right into Main street. It is the worst one in town. Just see! There is the post-office, looking as if it never would be able to pull itself out of the wreck. Across the street is the bank, with the soldiers guarding it. There, just ahead, you see a tall brick building lifting its head out of the midst of a pile of ruins. There is where many people were saved. The current carried scores of men, women and children past it, and those who had strength deserted their rafts and wrecks of houses and crawled into its windows.

"Now our progress is blocked. That immense pile of wreckage is by no means as high as it was; but you don't want to crawl over it yet. Phew! Let's get out of this. How those piles of rubbish do smell. You know the Board of Health says there is nothing the matter with Johnstown, but if the Board of Health would only take the trouble to nose about a bit it might learn a thing or two. You notice there have been grocery stores and markets around here, and you notice, too, the pile of decaying vegetable matter from them. These are worse than the dead bodies.

Horrible Scenes.

"Are there bodies under these ruins? Lots of them. There! what do you see this minute? Those workmen have discovered one in the ruins of the Merchants' Hotel. Poor fellow. He was pinned by falling walls, probably. A man was found there the other day with his pockets full of money. He had tried to save his fortune and lost his life. Near by a man was found alive after an experience of a week in the débris. He called for water, but never drank it. His tongue was too stiff, and he had not strength to move a muscle. He died almost as soon as he was found.

"Well, did you ever see such a mass of wreckage? It doesn't look as if there were twenty houses fit to live in all over this flat. But a good many will be patched up after a fashion, no doubt. And this is only one street out of several in the same condition.

"Hello! Those workmen are digging out of a cellar some barrels of whisky. That liquor will be guarded, for the old policemen and the 'tin' deputies have been having high old times with the liquor they have unearthed. There were formerly forty-five saloons in this town. Do you know how many there are left? Three. That's all. One saloon-keeper found $1,700 in the ruins of his place.

"Gracious! There is a freight car. It was caught

up half a mile or more away and dumped down in this street. And there is a piano sticking out. Hello! What have you found there? Oh, a looking glass. Yes, you find plenty of them in the rubbish almost as good as new. A friend of mine pulled out a glass pitcher and two goblets from that terrible mass at the bridge, and there wasn't a crack upon them. Queer, isn't it? But so it goes. Fragile things are not injured and stoves and iron are twisted and broken. The vagaries of this flood are many.

"I Thought You Were Dead."

"Turn this corner. Now, will you look at that? There is a house with the back all knocked out. The furniture has disappeared, but on the wall you see a picture hanging, and as I am alive it is a picture of a flood. What did I tell you a little while ago? Here is a house with its walls nearly intact. Next it is nothing but a heap of rubbish. Here is nothing but a cellar full of débris. Next it is a wooden dwelling. A man sits on the piazza with his clothing hung about him for an airing. And so it goes right here in the neigborhood of the main street, but if we pull out a bit from this place we shall see that the damage is a great deal greater. Through this break you can see the Presbyterian church. It is about ruined, but it still stands. If you go up stairs, what do you think you will see in that cold, dark, damp room? Stretched upon the tops of the pews are long boards, and stretched upon the boards are corpses. They have been embalmed, and are awaiting identification. But we won't go in there. All the morgues are alike, and we shall find another before long.

"Hark! There are two women greeting each other. Let's hear what they say.

"'Why, Eliza, I thought you were dead. How's all the folks? Are they all saved?'

"'Yes; they are all saved—all but sister and her little girl.'

"Well, that was cool, wasn't it? But you hear that on every corner. As I told you, in the presence of so much death the sensibilities are blunted. People do not yet realize their great grief.

"There, we are safely by the main street with its dangers of pestilence, for you noticed that it was reeking with filth and bad smells, and safely by the falling walls, for the workmen are tearing down everything shaky. Look out, there, or you will get scorched by that huge bonfire. They are burning all over town. Everything that the men can lift is dragged to these fires and burned. This is the plan for clearing the town. You noticed it at the bridge and you notice it here. Men with axes and -saws are cutting timbers too big to be moved, and men with ropes and horses and even stationary engines are pressed into service to tug at the ruins. Slowly the débris is yielding to the flames.

An Awful Sepulchre.

"Ha! now we are getting over by the hills into what is known as the Fourth ward. Here it is on our map —No. 7. What a sight! Most of the bodies are taken from the ruins here. As far as you can see there is nothing but wreckage—yes, wreckage, from which the foulest odors are continually rising and in the midst of which countless big fires are burning. Are you not almost discouraged at the idea of clearing so many acres up? Well, it does look like an endless task.

"There, you see that brick building? It is called the Fourth Ward School House. Do you want to go in? Piled up at one side are coffins—little coffins, medium sized coffins, large coffins—coffins for children, women and men. Oh! what a gloomy, horrible place. Stretched on these boards in this dismal room—what do you see? Corpses dragged from the river and from the débris. See how distorted and swollen are the faces. They are beyond recognition. Some have great bruises. Some are covered with blood. Some are black. Turn your head away. Such a sight you never saw before and pray God that you may never see it again. Nearly 250 bodies have been handled in this school house. Outside once more for a breath of air! Oh! the delightful change. But you are not yet away from the horrors. There is a tent in the school yard. What do you see? More coffins. Yes, and each one has a victim. Each is ready for shipment or burial.

20,000 to be Fed.

"Let's hurry along. Here on this corner is the temporary post-office. Over there is a supply station. There are eleven such departments now under the new management, and people are given not only provisions but clothing. You ought to see the women coming down from the hills in the morning for the supplies. Think of it! There are at least twenty thousand people in the flooded district to be fed for many weeks to come. You know there has been some comment because in the past all the money has not been used for food. I think it is a mistake. Where is charity to cease? In my opinion, the thing to do is to clean this town up, and give the business men and mills a chance to start up again. When this is done people can earn their own living, and charity ceases. I am backed up in this statement by Irwin Hurrell, who is a burgess of Johnstown, and knows everybody. Let me read you something from my note book that he said to me:

"'The people up in the hills have never had a better time. They won't work. They go around and get all the clothing they can and fill their houses with provisions.'

Thieves and Idlers.

"The burgess speaks the exact truth. Some of these houses are packed with flour and potatoes. The Hungarians and colored men and the "tin" deputies, now out of a job, have been the real thieves. They pulled trunks from the river, cut the locks and rifled them. There have been no professional thieves here. The thieves live here. Most of the respectable people were swept away by the flood, but nearly all the "toughs" were left. Now if I had my way I would make the survivors work. Some one said the other day: 'Why talk of sufferers? there are no sufferers. They are all dead.' This is true in a great measure. It is not charity to keep in idleness people who have lost nothing and won't work. I'd hunt them out and put them at it.

"Well, we will pass this supply depot, strike the Baltimore and Ohio track, and go up Stony Creek a bit. Notice the long lines of freight cars loaded with supplies. On our right runs the little river. On our left is Ward 7. I will note it as No. 8 on the map. You see there is a little stretch of plateau and then the ground rises rapidly. See what ravages the flood, made on the plateau. The houses are wrecked and filled with mud. The local name of this place is Hornertown. One man here had $60,000 in his house. It was wrecked. He dug away at the ruins and found $20,000. If we followed the stream up a mile or so we would come to the Stonyvale Cemetery. It is covered with logs and wrecks of houses. It was in one of these houses that the body of a woman was found last Saturday. She was sitting at a table. The house had floated here on the back water from down the river.

Red Cross Tents.

"There, I guess we have walked far enough. Here are the tents of the Red Cross Society, and by the side of them are those of the United States engineers. The engineers have thrown a pontoon bridge over the river, you see, to a place called Kernville. Here you are, No. 9 on our little map. Let us cross. By George! there is an old man on the bridge I have seen before. He lost his wife and two children in the flood, but he isn't crying for them. What bothers him most is the loss of a clock, but in the clock was $1,600.

"You see there is nothing new in Kernville. It is the same old story. Many lives have been lost here and the wreckage is something awful. The houses that remain are filled with mud and the ceilings still drip with water. People seem to have lost their senses. They are apparently paralyzed by their troubles. They sit around waiting for some one to come and clear the wreckage away.

"Well, it is a terrible sight and we will hurry through the place and cross to Johnstown flat, over another pontoon bridge further down. It brings us out, as you see, near the main street again. Hello! there is a man; there is his name on the sign—Kramer, isn't it? who is getting his grocery store open, the first in town. He was flooded, but carried some of his goods to an upper floor and saved them. Lucky Kramer! Here is a man selling photographs on the porch of a doctor's office. Dr. Brinkey. Oh, yes, he was drowned. His body was found last Monday.

"Well, we'll hurry by and get up to headquarters once more. It is 6 o'clock. See, the workmen are knocking off and are going to the river to wash up. Now, out comes the baseball, for recreation always follows work here.

"Once more on the platform of the freight station. Dusk settles down over the valley. An engine near by begins to throb and electric lights spring up here and there. All over the town the flames of the great bonfires leap out of the gloom. From the camps of the workmen come ribald songs and jests. The presence of death has no effect on the living.

"The songs gradually die away and the singers drop off into a deep sleep. The town becomes as silent as the graveyards which have been filled with its victims. Not a sound is heard save the crackling of the flames and the challenges of the sentries to some belated newspaper man or straggler.

"And thus another day draws to a close in ill-fated Johnstown."

CHAPTER XIX.

A Day of Work and Worship

Governor Beaver has assumed the command. He arrived in Johnstown yesterday, the 8th, and will take personal charge of the work of clearing the town and river. For that purpose $1,000,000 from the State Treasury will be made available immediately. This action means that the State will clear and clean the town.

It was a day of prayer but not a day of rest in Johnstown. Faith and works went hand in hand. The flood-smitten people of the Conemaugh, though they met in the very path of the torrent that swept their homes and families into ruin, offered up their prayers to Almighty God and besought His divine mercy. But all through the ruin-choked city the sound of the pick and the shovel mingled with the voice of prayer, and the challenge of the sentinel rang out above the voice of supplication. There was no cessation in the great task the flood has left them with its legacy of woe. Four charges of dynamite last night completed the wreck of the Catholic Church of St. John, which had been left by the flood in a worthless but dangerous condition.

The thousands of laborers continued their work just as on any week day, except that there was no dynamite used on the gorge and that the Cambria Iron Works were closed. There was the usual reward of the gleaners in the harvest-field of death, fifty eight bodies having been recovered. The most of those have been in Stony Creek, up which they were carried by the back rush of the current after the bridge broke the first wave.

Roman Catholic services were held in the open air.

Father Smith's Exhortation.

When the mass was over and Father Troutwine, who conducted it, had retired, Father Smith stood before them. "We have had enough of death lately," he said in a voice full of sympathy, "the calamity that has visited us is the greatest in the history of the United States. You must not be discouraged. Other places have been visited by disaster at times, yet we know that they have risen again. You must not look on the fearful past. The lives of the lost cannot be restored."

Here he paused because they were weeping around him, and his own voice was broken, but continuing with an effort, he told them to reflect for consolation upon the manner in which their friends had gone to death. They had looked to God, he said, and wafted in prayers and acts of contrition, their souls had left their bodies and appeared at the throne in heaven. "Surely never such prayers fell save from the lips of saints, and the lost of the valley are saints to-day while you mourn for them. God, who measures the acts of men by their opportunities, had pardoned their sins.

You who are left living must go to work with a will. Be men, be women. The eyes of the world are upon you, the eyes of all civilized nature. They listen, they wait to see what you are going to do."

Father Smith closed by telling them that the coming fast days of this week need not be observed in the midst of such destitution as this, and they might eat without sinning any food that would give them life and strength. When the father had finished the congregation filed slowly out past the high pile of coffins, for St. Columba's was a morgue in the days just passed.

The Protestant Services.

Chaplain Maguire held service in the camp of the 14th to-day. His pulpit was a drygoods box with the lid missing. It had been emptied of its freight into the wide lap of suffering. Before him stood the blue-coated guardsmen in a deep half circle. There was a shed at his back and a group of flood survivors, some in old clothing of their own, some in the new garments of charity. They were for the most part members of the Methodist congregation of Johnstown to which he had preached for three years.

"I hunted a long time yesterday for the foundations of my little home," he said, "but they were swept away, like the dear faces of the friends who used to gather around my table. But God doesn't own this side alone; He owns the other side too, and all is well whether we are on this side or the other. Are your dear ones saved or lost? The only answer to that question is found in whether they trusted in God or not. Trust in the Lord and verily ye shall dwell in the land and be fed."

It was not a sermon. Nobody had words or voice for preaching. Others spoke briefly and prayed. They sang, "Jesus, Lover of My Soul."

A Song in the Waters.

The shrill treble of the weeping women in the shed was almost lost in the strong bass of the soldiers. "Cora Moses, who used to sing in our church choir, sang that beautiful hymn as she drifted away to her death amid the wreck," said the chaplain. "She died singing it. There was only the crash of buildings between the interruption of the song of earth and its continuation in heaven."

Dr. Beale's Address.

Dr. Beale, whose own Presbyterian Church was one of the first morgues opened and who has lived among dead bodies ever since is the cheeriest man in Johnstown. He made a prayer and an address. It was all straight-from-the-shoulder kind of talk, garbed in homely phrase.

In the address he said: "I have been asked to say something about this disaster and its magnitude, but I haven't the heart. Besides I haven't the words. If I was the biggest truth teller in the world I could not tell the tale."

Then the preacher went hammer and tongs at the practical teachings of the flood. "That night in Alma Hall when we thought we would all die I heard men call on God in prayer and pledge themselves to lead better lives if life was given them. Since then I heard those same men cursing and swearing in these streets. Brethren, there was no real prayer in any of those petitions put up by those of godless lives that night. They were merely crying out to a higher power for protection. They were like the death-bed fears of the infidel, for I have seen seventeen infidels die and everyone showed the white feather. Nay, those prayers were unsanctified by the spirit, but let us who are here now living, dedicate ourselves to the service of Almighty God. There were those who were to be dedicated that night. I know one who, when it came, sent his family up the staircase, and taking up his Bible from his parlor table, opened at the 46th Psalm, first verse, and, following them, read, and the waters followed him closely. And through the flood he read the word of God and there was peace in that house while terror was all around it.

Mothering the Orphans.

Dr. Beale announced that Miss Walk wanted twenty-five children for the Northern Home and then began shaking hands with his congregation and pressing on them the lessons of his sermon. "Ah, old friend," he said, to a sandy moustached man in the grand army uniform, "You came safe out of the flood, now give that big heart of yours to Jesus."

The Baptist congregation also held an open-air service. The unfortunate Episcopal congregation is quite disorganized by the loss of their church and rector. They held no service, yet in a hundred temporary houses of the homeless the beautiful old litany of the faith was read by the devout churchmen.

The Soldiers' Sunday.

Sunday brought to the soldiers of the 14th no rest from the guard and police work which makes the Johnstown tour of duty everything but holiday soldiering. Even those who were in camp fared no better than those who were mounted guards over banks, stores and supply trains, or driving unwilling Italians to work down at Cambria City. There was no shade nor a blade of grass in sight. The wreck of the city was all their scenery, and the sun beat down upon their tents till they were like ovens. They policed the camp thoroughly, sweeping the bare ground until it was as clean as a Dutch kitchen. The boys had heard that Chaplain Maguire was to preach and they didn't leave a straw or a chip in his way.

A Young Guardsman's Suicide.

A sun-browned young soldier of C Company, 14th Regiment, sat on the river bank in front of the camp this afternoon and watched across the valley the fire-scarred tower of the Catholic Church, blown to complete ruin under the force of dynamite. After the front had sunk into a brick heap, he arose, looked down once at the sunny river and the groups of many soldiers doing there week's washing at the foot of the bank, and then strode slowly to his tent. A moment later there seemed to be a lingering echo of the fall of the tower in C Company's street. Captain Nesbitt, dozing in his quarters, heard the sound and

A RAILROAD TRAIN DELAYED BY THE FLOOD.

running in the direction of it found that **Private William B. Young**, aged 28, of Oakdale, had placed the muzzle of his rifle against his left temple and gone to swell by one the interminable list of the Conemaugh Valley's dead.

Despondency, caused by a slight illness and doubtless intensified by a night's guard duty among the gloomy ruins, is the only known cause of the soldier's act. He had been somewhat blue for a day, but there seemed to be no special weight upon his mind. His brother-in-law, private Stimmler, of the same company, said that he was always despondent when ill, but had never threatened or attempted his life. He was a farmhand, and leaves a wife and two children.

The Dinner "Shad" Jones Cooked.

The Sunday dinner was a great success. The bill of fare was vegetable soup, cold ham, beans, canned corn, pickled tripe and black coffee. It is worthy of note that the table in the officers' quarters did not have a delicacy upon it which was not shared by the men. The commissary ran short and had to borrow from the workmen's supplies. The dinner to-day was cooked by "Shad" Jones, a colored man known to every traveling man who has ever stopped at Johnstown for his ability to hold four eggs in his mouth and swallow a drink of water without cracking a shell. He lost his wife in the flood and the 14th has adopted him.

On this, the ninth day, the waters began to give up their dead. Stony Creek first showed their white faces and lifeless bodies floating on the surface, and men in skiffs went after them with their grappling rods. Several of them were taken ashore during the afternoon and carried to the Presbyterian Church morgue, which was the nearest. Then, too, the dead among the wreckage on shore came to light just the same as on other days. Their exhumation excites no notice here now. Dr. Beale, keeper of the records of morgues, counted the numbers on his finger tips and said there were more than fifty found to-day in Johnstown alone.

In one dead man's pocket was $3,133.62. He was Christopher Kimble, an undertaker and finisher, who, when he saw the water coming, rushed down stairs to the safe to save his gold and there he was lost. Several bodies were taken from the human raft burned beyond all recognition.

The body of Miss Bessie Bryan, the young Philadelphian, was identified to-day as it lay in a coffin by a grave from which it had been exhumed in Grand View Cemetery. "Returning home from a wedding in Pittsburgh with her friend, Miss Paulsen, caught by the flood on the day express, found dead and buried twice," will be the brief record of her wild sad fate.

Whiskey and Rioting.

Lieutenant Wright, Company I, with a detail of ninety-eight men, was called to the banks of Stony Creek over the raft to-night, to protect the employees of the Philadelphia Gas Company. There they found a gang of rioters. The rioters this afternoon found a barrel of whiskey in the field of débris, and before the militia could destroy it they had managed to take a large quantity of it up on the mountain. To-night they came down to the camp intoxicated, attacked the cook, cleared the supper table and were managing things with a high hand when a messenger was despatched for the guard. Before Lieutenant Wright's men reached there they had escaped. The Beaver Falls gang was surprised this afternoon by the militia, and gallons of whiskey, which they had hidden, were destroyed, A dozen saloons were swept into the creek at the bridge, and it is supposed that a hundred or more barrels are buried beneath the raft.

Among the most interesting relics of the flood is a small gold locket found in the ruins of the Hurlbut house yesterday. The locket contains a small coil of dark brown hair, and has engraved on the inside the following remarkable lines: "Lock of George Washington's hair, cut in Philadelphia while on his way to Yorktown, 1781." Mr. Benford, one of the proprietors of the house, states that the locket was the property of his sister, who was lost in the flood, and was presented to her by an old lady in Philadelphia, whose mother and herself cut the hair from the head of the "Father of His Country."

CHAPTER XX.

Millions of Money for Johnstown.

Never before in our country has there been such a magnificent exhibition of public sympathy and practical charity. As the occasion was the most urgent ever known, so the response has been the greatest. All classes have come to the rescue with a generosity, a thoughtfulness and heartfelt pity sufficient to convince the most stubborn misanthrope that religion is not dead and charity has not, like the fabled gods of Greece, forsaken the earth.

The following lines, cut from one of our popular journals, aptly represents the public feeling, and the warm sympathy that moved every heart:

I.

I stood with a mournful throng
  On the brink of a gloomy grave,
In a valley where grief had found relief
  On the breast of an angry wave!
I heard a tearful song
  That told of an orphan's love—
'Twas a song of woe from the valley below,
  To the Father of Heaven above!

II.

'Twas the wail of two lonely waifs—
  Two children who prayed for bread!
'Twas a pitiful cry—a mournful sigh—
  From the home of the silent dead!
'Twas a sad and soulful strain·
  It made the teardrops start;
'Twas an echo of pain—a weird refrain—
  And a song that touched my heart.

III.

Poor, fatherless, motherless waifs,
  Come, dry your tearful eyes!
Not in vain, not in vain, have ye sung your refrain;
  It's echo has pierced the skies!
The angels are watching you there,
  For your "home" is now above,
And your Father is He who forever shall be
  A Father of infinite love!

IV.

Blest be the noble throng,
  With generous impulse stirred,
Who are bringing relief to the Valley of Grief,
  Where the orphan's song was heard!
Peace to them while they live,
  Peace when their souls depart,
For a friend in need is a friend indeed
  And a friend that reaches my heart!

Among the first to start a fund for the sufferers was the New York *Herald*. The following is a specimen of the announcement made by that journal from day to day:

Great interest is being taken in the *Herald* fund for the Johnstown sufferers. In the city, employees of all sorts of business houses, and of railroad, steamboat and other companies, are striving to see who can collect the most money.

In the country, ministers, little girls, school children and busy workers are all collecting for the fund. It is being boomed by rich and poor, far and near.

With the checks for hundreds of dollars yesterday came this note, enclosing a dime:

" NEW YORK, June 8, 1889.
" MR. EDITOR:

"I am a little orphan girl. I saved ten cents, it is

all I have, but I should like to send it to the sufferers of the flood.

"ANNIE ABEL."

Another letter written in a lady's hand read this way:

"BROOKYN.

"DEAR HERALD:—

"Enclosed please find $1.17 left by little Hame Buckler in his purse when he died last September. Also twenty-five cents from Albert Buckler and twenty-five cents from Paul D. Buckler. Hoping their mites will help to feed or clothe some little ones, I am, with sympathy for the sufferers,

"S. A. B."

Felix Simonson, a twelve-year-old schoolboy, took it into his head on Friday to go among his friends and get help for the sufferers. Here is what he wrote on the top of his subscription paper:

"I am very sorry for the poor people who have lost everything by the flood, and I am trying to collect some money to send to them. Would you like to give something to help them?"

How Felix succeded is shown by a collection of $30.15 the first day.

A large amount of clothing for men, women and children is being sent to the *Herald* office, as well as liberal contributions of money.

The same story was, in effect, repeated from day to day. It only indicated what was going on throughout the country; in fact, throughout the world. London,

Paris, and other European towns, were only a few hours behind our American cities in starting funds for relief. The enthusiasm with which these responses were made is indicated by the following from one of the New York dailies:

Charity Running Rampant.

Everybody's business seems to be raising funds for Pennsylvania. The Mayor's office has been transformed into a counting room. More than a dozen clerks are employed in acknowledging the receipt of money for the Pennsylvania sufferers. A large number, many of them of the poorer class, bring their own contributions. Up to noon $145,257.18 had been subscribed. This does not include sums subscribed but not paid in. All the city departments are expected to respond nobly.

The Executive Committee of the Conemaugh Valley Relief Association met in the Governor's room at the City Hall yesterday, with General W. T. Sherman in the chair. Treasurer J. Edward Simmons announced that the fund in the Fourth National Bank amounted to $145,000 and that Governor Beaver's draft for $50,000 had been honored. John T. Crimmins reported that more than $70,000 had been received at the Mayor's office during the morning. He also reported that the Leake and Watts Orphan Asylum had offered, through the Rev. Dr. Morgan Dix, to take twenty-five of Johnstown's orphans, between the ages of five and twelve, and care for them until they were sixteen and then provide them with homes. H. C. Miner reported that many packages of clothing had been sent to Johnstown and that the theatrical guild was arranging for benefit performances.

Under date of Paris, June 5th, the following despatch conveyed intelligence of the gratifying response of Americans in that city:

Duty Nobly Done.

A meeting of Americans was held to-day at the United States Legation on a call in the morning papers by Mr. Whitelaw Reid, the United States Minister, to express the sympathy of the Americans in Paris with the sufferers by the Johnstown calamity. In spite of the short notice the rooms of the Legation were densely packed, and many went away unable to gain admittance. Mr. Reid was called to the chair and Mr. Ernest Lambert was appointed secretary. The following resolutions were offered by Mr. Andrew Carnegie and seconded by Mr. James N. Otis:

A Sympathetic Message.

"Resolved, That we send across the Atlantic to our brethren overwhelmed by the appalling disaster at Johnstown our most profound and heartfelt sympathy. Over their lost ones we mourn with them, and in every pang of all their misery we have our part.

"Resolved, That as American citizens we congratulate them upon and thank them for the numerous acts of noble heroism displayed under circumstances calculated to unnerve the bravest. Especially do we honor and admire them for the capacity shown for local self-government upon which the stability of republican institutions depends, the military organizations sent from distant points to preserve order during the chaos that supervened having heen returned to their homes as no longer required within forty-eight hours of the calamity. In these few hours the civil power recreated and asserted itself and resumed sway without the aid of counsel from distant authorities, but solely by and from the inherent power which remains in the people of Johnstown themselves."

Brief and touching speeches were made by General Layton, late United States Minister to Austria ; Mr. Abram S. Hewitt, General Meredith Read and others.

A Flow of Dollars.

The resolutions were then unanimously adopted and a committee was appointed to receive subscriptions. About 40,000f. were subscribed on the spot. The American bankers all agreed to open subscriptions the next day at their banking houses. "Buffalo Bill" subscribed the entire receipts of one entertainment to be given under the auspices of the committee.

As a sequel to the foregoing the following will be of interest to the reader:

NEW YORK, June 17.—John Monroe & Co. have received cable instructions from United States Minister Reid, at Paris, to pay Messrs. Drexel & Co., of Philadelphia, an additional sum of $2,266, received from the Treasurer of the Paris Johnstown Relief Committee. Of this sum $1066 are the proceeds of a special performance by the Wild West show, and with the previous contribution from Paris makes a total of $14,161.

THE JOHNSTOWN HORROR. 495

The pathetic story of sympathy and generous aid from every town and hamlet in the land can never be told; there is too much of it.

Philadelphia alone contributed over a million dollars, and New York showed equal generosity. In Philadelphia it was not uncommon to see glass jars in front of stores and at other places to receive con-

CONTRIBUTING TO THE RELIEF FUND IN PHILADELPHIA.

tributions from passers-by. In one of these an unknown man deposited $500 one day; this is indicative of the feeling pervading the whole community that stricken Johnstown must not suffer for houses, clothing, nor bread.

So rapidly did gifts pour in that within eight days after the disaster the following statement was made from Harrisburg:

The Governor's fund for the relief of the survivors of the flood in the Conemaugh Valley and other portions of the State is assuming large proportions and the disposition to contribute appears to be on the increase. To-day letters and telegrams were received requesting the Governor to draw for $68,000 additional, swelling the aggregate sum at his disposal to about $3,000,000. Many of the remittances are accompanied with statements that more may be expected. Governor Beaver telegraphed as follows from Johnstown:

"The situation is simply indescribable. The people have turned in with courage and heroism unparalleled. A decided impression has been made on the débris. The next week will do more, as they have many points opened for work. Everything is very quiet. People are returning to work again and gaining courage and hope as they return. There need be no fear of too much being contributed for the relief of the people. There is a long, steady pull ahead requiring every effort and determination on the part of the people here, which is already assured, and the continued systematic support and benefactions of this generous people."

Feeding the Hungry.

Three car loads of tents, enough to accommodate four thousand people, were sent to Johnstown to-day from the State arsenal at the request of General Hastings.

The following special dispatch bears date of June 5th:

Car loads of provisions and clothing are arriving hourly and being distributed. The cynic who said that charity and gratitude were articles seldom to be met with in Republics and among corporations would have had ample reason afforded him to-day to alter his warped philosophy several degrees had he been in this erstwhile town and seen train after train hourly rolling in, on both the Baltimore and Ohio and the Pennsylvania railroads, laden with clothing and provisions from every point of the compass. Each train bore messengers sent especially to distribute funds and provisions and clothing, volunteer physicians in large numbers, trained nurses and a corps of surgeons equipped with all needed instruments and medicines. Fortunately the latter are not needed.

Philadelphia's quota consists of clothes, boots, shoes, cotton sheeting, hard breads, salt fish, canned goods, etc., all of which will be gratefully received and supply the most pressing needs of the stricken people.

Relief Systematized.

The relief work has been so systematized that there is no danger of any confusion. At the several distributing depots hundreds assemble morning, noon and night, and, forming in line, are supplied with provisions. Men and women with families are given bread, butter, cheese, ham and canned meats, tea or coffee and sugar, and unmarried applicants sliced bread and butter or sandwiches.

The 900 army tents brought on by Adjutant-General Axline, of Ohio, have been divided, and two white-walled villages now afford shelter to nearly six thousand homeless people.

At the Main Commissary.

At the Johnstown station, on the east side of the river, everything is quiet, and considerable work is being done. This is the chief commissary station, and this morning by two o'lock 15,000 people were fed and about six hundred families were furnished with provisions. Five carloads of clothing were distributed, and now almost every one is provided with clothing.

The good work done by the relief committees in caring for the destitute can never be fully told. It was ready, generous and very successful.

The scenes at the distributing points through the week have been most interesting. Monday and Tuesday saw lines of men, women and children in the scantiest of clothing, blue with cold, unwashed and dishevelled, so pitifully destitute a company as one would wish to see. Since the clothing cars have come the people have assumed a more presentable appearance and food has brought life back to them and warmth, but their condition is still pitiful. The destitute ones are almost altogether from the well-to-do people of Johnstown, who have lost all and are as poor as the poorest.

Altoona to the Rescue.

Altoona has been so hemmed in by floods and the like, and her representatives have been so busy, that they had but little to say of the prompt action and excellent work done by open-handed citizens of that beautiful interior Pennsylvania city. Altoona first became alarmed by the non-arrival and reported loss of the day express east on the Pennsylvania Railroad Friday afternoon. Soon the station was thronged with an anxious crowd, and the excitement became intense as the scant news came slowly in. Saturday the anxiety was relieved by a telegram from Ebensburg, which a blundering telegraph operator made "three hundred lost," instead of "three thousand." That was soon corrected by later news, and the citizens immediately were called upon to meet for action. The Mayor presided, and at once $2,600 was subscribed and provisions offered. By three o'clock that afternoon a car had been loaded and started for Ebensburg, thirty-two miles away in charge of a committee. At Ebensburg that evening ten teams were secured after much trouble and the supplies sent overland seventeen miles to the desolated valley. The night was an awful one for the committee in charge. The roads were badly washed and all but impassable. The hours dragged on. At last, Sunday morning, the wagons drove into desolate Conemaugh. There were no cheers to greet them, no cries of pleasure. The wretched sufferers were too wretched, too dazed for that. They simply crowded around the wagons, pitifully begging for bread or anything to eat.

The committee report: " Impostors have not bothered us much, and, singular enough, the ones that have were chiefly women, though to-day we sent away a man who we thought came too frequently. On questioning he owned up to having fifteen sacks of flour and five hams in his house. On Tuesday we began to keep a record of those who received supplies, and we have given out supplies to fully 550 families, representing 2,500 homeless people. Our district is only for one side of the river. On the other is a commissary on Adams street, near the Baltimore and Ohio Railway station, another at Kernville, a third at Cambria City, a fourth at Morrellville and a fifth at Cambria. The people are very patient, though, of course, in their present condition they are apt to be querelous.

Wanted A Better Dress.

"One woman who came for a dress indignantly refused the one I offered her." 'I don't want that,' she said. 'I lost one that cost me $20, $15 for the cloth and $5 for making, and I want a $20 dress. You said you would make our losses good;' and she did not take the dress.

"A clergyman came to me and begged for anything in the shape of foot covering. I had nothing to give him. Men stand about ready to work, but barefooted. The clothing since the first day or two, when we got only worn stuff, fit only for bandages, has been good, and is now of excellent quality. Most of the children's garments are outgrown clothes, good for much service. Pittsburgh has sent from thirty to forty car loads of supplies, all of good quality and available, and in charge of local commissary men who had sense enough to go home when they turned over their supplies and did not stay and eat up the provisions they brought.

Ohio's Timely Work.

"But above all, I want to praise the supplies sent by the Ohio people in Cleveland and Columbus. These cities forwarded eight cars each. These were stocked with beautiful stuff, wisely chosen, and were in charge of Adjutant General Axline, sent by Governor Foraker, who worked like a wise man."

Grave Mental Conditions.

The mental condition of almost every former resident of Johnstown is one of the gravest character, and the reaction which will set in when the reality of the whole affair is fully comprehended can scarcely fail to produce many cases of permanent or temporary insanity. Most of the faces that one meets, both male and female, are those of the most profound melancholia, associated with an almost absolute disregard of the future. The nervous system shows the strain it has borne by a tremulousness of the hand and of the lip in man as well as in woman. This nervous state is further evidenced by a peculiar intonation of words, the persons speaking mechanically, while the voices of many rough looking men are changed into such tremulous notes of so high a pitch as to make one imagine that a child on the verge of tears is speaking. Crying is so rare that I saw not a tear on any face in Johnstown, but the women that are left are haggard, with pinched features and heavy, dark lines under their eyes. Indeed the evidence of systemic disturbance is so marked in almost every individual who was present at the time of the catastrophe that it is possible with the eye alone to separate the residents from those outside.

Everything required in the way of surgical appliances seem to be on hand, but medicines are scarce, and will probably be needed more in the next few days than heretofore.

A fact in favor of the controlling of any malady is to be found in the very general exodus of the town's people, who crowd the platforms of departing trains. There can be no doubt that this movement should be encouraged to the greatest possible extent, and it would be well if places away from Johnstown, at no too great distance, could be opened for the reception of those who, while not entirely disabled, are useless at home. The scarcity of pure spring water which is not tainted by dead animal matter is a pressing evil for consideration, but we doubt if this is as important a fact at Johnstown as it is further down the river, owing to the large amount of decomposing flesh in the water at this latter point. No disinfectant can reach such a cause of disease save the action of the large volume of water which dilutes all poisonous materials.

The Torch for Safety.

There is a strong movement on foot in favor of applying the torch to the wrecked buildings in Johnstown, and although the suggestion meets with strong opposition at this time, there is little doubt the ultimate solution of existing difficulties will be by this method. An army of men have been for two days employed in clearing up the wreck in the city proper, and although hundreds of bodies have been discovered, not one-fifth of the ground has yet been gone over. In many places the rubbish is piled twenty or thirty feet high, and not infrequently these great drifts cover an area of nearly an acre. Narrow passages have been cut through in every direction, but the herculean labor of removing the rubbish has yet hardly begun.

At a meeting of the Central Relief Committee this afternoon General Hastings suggested the advisability of drawing a cordon around the few houses that are not in ruins and applying the torch to the remaining great sea of waste. He explained briefly the great work yet to be accomplished if it were hoped to thoroughly overhaul every portion of the débris, and insisted that it would take 5,000 men to complete the task. Of the hundreds of bodies buried beneath the rubbish, sand and stones, the skeleton or putrid remains of many was all that could be hoped to be recovered.

A motion was made that after forty-eight hours' further search the débris of the city be consumed by fire, the engines to be on hand to play upon any valuable building that despite previous precautions, might become ignited by the general conflagration. This motion was debated pro and con for nearly half an hour. Those whose relatives or friends still rest beneath the wreck remonstrated strongly against any such summary action. They insisted that all the talk of threatened epidemic was only the sensation gossip of fertile brains and that the search for the bodies should only be abandoned as a last extremity. The physicians in attendance warned the committee that the further exposure of putrid bodies in the valley could have but one result—the typhus or some other epidemic equally fatal to its victims. It was a question whether the living should be sacrificed to the dead, or whether the sway of sentiment or the mandate of science should be the ruling impulse. Although the proposition to burn the wreck was defeated, it was evident that the movement was gaining many adherents, and the result will doubtless be that in a few days the torch will be applied, not only to the field of waste in Johnstown, but also to the avalanche of débris that chokes the stream above the Pennsylvania bridge.

CHAPTER XXI.

Order Out of Chaos.

The final acts in the great calamity, the horror which wrung the heart of the world, can be briefly told.

For many weeks the gigantic work of clearing away the ruins went on. No person who has not been an actual eye-witness of the awful havoc made by the rush of waters, can conceive of the labor and effort required to undo the devastation which presented its ghastly memorials everywhere throughout the fated valley. The flood was no respecter of places or buildings. Wherever there was a chance for a mad rush, the rush came, and consequences were left to themselves. How little was the time required to blast and destroy the fruits which patient industry had been accumulating for years!

Then came the very serious question, what could be done to repair the almost infinite damage, restore the homes of thousands who had suffered, and render Johnstown and other places as fit for habitation as they were before the dreadful disaster occurred? Could those mountainous piles of rubbish ever be cleared away? Could that immense mass of broken houses and debris lodged at the bridge, within which human beings were buried—no one could guess how many—ever be broken up? Of course it was not expected that Johnstown would ever appear just as it did before the flood. To reproduce a town that had been swept away with such awful fury would be impossible; the only thing to be attempted was to prepare places for new streets and buildings, and get ready to plant a new town on the ruins of the one that once was.

The reader, however, will understand that a considerable part of Johnstown remained, was not affected by the flood to any serious extent, and looks now very much as it did before the visitation came.

A Host of Workmen.

As soon as the first terrible shock was over and the extent of the calamity was known the whole country, the State of Pennsylvania especially, sprang to the rescue. There was money to pay the laborers, and there were men ready to work. Thousands were still looking for their dead, and day after day wandered aimlessly about, carrying a painful anxiety upon their faces, and an appearance of having been dazed and stunned by some overwhelming disaster, but other thousands who were not among the sufferers, coming from places near and remote, were prepared for action, and under the supervision of Gen. Hastings and various Relief Committees were set to work.

The Pennsylvania Railroad Company re-opened its regular office on June 10th. Meanwhile the Company put forth almost superhuman exertions to get its road in repair. One of the most important arteries of travel and freight transportation had been cut. One of the great belts binding the East and West together had been broken. The flood occurred at a time which was most unfortunate for the Company. The summer travel was commencing, and it was important that the road, so splendidly equipped, should be in good working order to meet the heavy demands.

Then, too, there were large manufacturing establishments under written contract to furnish goods to their customers on certain dates. The amount of business that would be disarranged and trouble that would be caused unless travel and traffic were immediately resumed could not be computed nor even imagined.

Labor Night and Day.

The Company was equal to the emergency, and in an incredibly brief space of time the great highway began to roar again with traffic. Temporary bridges were constructed for the passage of trains until permanent ones could be built. An army of workmen labored by day, and others, under electric lights, worked at night. There was an interruption in the operations of the road of only about a week's duration.

The Cambria Iron Works, of which the reader has heard so much, resumed operations on June 10th. Previous to this the company ordered two million feet of lumber to build houses for its employees. Happily the furnaces had suffered but little injury, and the hundreds of laborers who had survived the flood and reported for duty made short work of the ruins, and speedily put the works in condition to begin operations. At once matters began to assume a more hopeful aspect. This great concern had been a heavy loser, but resolved to face the calamity bravely, and such a resolve carried good cheer and hope throughout the stricken district.

Doings of the Relief Committee.

Under date of June 17th, a newspaper correspondent wrote as follows :

"The Relief Committee have decided to erect a hundred portable houses to shelter the survivors as soon as the buildings can be received from Chicago. The houses will be twelve by twenty-six feet, and will be large enough to accommodate six persons each. Each house will be furnished with a stove and utensils, six chairs, two beds and bedclothes, two spring mattresses, one pair pillows, two pairs of sheets for each bed, woolen blankets, a bureau, a table, and table-ware to set it. In fact, a family will be given everything necessary to go to housekeeping, and told to go ahead and paddle their own canoe. The object is to start the town on toward a rise from the ruins, but as the town is yet in chaos, it is impossible to make permanent arrangments. The grade of the town may be raised. If a man cannot find his own ground now, he can set his house up anywhere, and move it on to his land when it is found under the debris. If the houses give satisfaction, the Committee will not stop at buying a thousand of them, and building up the town. In conjunction with this move at building up the ruined city, General Hastings has purchased an immense quantity of lumber, and will next Tuesday begin building shanty stores for those who will set up in business again. Over a hundred have already made application.

"Arrangements are now being made for the erection of a lock-up, which Burgess Hovell says will be filled as soon as completed with persons who have been filling their houses with valuables from the wreckage. Many citizens, who have hitherto been considered honest, are known to have entered wrecked houses and carried off valuables by the armful. As soon as the Burgess can get his affairs straightened out, he says he will issue search-warrants, and every house that is suspected of containing booty will be turned wrongside up."

The Governor at the Front.

Two days later the situation was thus described: "Governor Beaver and the Flood Commission arrived here just before noon, and, accompanied by General Hastings, made a tour of the devastated district on horseback, dining afterward at headquarters. The visit of Governor Beaver and the Flood Commission has borne practical fruit. The visitors met the Finance Committee of the Citizens' Relief Committee at Alma Hall, and discussed the situation in all its details. The Commission expressed itself as amazed at the extent and completeness of the devastation, and pledged itself to render the citizens of the place all the aid in its power. The local Committee presented a list of their wants, and, after canvassing the demands, the

Commission authorized the immediate purchase of five hundred of the Chicago ready-made houses on its account, and also the erection of all the store buildings that may be asked for by local merchants. The Governor and Commission went immediately to their special train after the adjournment of the conference, and departed for Cresson, whence they will go on a trip through the other devasted districts of the State.

Trouble Brewing.

"A big strike is imminent among the laborers employed upon the public works here. Trouble has been brewing for several days, in consequence not only of the scarcity of the food supply, but of the poor quality of the rations furnished, as well as dissatisfaction with the pay. This trouble culminated to-night at a meeting of the Booth and Flinn men, who are especially dissatisfied. They appointed a committee of five to wait upon General Hastings and request his good offices on their behalf. The committee made a long statement of their grievances. They claim that they had had nothing to eat since morning, and that the food they do get is of an inferior quality. They also say that although they engaged to do work at the rate of one dollar and fifty cents per day, they are required to work on the drift at night without extra pay. They said that they should have one dollar and seventy-five cents per day, and requested General Hastings to intercede with their employers in their behalf, threatening to strike if their demands are not complied with. General Hastings promised to bring the matter to the

THE JOHNSTOWN HORROR.

attention of the contractors, but said that was all he could do. It is generally believed that the action taken presages a general strike unless the demand for one dollar and seventy-five cents per day is conceded." The strike, it should be added, did not occur.

A Later Report.

More than six weeks after the catastrophe, another careful recorder made these observations: "Though the work already accomplished is great, as much or more remains undone. Only the lumber has been removed from the debris, while sand, dirt, bricks and stones form a mass several feet thick over the whole town. Railroad cars and wrecked houses that were washed away from their foundations are still seen in various parts of town.

"The rivers are half filled with debris, which has withstood all efforts to move it, and the wreck at the stone bridge is as bad in the bed of the stream now as it was against the bridge immediately after the flood. A few business houses have been erected in addition to the Park stands, but these are mostly plank structures composed of flood lumber, and fit only for stables. The people themselves have shelter for the present in one-story ten-by-twenty houses without plastering or any other provision against the elements.

Promoting the General Good.

"All these facts combine to make the most prominent citizens anxious as to the outcome, But notwithstanding this, there seems to be more than a desire on the part of the citizens to do their utmost to restore their homes and business. To this end some of the leading spirits are working to secure the consolidation of the fourteen boroughs. A report from the committee on this subject was to have been made last Monday, but was withheld or not made for good reasons. These reasons appear to be that Conemaugh borough opposes the scheme, and that some of the politicians in the others fear to let go their hold lest they never recover it. Nobody denies that it would inure to the benefit of all the boroughs to consolidate. It seems to be the only method by which the town will ever become what it was. Within the past few days the greatest barrier to consolidation has been overcome and, it is said, the committee will soon present a report that will meet with general approval.

"Moxham, where are situated the Johnson Company steel rail works, has had a boom since the flood. The place, situated about two miles south of the town, was but slightly injured by the water, and is connected with Johnstown by a rapid transit railroad. Most of the professional men have ordered houses to be erected here immediately. A select school will be opened, and all preparations are being made to accommodate the increased population.

"Superintendent Duncan, of the street railway, is authority for the statement that the horse railway will be replaced by one operated by electricity. This was probably brought about by negotiations with T. L. Johnson, of the Johnson Steel Rail Company, who has been known to favor such a plan for some time, and who will likely become a heavy stockholder in the new arrangement."

Fire Added to Flood.

Troubles, it is said, never come singly; for some singular reason they come in groups and clusters; one appears to draw on another, and that a third, until one would think all the vials of wrath were suddenly emptied. Poor Johnstown had already suffered the direst woes; the bitter cup of agony had been pressed to her lips, but, as if one element in nature had been exhausted, another came to complete the work of destruction.

Fire broke out on the 24th of June, and for a time threatened to reduce to ashes that part of the town which had been spared by the angry waters. Some children were playing that they were workmen, and were clearing up the wreck. In their play they attempted to burn up some loose rubbish, and, as is often the case, did more than they intended. The fire caught and spread.

The facilities at this time for stopping a conflagration were very meagre. Where a few days before there had been resistless torrents of water, there was now scarcely any to be had. The fire crackled, leaped up with threatening glare, reached out its red tongue for fresh fuel, jumped from one building to another, and rolled great clouds of smoke skyward, completing the pall of gloom which for more than three weeks had hung over the fated city. A small force of firemen from Philadelphia was on the ground, but their efforts were sadly crippled. It is often hard work to fight devouring flames even with abundant facilities; when these are wanting the task becomes quite hopeless. The progress of the flames was finally stayed by blowing up buildings; yet before this could be done twenty-five houses were destroyed, a part of which were so badly wrecked that they would have been removed without any attempt to reconstruct them, while others, several of them comfortable residences, would have been moved to the old sites from which the flood swept them, and would have served for further use.

The loss, some $30,000, was trifling compared with that suffered by the flood; still it assumed serious proportions on account of the great destruction of property which had already taken place. Stricken Johnstown needed every dwelling, every barn, every roof for the thousands of homeless wanderers that thronged the streets, and this new calamity was indeed deplorable. The country heard the intelligence with a fresh thrill of horror and sympathy, and wondered whether utter annihilation would not overtake the city, so large a part of which had been plowed by the river of death.

A New City.

Through the summer months the work of removing the vast masses of debris caused by the flood was carried forward vigorously. Where the accumulation was greatest dynamite was finally brought into use. Some persons objected to this, just as before they objected to applying the torch. Love clings even to its dead, and shrinks from any disfigurement of the form that was cherished tenderly in life.

It was not uncommon after a heavy blast of dynamite had been exploded, to see whole bodies, or fragments of bodies, suddenly brought into view, released from the wreckage in which they had been buried. The spectacle was appalling, and would have been even more so but for the fact that death in the most haggard forms had become a familiar sight to the survivors.

How many bodies have been torn, crushed, scattered in fragments, ground into dirt and sand and mixed with their mother earth, can never be known. Neither can it be known with any accuracy how many thousands perished in the terrible calamity.

As fast as the streets and building sites could be cleared of the immense deposits with which they were overlaid, new dwellings were erected.

Homes for the People.

These houses are perhaps as good as could be expected under the circumstances. The first necessity was to furnish a shelter for the homeless. How different these plain dwellings from the comfortable, and in some instances elegant homes which remain now only in the memory of their occupants! It was wisely thought that the best use which could be made of a large part of the money given so lavishly for Johnstown would be to provide good, comfortable houses for families, or the remnants of families, who had been rendered homeless. This work was carried on as fast as circumstances would permit, and soon the place began to put on a new appearance.

Meantime the large force of men employed in removing the debris worked with good effect. Reports from time to time appeared in the newspaper press as to the progress made. At first it seemed a herculean task, and probably after the work shall have ceased there will remain much that might have been done but never will be. Very likely many years from now, when the pick and shovel are put into the ground, and the earth is thrown up, the bones of the dead will be there to remind the living of the awful visitation which engulfed thousands of human beings.

Thanks where they were Due.

While credit is due many persons and organizations, particularly the Red Cross brigade, mention should be made of the efficient services of Gen. Hastings. Few men were ever placed in a more trying position—a position which required great tact, consideration, sympathy, firmness, and energy. He acquitted himself in such a way as to secure the good opinion of those immediately surrounding him, and of the public at large.

Gen. Hastings left Johnstown on July 8th. That evening the Fourteenth Pennsylvania Regiment, which had been assigned to him for duty, was drawn up before his headquarters. The various heads of departments were there, also several hundred of the townspeople, and there was a stir which indicated that something unusual was going on. Colonel Perchment, of the Fourteenth Regiment, had come with his command to thank Gen. Hastings for his efficient leadership, and the uniform kindness and courtesy they had received from his hands. A high compliment was also paid to Gen. Wiley, director of the department of public safety.

In his reply Gen. Hastings paid a fitting tribute to the services rendered by the Fourteenth Regiment, and said they had done honor to the National Guard of the State.

Colonel Stewart then stepped forward, and on behalf of the Grand Army of the Republic, presented Gen. Hastings with a beautiful gold and diamond badge. It bore on one side the words "From the Department of Pennsylvania of the G. A. R." On the reverse side was the inscription: "To Adjutant-General D. H. Hastings for many favors and earnest help to the Grand Army of the Republic."

In his response General Hastings said:

"Colonel Stewart, I cannot find words to express the gratitude I feel to the old soldiers who are here and whom you represent, for this most unmerited compliment. I want to assure you that I am entitled to no such compliment as you have bestowed upon me. I want to say to you that I would not have one of my hearers go away from here with any other thought in his mind than that I only wanted to do my duty to my fellow-men in this stricken region.

"The Grand Army of the Republic, as an organization, and many of them as individuals, have been very kind to me, and if I have, by official action or otherwise, been enabled to instill in the minds of the youth of this commonwealth a soldierly spirit, a patriotic love of country, which I hope I have, I have only been able to point to the example that has been set to the people of this State and nation by the boys who wore the blue. When I had an opportunity to cross this river for the first time, and go down into the heart of the town, there I found your able commander with his coat off busy at work distributing clothing, comfort, consolation, and kind words to the bereaved ones whose parents had followed with him the flag of the country. By his side were gathered some of the men who are gathered with him here to-night."

Mr. Cyrus Elder and Colonel John P. Linton spoke for the citizens. Mr. Elder said that the Citizens' Committee had, at its meeting that day, adopted this resolution: "General D. H. Hastings having advised the Finance Committee that other official duties will oblige him to leave Johnstown to-morrow, we desire to put upon our records, in an informal way, our high appreciation of his services to this suffering community. Coming to us in the earliest and worst days of our distress, he made himself one with us, he voluntarily partook of the hardships which we endured, and he has devoted himself unreservedly to the work of making the remnant of our ruined city habitable, and of comforting, strengthening, and encouraging the helpless people. We shall not attempt any commendation of his great labors, or try to say how thoughtful he has been for us, how wise and how kind. It is best stated in saying that he has endeared himself to all our people, who will join us in saying, 'God bless him.'"

General Hastings and Colonel J. L. Spangler returned to their homes at Bellefonte, Pa., on July 10th. A great public reception was given to them in Bush's Arcade Hall amid cheers and music. Mr. George C. Potts, a prominent iron-ore operator, was made President. Mr. E. C. Humes, President of the First National Bank, delivered the address of welcome to the distinguished guests. General Hastings was loudly called for. The General was pretty well exhausted physically, but responded as follows:

"MR. CHAIRMAN AND NEIGHBORS: I thank you more than I can find words to express for this most unmerited compliment. It has always been my ambition to merit the approval and good-will and kindly feeling of my neighbors and fellow-townsmen. If we have done anything within the past few weeks that merits your approval, I am duly thankful, and it shall always be my ambition to merit the good-will of my neighbors in Bellefonte. I will have to ask you to excuse me from making any extended remarks at this time, and for this compliment paid me this evening I thank you from the bottom of my heart. My friend, Colonel Spangler, who was with me all through the troubles, is here, and he can make more extended remarks of our labors there."

As early as June 14th Governor Beaver issued a proclamation in which he said: "The propriety of using the money contributed by generous donors for the benefit of individual sufferers, for the purpose of starting men in business, might be questioned, particularly if that business should prove remunerative hereafter. There can be little doubt, however, that the most useful and judicious expenditure at the present moment for the entire people of the region would be a fund which could be used for putting up simple board shanties in which business might be commenced by the courageous business men of Johnstown, who have signified their intention of remaining where they are and assisting in building up the ruins that speak so eloquently in their behalf. Credit is tendered them to any extent by merchants in our great trading centres. What they need is simply a cover for their goods and wares."

Thus it will be seen that the stricken city is taking on a new life, is slowly rising from the terrible disaster, and bids fair in due time to partially recover from the deadly shock. For such a consumation all persons will devoutly wish, and will rejoice at every sign of restored business, homes, industries and domestic comfort.